DISSERTATIONS

DISSERTATIONS

ON

SUBJECTS CONNECTED WITH

THE INCARNATION

BY

CHARLES GORE, M A

CANON OF WESTMINSTER
OF THE COMMUNITY OF THE RESURRECTION, RADLEY

Neque sit mihi inutilis pugna verborum
sed incunctantis fidei constans professio

WIPF & STOCK · Eugene, Oregon

Wipf and Stock Publishers
199 W 8th Ave, Suite 3
Eugene, OR 97401

Dissertations on Subjects Connected with the Incarnation
By Gore, Charles
Softcover ISBN-13: 978-1-6667-3422-5
Hardcover ISBN-13: 978-1-6667-2985-6
eBook ISBN-13: 978-1-6667-2986-3
Publication date 8/19/2021
Previously published by John Murray, 1895

This edition is a scanned facsimile of the original edition published in 1895.

FRATRI ADMODUM DILECTO

RICARDO RACKHAM

BENEVOLENTISSIMO LABORUM ADIUTORI

IN VERITATE EXPLORANDA CURIOSISSIMO

PREFACE

THESE dissertations are the fulfilment, after a much longer delay than I anticipated, of an intention expressed in the preface to the *Bampton Lectures* of 1891 to prepare a supplementary volume addressed to a more strictly theological public. Circumstances however have now led to the selection of a set of subjects not altogether identical with those then indicated. The amount of discussion which arose in connexion with my lectures as to our Lord's human consciousness has rendered necessary a prolonged treatment of the theology of the New Testament and of the Church on this subject. A dissertation on the rise of the transubstantiation dogma followed naturally from this special treatment of the theology of the Incarnation; and recent controversy has rendered desirable a more elaborate discussion of our Lord's birth of a virgin. Under these circumstances 'the early Greek theology of the supernatural in its relation to nature' and 'the relation of Ebionism and Gnosticism to the theology of the New Testament and of the second century' only come in for incidental treatment.

In the first dissertation—on our Lord's birth of a virgin—I have tried to give the first place to the presentation of the positive case for this article of the Christian creed, and only the second to resolving objections or considering possible rival theories. Hence I have said nothing about such a theory as that of Holtzmann[1], of different documents used by St Luke in his first two chapters and of interpolations and alterations made in the use of them—a theory which seems to rest on purely *a priori* grounds. It seems to me that, to justify a distinction of various 'sources' used by a compiler, we need either very distinct evidences of style (such as the difference between St Luke's own style, i. 1-4, and that of his 'source' beginning at i. 5), or very violent inconsistencies, or phenomena apparent over a large area, as in the case of the Hexateuch. If the area is small, the difference of style not plain, and the narrative fairly self-consistent, the proposed distinction becomes at once arbitrary. Critics of

[1] *Handcommentar zum N T* (Freiburg, 1889) bd 1 pp 13, 46

Preface.

documents, especially biblical documents, appear to me very seldom to know where to stop in their analysis.

I owe to the Rev. G. A Cooke, of Magdalen, the substance of the note on pp. 39-40 His diligent investigation of the sources of a statement current in modern apologetic literature has, I fear, decisively pricked a small but somewhat interesting bubble.

In the second dissertation—on our Lord's consciousness as man—my excuse for so much quotation lies in the necessity for bringing under the eye of the reader the inadequacy *in one respect* of much of the patristic and all the mediaeval theology There has not hitherto existed any adequate *catena* of theologians on this subject I hope I shall be pardoned if a lack of complete consistency is noticed in regard to the translation of patristic passages. In any case I have produced all important passages or phrases in the original language I cannot but hope that in this dissertation I shall have satisfied one or two of those whose approval I am most anxious to keep or to regain.

In regard to the third essay, I have thought that the lack of sufficiently exact histories of eucharistic doctrine justified a detailed statement of the rise of the theory and dogma of transubstantiation But I must ask that it should be remembered that, if information outside the period professedly covered is incidentally given, I do not profess to cover more in detail than the period from A.D 800 to 1215.

In the preparation of these dissertations for the press I owe thanks for help to my brothers, the Rev. Thomas Barnes and the Rev. Richard Rackham. To the latter I owe more than I can well express, and particularly the appended note on the *Codex Sinaiticus* and the preparation of the Table of Contents and of the indices of scriptural passages and of names He has added to the latter a few dates which will, it is hoped, increase its usefulness.

C. G

RADLEY VICARAGE,
 St. James' Day, 1895

CONTENTS

THE VIRGIN BIRTH OF OUR LORD

	PAGE
Subject and aim	3
§ 1. The silence of St. Mark, St. John, and St. Paul	
St. Mark	6
St. John	7
St. Paul	10
§ 2 The narrative of St. Luke	
its origin and trustworthiness	12
objections. (1) the census	19
(2) angelic appearances	21
§ 3 The narrative of St. Matthew	
its origin	28
objections. (1) massacre of the innocents	29
(2) influence of prophecy	31
§ 4 The relation of the two narratives	
(1) the historical outline	36
(2) the genealogies	37
§ 5 The tradition of the churches	
importance of tradition	41
consensus of tradition found in	
Irenaeus Justin	43
Ignatius Aristides	46
Alexandrians non-Catholic writings	47
discordant teaching found in	
Cerinthus Ebionism	49
§ 6 The theory of legend	
the miraculous birth not	
due to legendary tendency	55
a repetition of O. T. incident	60
derived from Philo's language	61

xii   *Contents.*

PAGE

§ 7 The connexion of doctrine and fact
     is inevitable . . 63
     (α) birth and personality . 64
     (β) the Second Adam and a new creation 65
Conclusion
     and its relation to church authority 67

THE CONSCIOUSNESS OF OUR LORD IN HIS MORTAL LIFE

The subject 71
     its relation to Christian faith . . 72
     spirit in which it should be studied (Hilary) 73

I.

THE VIEW OF OUR LORD'S CONSCIOUSNESS DURING HIS HUMAN AND MORTAL LIFE WHICH IS PRESENTED IN THE NEW TESTAMENT

§ 1. The evidence of the Gospels
     picture of a human growth . . 77
     with assertion of divine sonship and infallibility 78
     but evidence of a limitation of knowledge
          (1) human experiences—interrogation, prayer 81
          (2) St. Matt. xxiv 36 *neither the Son* 83
          (3) testimony of St. John's Gospel 84
          (4) argument from silence . 87
§ 2 The language of St Paul
     self-emptying (Phil ii 5–11) . 88
     self-beggary (2 Cor. viii. 9) 89
§ 3 An absolute κένωσις not affirmed in the N. T.
     the eternal Word in St. John, St Paul, the Hebrews 91
     silence as to an arrest of the Word's divine functions 93
§ 4 Provisional conclusion
     the Incarnation involves a real limitation . 94
     as opposed to
          dogmatical repudiation of ignorance 95
          humanitarian assertion of fallibility . 95

II.

THE HISTORY OF CHRISTIAN OPINION OUTSIDE THE CANON ON THE SUBJECT OF OUR LORD'S HUMAN CONSCIOUSNESS.

	PAGE
§ 1. Preliminary. On the permanence in the Incarnation of the Godhead of Christ	
as taught by Irenaeus	98
Origen	100
Eusebius	100
Athanasius	103
Proclus	104
§ 2. Early tradition and speculation on the special subject of the human consciousness of Christ	
tradition not definite on the subject	106
doctrine of Irenaeus	108
Clement of Alexandria	113
Origen	114
§ 3 The anti-Arian writers who admit a human ignorance	
Trinitarian controversies	122
doctrine of Athanasius	123
Gregory Nazianzen	126
Basil	127
Ambrose	127
§ 4 Anti-Arian writers, especially of the west	
tendency of anti-Arian theology	130
protest of Theodoret	131
doctrine of Hilary	133
Jerome	135
Augustine	136
§ 5 The Apollinarian controversy	
lack of interest among Catholics	138
doctrine of Gregory Nyssen	140
§ 6 The Nestorian controversy	
Theodore of Mopsuestia	144
zealous repudiation of Nestorianism	145
doctrine of Hilary	147
Cyril	149

xiv   *Contents.*

                                                                    PAGE
§ 7. The Monophysite controversy
        (1) vindication of the manhood not fruitful in result   154
                the Agnoetae and Leontius   155
                        Eulogius   . 158
                        Gregory .   159
                John Damascene   .   .   .   160
                Agobard and the Adoptionists in the west   161
        (2) the Definition of Chalcedon leaves the two
                natures in simple juxtaposition   .   162

§ 8. Mediaeval and scholastic theology
        determined against a real ignorance   .   166
        refinements of Thomas Aquinas   168
        qualifications
                (1) hesitation as to what is *de fide*   169
                (2) decisions only as to matter of fact   169
        scholastic theology
                (1) mistaken in its use of church dogmas   170
                (2) based on one-sided metaphysical idea of God 171
                        derived from Greek philosophy   .   .   173
                        through Dionysius Areop and Erigena   173
                        resulting in nihilianism   .   .   175
                        as expressed in Peter Lombard   .   175

§ 9. The theology of the Reformation
        a return to Scripture   179
        theories of Luther   .   .   181
                the Reformed   .   .   .   182
        modern views
                (1) absolute kenotic—   Godet .   184
                (2) partial kenotic—   Fairbairn   189
                (3) double life—   Martensen   192
                (4) gradual incarnation—Dorner   .   193

§ 10. Anglican theology
        its characteristics   196
        utterances of
                Hooker   Andrewes   Jeremy Taylor   .   .   196
                Bull   Beveridge Waterland   .   198
        modern authorities
                Church   Westcott   Bright   .   .   199

Contents.

III.

THE CONCLUSION OF THIS INQUIRY. THE RELATION OF THIS CONCLUSION TO CHURCH AUTHORITY: ITS RATIONALITY

	PAGE
§ 1 Conclusion from our inquiry	
a real self-limitation in the Incarnation	202
without abandonment of the divine functions in another sphere	206
fourfold appeal to opponents	205
§ 2. The relation of our conclusion to ecclesiastical authority	
its consistence with ecumenical decrees	207
in particular those of Nicaea	208
Chalcedon and CP III	210
reasons for defectiveness in patristic and scholastic theology	213
§ 3 The rationality of our conclusion	
(1) the inconceivable not necessarily the irrational	216
(2) the power of sympathy	218
(3) difference between divine and human knowledge	220
(4) modern view of God's relation to His creation	222

TRANSUBSTANTIATION AND NIHILIANISM

Subject and aim	229
I The growth of the doctrine of transubstantiation	
§ viii in the east, John of Damascus	230
in the west	
retarding influence of Augustine	232
reflected in Caroline theologians	234
§ ix Paschasius Radbert's teaching	236
Rabanus Maurus opposes it	239
Ratramn "	240
Hincmar, Haimo support it	246
§ xi the Berengarian controversy	247
Berengar's position	248
Humbert's decree (A. D. 1059)	257

Contents.

		PAGE
	Lanfranc and Hugh of Langres	258
	Witmund	258
	Durandus of Troarn	263
S XII	Alger	264
	Gregory of Bergamo	265
	Hildebert	266
	Peter Lombard	267
A.D 1215	the Lateran decree	268

II The metaphysical theory and philosophical principle involved three objections
    (1) no scriptural or primitive authority . . . 269
    (2) metaphysical difficulty . . 270
        not the same with the *homoousion* doctrine . 272
        doctrinal outcome of materialistic conception . 271
    (3) it violates the principle of the Incarnation 272
        as stated by Irenaeus 273
        Leontius . . . 277

III Nihilianism the background of the theory of transubstantiation
    nihilianism prevalent in early middle ages . . . 279
    = transubstantiation in relation to the Incarnation . 281
    the dogmatic barriers of the Incarnation doctrine were wanting in the case of the eucharist . . 283
    reasons for not accepting transubstantiation even in a refined sense . . . 284

APPENDED NOTES

A. Supposed Jewish expectation of the virgin birth . . 289
B. The readings of Codex Sinaiticus . . 292
C. On the patristic interpretation of St. John vi. 63 . 303
D. Tertullian's doctrine of the eucharist . 308

DISSERTATION I

THE VIRGIN BIRTH OF OUR LORD

AMONG subjects of present controversy not the least important is the Virgin Birth of Jesus Christ. It is not only that naturalistic writers frequently speak as if it were unmistakeably a fable; but writers who do in some sense believe in the Incarnation are found at times to imply that, while the Resurrection must be held to, the Virgin Birth had better be discarded from the position of an historical fact. And even writers of a more orthodox character are occasionally found to speak of it with some considerable degree of doubt or disparagement[1]. Such rejection or doubt is in part based upon the silence, or presumed silence, on the subject of two of the evangelists, St. Mark and St. John, also of the apostolic epistles, especially those of St. Paul. In part it is held to be justified by discrepancies between the accounts of the birth

[1] See, as examples of these classes, Renan, *Les Évangiles* (Paris, 1877) pp 188 ff, 278 ff ; Meyer, *Commentary on St Matthew*, 1. 18 (Clark's trans); *The Kernel and the Husk* (Macmillan, 1886) pp. 267 ff ; Dr A Harnack, *Das Apost. Glaubensbekenntniss* (Berlin, 1892) pp. 35 ff This pamphlet is part of a considerable agitation in Germany, and represents a widespread tendency in that country. The tendency is certainly abroad among Christians at home, though perhaps at present more in conversation than in literature.

in St. Matthew and St. Luke; and by circumstances which are supposed to render those accounts unworthy of the credit of serious critics. At the same time it is often maintained that the belief in the Incarnation is not bound up with the belief in the virginity of Mary: and that, even if this latter point were rejected or held an open question, we could still believe Jesus Christ to be not as other men, but the Son of God incarnate[1]. This latter belief in the person of Christ is, it is maintained, legitimate as warranted by His claims, His miracles, His resurrection, His kingdom; but it does not therefore follow that legend may not have gathered around the circumstances of His birth. There is analogy, it is suggested, for such an accretion in the birth-stories of innumerable heroes, both Jewish and Gentile, from Buddha, Zoroaster, and Samson downwards to Augustus and John the Baptist.

In view of this tendency of thought, I will endeavour—

(1) to account for the silence of St. Mark, St. John, and St Paul, so far as it is a fact, while at the same time indicating evidence which goes to show that these writers did in reality recognize the fact of the Virgin Birth;

(2) to justify the claim of Luke i–ii to contain serious history;

(3) to do the same for Matt. i–ii taken by itself;

(4) to indicate the relation of the two accounts;

---

[1] See quotations in Dr A B Bruce's *Apologetics* (Clark, 1892) pp 408, 409; and cf. Dr. Fairbairn, *Christ in Modern Theology* (Hodder & Stoughton, 1893) pp 346, 347 I do not understand Dr Fairbairn to express any doubt as to the fact of the virgin birth.

(5) to show cause for believing that the Virgin Birth has in Christian tradition from the first been held inseparable from the truth of the Incarnation;

(6) to deal with the argument derived from the birth-legends of heroes;

(7) to show cause for believing that the doctrine of the person of Christ is in reality inseparable from the fact of His birth of a virgin.

First however it is necessary to make plain the point at which this argument begins, and the class of persons towards whom it is addressed. I am assuming the substantial historical truth of the evangelical narrative common to the three synoptists and supplemented by St. John: I am assuming the reality of the physical resurrection and, accordingly, the possibility of miracles and their credibility on evidence: I am assuming that Jesus Christ really was the Son of God incarnate. One who entertains doubts on these matters must satisfy himself by considerations preliminary to our present undertaking [1], just as in the beginning of Christianity the belief in Jesus as the Son of God was, as will be presently explained, prior to the knowledge of His Virgin Birth. The question now is,—granted the miraculous personality of Christ and His resurrection, granted the idea of the Incarnation to be the right interpretation of His person, is there still reason to doubt the historical character of the miracle of the birth, and is it reasonable to imagine that such doubt will be compatible with a prolonged hold on the belief in the Incarnation itself?

[1] Such considerations I have endeavoured to present in summary in the *Bampton Lectures for* 1891 (Murray) lect. i, ii, iii.

§ 1.

The silence of St. Mark, St. John, and St. Paul.

The original function of the apostles was mainly that of eye-witnesses. It was therefore necessarily limited by the period of the public ministry of our Lord, during which period alone they had 'companied with him,' i. e. from the days of John the Baptist till the time when He was taken up into heaven [1]. To have allowed their original preaching to go behind the limit of this period would have been to abandon a real principle of Christianity, the principle that it was to rest upon the personal testimony of men who in company with one another had passed through a prolonged experience of the words and works of Jesus of Nazareth, of the circumstances of His death and the reality of His resurrection. To have gone outside this period of personal witness would have been, I say, to abandon a principle; and there can therefore be no question that the original 'teaching of the apostles' did not and could not include the Virgin Birth [2]. If we accept the trustworthy tradition which

---

[1] See Acts i. 8, 21, ii 32, iii 15, x 39, St Luke i 2, St John i 14, xv 27, xxi 24, Hebr ii 3

[2] It is plain that Joseph and Mary must have kept this event secret from the world and their neighbours When it was known through Christian preaching, it led to slander, disagreeable even to think of, but widely current in the second century. See Renan, *Les Évangiles*, p. 189 'La fable grossière inventée par les adversaires du christianisme, qui faisait naître Jésus d'une aventure scandaleuse avec le soldat Panthère (*Acta Pilati*,

The Virgin Birth of our Lord. 7

makes St. Mark's Gospel represent the preaching of Peter —the part of his experience which he embodied in his primary instruction — we shall see at once why the Gospel of Mark does not carry us behind the preaching of John the Baptist. It needs to be remarked, over and above this, that St. Mark in one passage exhibits a noticeable difference as compared with St. Matthew and St Luke. Where St. Matthew has 'Is not this the carpenter's son?' and St. Luke 'Is not this the son of Joseph?' St. Mark writes 'Is not this the carpenter?'[1] It is probable that of these two expressions, St. Matthew's (as corroborated by St. Luke) is primary, and St. Mark's secondary; and that the alteration in St. Mark must be attributed to an unwillingness to suggest —even in the surprised questioning of the Jews—the proper parentage of Joseph, where nothing had been previously given to prevent misunderstanding, as in St. Matthew's and St. Luke's Gospels[2]

As to St John, it seems to me quite impossible to

A 2, Celse, dans Origène, *Contre Celse*, 1 28, 32, Talm de Jér *Schabbath*, XIV 4, *Aboda zara*, II. 2; Midrasch *Koh* x 5, &c), sortit sans trop d'effort du récit chrétien, récit qui presentait à l'imagination le tableau choquant d'une naissance où le père n'avait qu'un rôle apparent Cette fable ne se montre clairement qu'au II⁰ siècle; dès le I⁰ʳ, cependant, les juifs paraissent avoir malignement présenté la naissance de Jésus comme illégitime.' It appears that *Panthera* is only in fact an anagram for *Parthenos*. see Rendel Harris, *Texts and Studies* (Cambridge, 1891), vol. 1. no 1 p 25

[1] St Matt xiii 55, St. Mark vi 3; St Luke iv 22

[2] So Baur, Hilgenfeld, and Bleek, quoted by Weiss, *Handbuch uber Evang Markus und Lukas*, on Mark vi 3 St. Luke (ii 48) allows a parallel expression, 'Thy father and I,' where it is liable to no misconception. So also St John (1 45 'Jesus of Nazareth, the son of Joseph'), writing at a later period, when, I believe, the common teaching of the Church was well established.

believe that he was ignorant of the Virgin Birth of our Lord. Ignatius, who was bishop of Antioch in Syria a very few years after the writing of the fourth Gospel, calls the virginity of Mary a 'mystery of loud proclamation' in the Church[1]: it could not have been otherwise considering the currency which the first and third Gospels, and still more the materials of those Gospels, had already obtained. More than this: we know on very high authority (that of Polycarp, John's disciple, as quoted by Irenaeus[2]) that St. John was in sharp opposition to the gnostic teacher, Cerinthus. Cerinthus, like all Gnostics, denied the real Incarnation. He distinguished between the higher being, the spiritual Christ, and the human Jesus. He supposed the man Jesus to have been born in the ordinary way of Joseph and Mary, and to have been the most perfect of all men; he supposed the divine Christ to have descended upon him after his baptism and to have left him before his passion[3]. Cerinthus thus denied both the real Incarnation and the miraculous birth. St John's whole force is thrown into the affirmation of the real Incarnation. He cannot have been ignorant that the denial of the Incarnation was associated with the denial of the miraculous birth. We may ask then, (1) Was he indifferent to this latter? (2) If not, does he give any indications that he believed in it? (3) Why did he not narrate it at length? I should answer thus: (1) He was not indifferent to it, but, as in the case of the institution of baptism and of the eucharist[4], he supplies the justifying

---

[1] See below, p 46
[2] con. Haer. iii. 3 4.
[3] Iren. con Haer. i. 26. 1
[4] St John iii 3-8, vi 53-65

The Virgin Birth of our Lord.

principle—in this case the principle of the Incarnation—without supplying what was already current and well known, the record of the fact. The denial of the fact had been but the result of the denial of the principle. Granted the principle, the belief in the fact would follow inevitably. (2) He does give indications that he recognized the fact. In the scene of the marriage-supper at Cana, before the first miracle had yet been wrought, he shows Mary, our Lord's mother, manifestly expecting of her son miraculous action manifestly regarding Him as a miraculous person[1]. There is no such natural explanation of this as that St. John regarded her as conscious from the first of His miraculous origin and nature. Once more· St. John's mind is full of the correspondence between 'the Son' and the other 'sons' of God, between Christ and the Church. One main motive of his Apocalypse is to exhibit the Church passing through the phases of the life of Christ. Like Him it is born, suffers, dies, rises, ascends[2]. When St. John then gives us the picture of 'a woman arrayed with the sun and the moon under her feet,' who brings forth 'a son, a male thing,' and other 'seed' besides[3], he is probably presenting the idea of the true Jerusalem, 'the mother of us all,' bringing forth into the world the Christ and His people. But there is a retrospect, or dependence, which can hardly be disputed, upon Mary the actual mother of Jesus, the Christ. The more sure one feels of this, and the more one dwells upon the parallelism exhibited throughout these chapters between the Head

---

[1] St. John ii. 3-5. [2] Rev. xii 5, 17, xi. 7-12
[3] Rev. xii 1, 5, 17

and His body, the more disposed one is to see in the picture of the dragon who watches to destroy the newborn child and the flight of the woman into the wilderness[1] a mystically-worded[2] retrospect upon the hostile action of Herod who sought the young child's life to destroy him[3], i.e. a recognition of the history of the nativity as given in St. Matthew. (3) It would have been impossible for St. John, consistently with the main purpose of his Gospel, to have recorded the Virgin Birth, for his Gospel is, before all else, a personal testimony. It is the old man's witness to what he saw and heard when he was young, and had brooded and meditated upon through his long life. This witness he now leaves on record, at the earnest request of those about him, and for the necessities of the Church. Such a Gospel must have begun where personal experience began.

Once more with regard to St. Paul—it is a well-known fact that his epistles are almost exclusively occupied in contending for Christian principles, not in recalling facts of our Lord's life. His function was that of the theologian rather than that of the witness. One conclusion from this might be that St. Paul was ignorant of, or indifferent to, the facts of our Lord's life. But we are restrained from this conclusion by the evidence which

---

[1] Rev xii 13, 14

[2] It should be noticed that the account of the death, resurrection, &c. of the 'two witnesses' who represent the Church in xi. 7–12 contains many points of *difference* from the actual history of the parallel events in our Lord's case, as well as many points of similarity. The relation of the 'mystical' and actual accounts of the death and resurrection is similar to the relation of the two accounts of the birth and early persecution.

[3] St. Matt ii 13.

The Virgin Birth of our Lord.

he gives at least on two occasions when his argument compels him to recall to the Corinthians his first preaching and he recalls it each time in the form of an evangelical narrative [1]. We learn from this that St. Paul's first preaching contained at least a considerable element of evangelical narrative. Of all the contents of this narrative we cannot be sure: it is not impossible that it made reference to the miraculous birth of Jesus. But it would be foolish to maintain this in the absence of direct evidence. What we can maintain, with great boldness, is that St. Paul's conception of the 'Second Adam' postulates His miraculous birth. 'Born of a woman,' 'born of the seed of David according to the flesh [2],' He was yet 'from heaven [3]': born of a woman, He was yet a new head of the race, sinless, free from Adam's sin; a new starting-point for humanity [4]. Now considering how strongly St. Paul expresses the idea of the solidarity of man by natural descent, and the consequent implication of the whole human race in Adam's fall [5], his belief in the sinless Second Adam seems to me to postulate the fact of His Virgin Birth; the fact, that is, that He was born in such a way that His birth was a new creative act of God. On this connexion of ideas,

---

[1] 1 Cor. xi 23-25, xv 3-8   [2] Gal. iv. 4, Rom 1 3

[3] 1 Cor xv. 47. ὁ δεύτερος ἄνθρωπος ἐξ οὐρανοῦ has been interpreted of Christ at His second coming But it describes the *origin* of the second man, being parallel to 'the first man is of the earth earthy,' and must therefore be referred to His first coming

[4] 2 Cor. v. 21, Rom. v 12-21; 1 Tim ii 5

[5] Rom v. 12-21, especially the phrase ἐφ' ᾧ πάντες ἥμαρτον. Cf. Acts xvii 26 ἐποίησεν ἐξ ἑνὸς πᾶν ἔθνος ἀνθρώπων 1 Cor xv. 48 οἷος ὁ χοικός, τοιοῦτοι καὶ οἱ χοικοί· Eph iv. 22, and Col iii 9 ὁ παλαιὸς ἄνθρωπος, which is morally corrupt.

however, more will need to be said when we come to deal with the relation of the Virgin Birth to the idea of the Incarnation.

The 'argument from silence' then, so far as it is based on the facts, appears to be a weak argument, because it gains its strength from ignoring the character and conditions of the 'silent' records. At least their silence suggests no presumption against the veracity of the records that are not silent, supposing that they present valid credentials, considered in themselves. Accordingly we proceed to the consideration of these records, that is, the narratives of the Virgin Birth in the first two chapters of the first and third Gospels.

§ 2.

The narrative of St. Luke.

Suppose a Christian of the earliest period instructed, like Theophilus, in the primitive oral 'tradition' of the Christian society; suppose him familiar with the sort of narrative that is presented to us in St. Mark's Gospel of the words and deeds of Jesus, and convinced of His Messiahship and divine sonship,— such an one would beyond all question have become inquisitive about the circumstances of the Master's birth. The inquiry must have been general and must have arisen very speedily. Let us transfer ourselves in imagination to that earliest

The Virgin Birth of our Lord.

period, of not less than about five years, before the persecution which arose about the death of Stephen, when the band of Christians in Jerusalem were continuing steadfastly and quietly in the 'apostles' teaching,' and constant repetition was forming the oral Gospel which underlies the earliest evangelical documents; we cannot conceive that period passing without inquiry, systematic inquiry, into the circumstances of our Lord's birth. Now at the beginning of that period the Mother was with the apostolic company. She may well—for all we know—have continued with them to the end of it. The Lord's 'brethren' too were there[1]. There was no difficulty, then, in obtaining trustworthy information. Joseph and Mary *must* have been silent originally as to the conditions of the birth of Jesus, for reasons obvious enough. They could only have 'kept the things and pondered them in their hearts.' But in the apostolic circle, in the circle of witnesses and believers, the reasons for silence were gone: Mary would have told the tale of His birth.

Now in St. Luke's Gospel—to take that Gospel first—we are presented with an obviously early and Jewish narrative containing an account of the birth of Jesus, incorporated and used by St. Luke. If then St. Luke is believed to be trustworthy in his use of documents, if the account given is credible considered in itself, there is no difficulty at all in perceiving from what source

[1] There is, however, nothing improbable in the hypothesis that the 'brethren' did not originally share the secret of Joseph and Mary as to the virgin birth (The more probable view, as it seems to me, is that which makes the 'brethren' half-brothers of our Lord, children of Joseph by a former marriage.)

originally it could have been derived and from what epoch its information could date.

Now when we examine the opening chapters of St. Luke, almost the first thing that strikes us is the contrast in style between the elaborate preface of the evangelist's own writing and the narrative to which he immediately passes. There can be no doubt that in the narrative of the nativity, St. Luke—writing, shall we say with Dr. Sanday, about A.D. 80[1]—is using an Aramaic document[2]. But is St. Luke trustworthy in his use of early documents? The ground on which we can best test this is the Acts of the Apostles. I assume—what I think is the only reasonable view—that St. Luke wrote the Acts as a whole: that he is the fellow-traveller of St Paul in the later portion[3], and that for the earlier portion, the Jerusalem period, he has been dependent upon information and documents supplied by others—probably by Philip the Evangelist and by some one—possibly Manaen or Joanna the wife of Chuza—connected with the court of the Herods[4]. Has he then

[1] See Sanday, *Bampton Lectures for* 1893 (Longmans) pp 277 ff., *Book by Book* (Isbister, 1892) pp. 366, 404

[2] See Weiss, *Markus und Lukas*, p. 239 'Die hebraisirende Diction der Vorgeschichte sticht gegen das classische Griechisch des Vorworts so augenfallig ab, dass hier die Benutzung einer schriftlichen Quelle kaum geleugnet werden kann.' Godet, *Saint Luc*, 1 85 'Il travaille sur des documents antiques, dont il tient à conserver aussi fidèlement que possible le coloris araméen.' Sanday, *Book by Book*, p. 399 Cf. also Ryle and James, *Psalms of Solomon* (Cambridge Univ. Press, 1891), p. lx 'The writings which, in our opinion, most nearly approach our Psalms in style and character are the hymns preserved in the early chapters of St Luke's Gospel, which in point of date of composition probably stand nearer to the Psalms of Solomon (B.C. 70-40) than any other portion of the New Testament' [3] Acts xvi 10-18, xx 6 to the end.

[4] Cf. Sanday, *Book by Book*, p 399 'Most of the occasions on which

shown himself in this collection and use of documents a trustworthy historian? This question we answer with a very emphatic affirmative. If Prof. Ramsay has summed up the verdict of recent inquiry as to the historical trustworthiness of the Pauline period of the Acts, not less certainly does it seem to me that recent inquiry has gone to confirm the historical worth of the early chapters The situation of the first Christians in Jerusalem: their preoccupation, not with the questions of Pauline or Johannine theology, but simply with Jesus as Messiah, and as fulfilling in His death and resurrection the prophecies of the Messiah: the moral brilliancy and yet simplicity of the first development of the Church: the exact relation in which Pharisees with their zeal for the law, and Sadducees in their hostility to a resurrection doctrine, and their preoccupation with the political situation, would stand to the new movement[1] ·

we hear of St Luke have their scene at a distance from Palestine, but at one time he would seem to have been for fully two years within the limits of the Roman province which bore that name He accompanied St. Paul on his last recorded journey to Jerusalem, stayed with him for some time at the house of Philip the "Evangelist" at Caesarea, went up with him to Jerusalem, and, as we infer, remained not far away from his person during the time of his later confinement at Caesarea' Philip the Evangelist—one of the Seven—must have had an intimate acquaintance with the events of the early period of the Jerusalem Church. Again, 'St Luke displays a special knowledge of matters relating to the court of the Herods He mentions by name a woman whom none of the other evangelists mentions, "Joanna the wife of Chuza, Herod's steward" [Luke viii 3], and in like manner in the Acts he speaks of Manaen, "foster-brother of Herod" [Acts xiii 1, one of the "prophets" or "teachers" at Antioch]. Here we have a glimpse of a circle from which St Luke probably got his account of' events connected with the Herods

[1] See, for the Sadducees, Acts iv. 1, v. 17, 24; for the Pharisees, with the scribes and common people, v 34, vi. 12 f, vii. 54 ff; for both together, ix. 1; for their divergence, xxiii. 6 ff.

the circumstances out of which arose the appointment of the Seven: the personality, work, and speech of Stephen—all this is represented in such a way as guarantees the faithful correspondence of the narrative with the actual situation; in other words, in such a way as guarantees that St. Luke is trustworthy in his use of his information and his documents. The study of the Acts, then, sends us back to the Gospel with a greatly invigorated belief in St. Luke's trustworthiness in his use of documents. We examine further the document of the nativity, and we find not only that it is Aramaic, but that it breathes the spirit of the Messianic hope, before it had received the rude and crushing blow involved in the rejection of the Messiah. The Forerunner is 'to make ready a people prepared for the Lord[1].' The Child is to have 'the throne of his father David,' and to 'reign over the house of Jacob for ever[2].' God hath 'holpen Israel his servant, that he might remember mercy (as he spake unto our fathers) toward Abraham and his seed for ever[3].' He hath 'visited and wrought redemption for his people, and hath raised up a horn of salvation for us in the house of his servant David, salvation from our enemies and from the hand of all that hate us[4].' It is the hope of 'the redemption of Jerusalem[5]' that is to be gratified. Now all this language of prophecy does indeed admit of interpretation in the light of subsequent facts. St. Paul could justify to the Jews the actual result out of their own Scriptures[6]. But it is not the sort of language that early Jewish Christians

[1] i 17. [2] i 32, 33. [3] i. 54, 55.
[4] i. 68–71. [5] ii. 38. [6] Romans ix–xi.

The Virgin Birth of our Lord. 17

would have invented after the rejection of the Christ. It contrasts very markedly with the language of St. Peter's speeches in the Acts[1], or of St. Stephen[2], or of St. Paul[3], or of St. James[4], or of St. John[5]. No doubt in the language of Simeon the coming of the Christ is 'a light for revelation to the Gentiles,' as well as 'the glory of God's people Israel.' He too alone among the speakers of these opening chapters sees that the crisis is to be anxious and searching. He 'said unto Mary his mother, Behold, this child is set for the falling and rising up of many in Israel; and for a sign which is spoken against; yea and a sword shall pierce through thine own soul; that thoughts out of many hearts may be revealed[6].' But these are notes so often struck in the Old Testament that they must have found some echo in the immediate anticipation of the work of the Child. They are like the warnings of John the Baptist[7]. But they do not anticipate the disastrous result. They do not forecast wholesale rejection; they only just interpose a note of moral anxiety in the general tone of hopeful exaltation. Nor is it unnecessary to observe that the conception of the person of our Lord in these chapters is purely Messianic[8]. He is to 'be great and shall be called the Son of

---

[1] See iii. 12-26, iv. 11, 25-28. [2] Acts vii. 51, 52.
[3] Acts xiii. 46, 1 Thess. ii. 14-16.
[4] St James v. 6. [5] St John xii. 37-43.
[6] St Luke ii. 31-35. [7] St Luke iii. 8.
[8] The distinction however between the Messianic and the divine conception of our Lord must not be pressed too far. It is true that the Jewish thought of our Lord's time did not anticipate a divine Messiah. The Messianic king of the Pharisaic *Psalms of Solomon* (c. 60 B.C.) does not rise above the human limit and the 'Son of Man' coming in glory as found in the *Book of Enoch* (by interpretation of Daniel vii 13)—probably

the Highest.' He shall be called 'holy, the Son of God,' because 'the Holy Ghost shall come upon' His mother, 'and the power of the Most High shall overshadow' her[1]. Mary is made to understand that the child whom she is to bear is to be the product of miraculous divine agency and is to be the exalted Messiah, but the doctrine of the Incarnation, strictly speaking, is not more to be found here than in the early speeches of the Acts.

Here then is an account which presents phenomena practically irreconcilable with the hypothesis that it was an invention of the early Jewish Christian imagination; an account which may well be Mary's account; which must be Mary's, in origin, if it is genuine; and which is given to us by a recorder of proved trustworthiness, who moreover makes a point of 'having traced the course of all things *accurately from the first.*' Finally it is an account which there is no evidence to show the *imagination* of any early Christian capable of producing, for its consummate fitness, reserve, sobriety and loftiness are unquestionable. Is there then any good reason against accepting it[2]?

a pre-Christian idea—is neither properly divine nor properly human. But the highest Old Testament idea of the divine and human Messiah could not, we may venture to say, have been realized and combined with the idea of the servant of Jehovah, except by the eternal Son of God made very man. *Thus in our Lord's own thought and language there is no line of demarcation between the Messianic and the Divine claim.* To go no further, a strictly divine meaning is given to the function of the Son of Man as judge of the world. And the apostles and first disciples were carried on insensibly from the confession 'Thou art the Christ of God' to the further confession 'My Lord and my God.' See on the subject generally Stanton's *Jewish and Christian Messiah* (Clark, 1886).

[1] St Luke i. 32, 35.
[2] Of course discrepancies with St. Matthew might discredit either it *or* St. Matthew's account, but these are considered later.

The Virgin Birth of our Lord.

1. It is often alleged that the notice of 'the first enrolment (or census), made when Quirinius was governor of Syria [1],' is unhistorical.

This objection had its full force when secular history recognized no Syrian governorship of Quirinius until just before the time when Judaea became a Roman province, when a 'census' was certainly made (A D. 6)[2]. But Quirinius' earlier governorship is now, chiefly through the labours of Bergmann and Mommsen, recognized as probable. The case may be fairly stated thus [3].

Publius Sulpicius Quirinius was probably governor of Syria (*legatus Augusti pro praetore*) for the first time between B. C. 4–2, but certainly after, not before, the death of Herod (which occurred in B C. 4)[4].

There is no record, independent of St. Luke's, of any 'census' (ἀπογραφή) of the Jews till that which took place during Quirinius' *second* legation, and is mentioned by Josephus. But St. Luke elsewhere alludes to this later census [5], and apparently intends to distinguish an earlier one from the later by the phrase he here uses, 'the *first* census [6] under Quirinius.'

The phrase 'there went out a decree from Caesar

---

[1] St Luke ii. 2
[2] Mommsen, *Provinces of the Roman Empire* (Eng trans., Bentley, 1886) ii 185–7
[3] The matter has been discussed *ad nauseam*, as by Zumpt, Godet, Keim, Edersheim, Farrar, Geikie, Didon See *Dict of Bible*, s. v. CYRENIUS. In Farrar's *St Luke* ('Cambridge G. T. for Schools') there is an excellent brief discussion of the matter.
[4] Mommsen, *Res gestae D Augusti* (Berlin, 1883) p 177; Keim, *Jesus of Nazara* (Eng. trans, Williams & Norgate) ii pp. 116 f.
[5] Acts v. 37 ἐν ταῖς ἡμέραις τῆς ἀπογραφῆς
[6] St Luke ii 2 αὕτη ἀπογραφὴ πρώτη ἐγένετο ἡγεμονεύοντος τῆς Συριας Κυρηνίου.

Augustus that a census be taken of all the world' may well refer to the *rationarium* or *breviarium* of the empire which Augustus busied himself in drawing up, and which included allied kingdoms¹. Herod, who was not only a 'rex socius,' but wholly dependent on the emperor², may well have been forward to supply a census of his kingdom to please his master. At a somewhat later date we read in Tacitus of the subjects of an allied king (of Cappadocia) who were 'compelled to submit to a census after our [the Romans'] fashion and to pay tribute³.' On the other hand, it is exceedingly improbable that any Christians would have *invented* such an ignoble reason as an imperial census for bringing Joseph and Mary up to 'the city of David.'

It must be remembered that the chronological data of St. Luke ii and iii were in all probability supplied by himself and not by his 'sources.' We are, therefore, not at all concerned to deny that St. Luke may have been slightly wrong in his date; for our Lord must have been born some months before the death of Herod and

---

¹ Cf. Suet. *Augustus*, cc 28, 101 'rationarium imperii; breviarium totius imperii.' Tac. *Ann* 1. 11 'opes publicae continebantur, quantum civium sociorumque in armis, quot classes, regna, provinciae, tributa aut vectigalia, et necessitates ac largitiones, quae cuncta sua manu perscripserat Augustus.'

² The evidence of the entire subjection of Herod to Augustus may be found in Josephus, *Ant.* xvi. 4. 1, 11 1 (he seeks leave to try his sons, &c.), xvii. 2. 6 (παντὸς γοῦν τοῦ Ἰουδαικοῦ βεβαιώσαντος δι' ὅρκων ἦ μὴν εὐνοῆσαι Καίσαρι καὶ τοῖς βασιλέως πράγμασιν). Herod was often under the displeasure of Augustus, cf. xvi. 9 3-4 (he threatens that having treated him as a friend, he shall in future treat him as a subject).

³ Tac *Ann*. vi. 41 (A D 36) 'Clitarum natio Cappadoci Archelao sub-iecta, quia nostrum in modum deferre census, pati tributa adigebatur, in iuga Tauri montis abscessit.'

therefore, as would seem certain, before the first governorship of Quirinius It is noticeable that Tertullian[1] in fact attributes the 'census' to Sentius Saturninus, not to Quirinius But it seems to me, especially in view of the deficiency of historical authorities for the period, that we display an exaggerated scepticism if we deny that so well-informed a writer as St. Luke may have been quite correct in ascribing the movement to Bethlehem of Joseph and Mary to some necessity connected with a 'census' of Judaea which Herod was supplying at the demand of Augustus[2].

2. Again, angelic appearances such as occur thrice in these chapters—to Zacharias, to Mary, and to the shepherds, are a scandal to some minds, and tend to discredit the whole narrative by giving it an air of ideality, that is, unreality.

Now it is important not to allow this matter to assume an exaggerated importance. For to suppose such angelic appearances and communications as are related in these chapters to be imaginative outward representations of what were in fact real but merely inward communications of the 'divine word' to human souls, is both a

---

[1] *adv Marc* iv 19 'Census constat actos tunc [at the time of our Lord's birth] in Iudaea per Sentium Saturninum' [B C 8-6].

[2] It is remarkable how critics, like apologists, are apt to go for 'everything or nothing' St Luke's credibility is not disproved, if it is made probable that our Lord's birth took place not at the beginning of Quirinius' governorship but at the end of that of his predecessor I ought to add, as I have quoted Mommsen in proof of the earlier governorship of Quirinius, that he denies that any census took place at that time Indeed he uses somewhat strong language to express his resentment at his labours having become in any way available for apologists—'homines theologi vel non theologi sed ad instar theologorum ex vinculis sermocinantes' (*op cit.* p 176)

possible course and one which is quite consistent with accepting the narrative as substantially historical and true. No one who believes in God and His dealings with men, and who accepts the testimony of all the prophets as to 'the word of the Lord' coming to them [1], can doubt the reality of substantive divine communications to man of a purely inward sort. Such an inward communication is recorded in these chapters to have been made to Elisabeth [2] and the angelic appearances to Joseph, recorded by St. Matthew [3], are merely inward occurrences, i e. they are intimations conveyed to his mind in sleep No one, moreover, who knows human nature can doubt that such inward communications could be easily transformed by the imagination into outward forms. It is then quite conceivable that Zacharias on the solemn, the unique, occasion of his approaching God to offer the incense in the holy place [4], did in answer to his earnest prayer [5], receive inwardly a divine intimation of a mysterious sort as to what was to befall him, such as made a vivid impression upon his mind, and even took effect upon his organs of speech—as mental shocks do produce physical effects—and that this divine intimation represented itself to his imagination in the outward form and voice of an angel. It is possible to give a similar interpretation to Mary's vision, and to that of the shepherds, though in this case the account would have to be more freely dealt with. There are no insuperable objec-

---

[1] Sanday, *Bampton Lectures*, lect III
[2] St Luke 1 41-45   [3] St Matt 1 20, 11 13, 19
[4] See Edersheim, *Jesus the Messiah* (Longmans, 1884) 1 p 134 'only once in a lifetime might any one enjoy that privilege'
[5] St. Luke 1 13.

The Virgin Birth of our Lord. 23

tions to a 'subjective vision' theory in these cases such as do, unmistakeably, present themselves when the same theory is applied to the appearances of our Lord after the resurrection[1], nor, as was said above, would such a theory, if accepted, affect the credibility of the narrative as a whole. The truth of the inward intimation was, on the hypothesis, proved by the subsequent facts: its form was recorded as it presented itself to the subject of it.

And here, in a discussion which is concerned only with the substantial truth of these evangelical narratives it might be wiser for me to leave the matter. But the present seems a suitable occasion to go on to ask whether it is really reasonable to find a scandal in angelic appearances? There can be no *a priori* objection against the existence of such spiritual beings, good and bad, as angels and devils. Many of us would say that the phenomena of temptation, as experienced by themselves, cannot be interpreted without a belief at least in the latter[2] Above all, our Lord's language certainly

---

[1] e g the empty tomb the importance attached to the actual body and its peculiar features the appearance to great groups of men simultaneously more than all, the fact that what reassured the disciples after the death and burial of their master—and in fact transformed their character and fundamentally altered their point of view—was no communication from God, but the actual and repeated appearance of the person of Jesus in the body. All the stress is on the fact

[2] Cf Dale, *Lect. on the Ephesians* (Hodder & Stoughton) pp. 422 f 'Evil thoughts come to us which are alien from all our convictions and all our sympathies There is nothing to account for them in our external circumstances or in the laws of our intellectual life We abhor them and repel them, but they are pressed upon us with cruel persistency They come to us at times when their presence is most hateful, they cross and trouble the current of devotion; they gather like thick clouds between our souls and God, and suddenly darken the glory of the divine righteousness and love.

reaches the level of positive teaching about good, and still more about bad, spirits. As regards good spirits, not only does His language constantly associate angels with Himself in the coming and judicial work of the last day[1], but He talks of them with explicit distinctness as beholding the face of God, as limited in knowledge of the great day, as without sensual natures, as attached to children, ministering to the souls of the dead, attendant on Himself at His request[2]. As regards evil spirits, He must Himself have related His own temptation to His disciples, in which the personal agency of Satan is vividly presented. He speaks with great simplicity of the devil as disseminating evil and hindering good[3]. He warns Peter of an explicit demand made by him upon the souls of the apostles[4]. He deals with demons with unmistakeable seriousness, emphasis, and frequency. He sees Satan behind moral and physical evil[5]. He

We are sometimes pursued and harassed by doubts which we have deliberately confronted, examined, and concluded to be absolutely destitute of force, doubts about the very existence of God, or about the authority of Christ, or about the reality of our own redemption. Sometimes the assaults take another form. Evil fires which we thought we had quenched are suddenly rekindled by unseen hands we have to renew the fight with forms of moral and spiritual evil which we thought we had completely destroyed.' Cf. also Trench, *Studies in the Gospels* (Macmillan, 1878) p 18 'Assuredly this doctrine of an evil spirit . . . so far from casting a deeper gloom on the mysterious destinies of humanity . . . lights up with a gleam and glimpse of hope regions which would seem utterly dark without it' And F D Maurice, *The Gospel of the Kingdom of Heaven* (Macmillan) lect vi

[1] St Matt. xiii. 41, 49, xvi 27, xxv 31, and parallel passages, cf St. Luke xii. 8

[2] St. Matt. xviii. 10, xxiv 36, xxvi. 53, St. Mark xii. 25; St. Luke xvi 22

[3] St. Matt xiii 39; St. Luke viii 12.   [4] St Luke xxii. 31.

[5] St Luke xiii. 16; St John viii. 44.

looks out upon the antagonism to good which the world presents and says 'An enemy hath done this[1].' He recognizes the approach of evil spirits in the trial of the passion[2]. But He knows that the power of the forces of evil is really overthrown and their doom certain[3].

Now the question of diabolic agency and temptation is one which really concerns the permanent spiritual struggle of mankind. It is not, like questions of literature and science, one with which religion is not primarily mixed up. It is a matter of profoundly practical religious interest. Is that which opposes itself to our efforts after God, whether individual or social, that which seems to lie behind all the wickednesses of particular men, and to organize evil broadly and continuously—is it inevitable nature, an essential element in the constitution of things, is it in effect a rival God? or is it, on the other hand, an evil will, or kingdom of evil wills, hostile and active, but wholly subordinate to God and destined to be overthrown? To teach ignorantly on such a matter, or to inculcate false impressions about it, would be most seriously inconsistent, I do not say with the personality of the incarnate Son of God, but even with the office of the Son of Man as spiritual teacher of all mankind, having a perfect insight into the spiritual condition of our human life. Nor is it possible to suppose that our Lord, without emphasizing the existence of 'spirits,' connived in regard to it at popular belief and language, and, as it were, used the

---

[1] St Matt xiii 28 See a very striking sermon in H S. Holland's *God's City* (Longmans, 1894)
[2] St Luke xxii 53, St John xiv 30
[3] St Luke x 18, St Matt xii 28, 29, xxv. 41

belief only so far as was necessary to render Himself intelligible He did much more than this. On a matter —the existence of angels and spirits—which appears to have been in controversy between Pharisees and Sadducees[1], He must be regarded as having taken a side. Further, the teaching and method of Jesus Christ with regard to Satan and the 'demons,' when compared with current Jewish lore, exhibits a marked independence and originality owing to its entire freedom from elements of superstition Our Lord in 'exorcising' demons appears as doing by simple moral authority what the Jewish exorcists did by incantations and charms[2] On the whole, it is impossible to treat His language about spirits as 'economical' without giving profound unreality to His teaching as a whole.

The present writer then does not see how doubt about the existence and action of good and bad spirits is compatible with a real faith in Jesus Christ as the absolutely trustworthy teacher. There is nothing contrary to reason in such a belief. That it should have been associated with a vast amount of superstition and credulity is no more an argument against its validity

---

[1] Acts xxiii 8

[2] For Jewish exorcisms cf Tobit vi 16, 17 (Neubauer's trans from the Chaldee) 'And when thou shalt come into the marriage-chamber with her, take the heart of the fish, and smoke thereof under her garments; and the demon shall smell it and he shall run away and never come again.' Cf Joseph *Ant* viii 2 5, *Bell Jud* vii 6 3. See further on Jewish belief in angels and demons, Charles' *Book of Enoch* (Clar Press, 1893) p 52. That our Lord does at times use merely popular language about spirits is certain, as in St. Matt xii 43–45 There, however, He is plainly speaking in metaphor. The 'waterless places' through which the demon walks are as metaphorical as the 'empty, swept, and garnished house' of the soul

The Virgin Birth of our Lord. 27

than against religion as a whole No one can deny that in our Lord's case, the teaching which He gave about spirits is guarded from superstition by His teaching about God and human responsibility. Now, granted the existence of devils and angels[1], there is no reason for doubting that they have from time to time made their presence perceptible to men—in the case of angels, as messengers of God and instruments of His redemptive purpose[2]—and to return to St. Luke's narrative of the nativity, there is no reason for doubting that angelic ministrations were actually employed to announce the birth of the Forerunner and the incarnation and birth of the Christ.

No other considerable objections than these two, which have now been examined and set aside, have been urged against the historical character of the first two chapters of St Luke's Gospel: we are justified therefore in falling back upon the positive considerations which indicate that the account in these chapters is derived from no other person than the Virgin Mother herself.

---

[1] The belief in the existence and appearance of 'spirits' is quite consistent with the recognition that we know hardly anything about them The amount of pretended knowledge on the subject in Jewish and Christian writers is appalling. But in the Bible they are, we may say, never the subjects of divine revelation for their own sake Their 'persons' are merged in their offices of adoration and service Where angels appear in the Bible they appear in the form of men

[2] The objection made against the early chapters of St Luke on the score of the similarity of their contents to the birth-legends of heroes is met later on, § 6, p 55.

§ 3.

The narrative of St. Matthew.

Now we approach St. Matthew's account of the nativity. The narrative of St Luke, if it is authentic, must, as was said above, have come from Mary. The narrative of St. Matthew, on the other hand, bears upon it undesigned but evident traces of coming from the information of Joseph. It is Joseph's perplexities that are in question[1]. Divine intimations are recorded as given to Joseph on three occasions, leading him to act for the protection of the Mother and Child from external perils[2]. Now supposing the conception of Jesus really to have taken place without the intervention of Joseph, and supposing Joseph to have been, as the evangelist says, a 'just man' and to have died, as appears to have been the case, before the public ministry of our Lord began—it is only natural to suppose that he would have left behind him some document[3] clearing up, by his own testimony, the circumstances of the birth of Jesus. If the miraculous birth was ever to have been made public, his testimony would have been imperatively needed This document he must, we should suppose, have given to Mary to vindicate by means of it, when occasion demanded, her own virginity. Why should she not, after the establishment of the

---

[1] i 19   [2] i 20, ii 13, 19, 22
[3] Joseph, like Zacharias (Luke i 63), would have been able to write.

Church at Pentecost, have given it to the family of Joseph, the now believing 'brethren of the Lord'? Why should it not have passed from their hands to the evangelist of the first Gospel, and have been worked over by him in view of his predominant interest—that of calling attention to fulfilments of prophecies? This theory of the origin of the first two chapters of St. Matthew's Gospel at once accounts for the phenomena they present and vindicates, in substance, their historical character. That the narrative did pass through the hands of our Lord's family is more than likely, for Julius Africanus, a Christian writer of the beginning of the third century, who lived at Emmaus, informs us, and probably rightly, that it is to the relations of our Lord (οἱ δεσπόσυνοι καλούμενοι) that we owe the attempts to construct genealogies of Christ [1].

Is there then anything internal to the narrative prohibiting such a view? It is a certain historical fact that Herod was, from circumstances and disposition, acutely jealous of any royal claim which might imperil his own position and that of his family [2]. It is certain that his

[1] In Euseb. *H E.* 1 7. Cf Renan, *Évang* pp 60, 61, 186 'Le tour de la généalogie de Matthieu est hébraique, les transcriptions des noms propres ne sont pas celles des Septante (Boés, et non Booζ). Nous avons vu d'ailleurs que les généalogies furent probablement l'œuvre des parents de Jésus, retirés en Batanée et parlant hébreu.'

[2] See Joseph *Bell. Jud.* 1. 30 4 ἐπτόητο τῷ φόβῳ καὶ πρὸς πᾶσαν ὑπόνοιαν ἐξερριπτέζετο. *Ant* xvii 2. 7 [the Pharisees] προὔλεγον ὡς Ἡρώδη μὲν καταπαύσεως ἀρχῆς ὑπὸ θεοῦ ἐψηφισμένης αὐτῷ τε καὶ γένει τῷ ἀπ' αὐτοῦ τῆς τε βασιλείας εἰς τε ἐκείνην [Pheroras' wife] περιηξούσης καὶ Φερώραν, παῖδάς τε οἳ εἶεν αὐτοῖς .. καὶ ὁ βασιλεὺς τῶν τε Φαρισαίων τοὺς αἰτιωτάτους ἀναιρεῖ καὶ Βαγώαν τὸν εὐνοῦχον, κ.τ.λ. κτείνει δὲ καὶ πᾶν ὅτι τοῦ οἰκείου συνειστήκει οἷς ὁ Φαρισαῖος ἔλεγεν. This incident was shortly before Herod's death 'The momentary glimpses which we gain of him in the New Testament,' says the late Dean Stanley, 'through the story of his conversation with the

last days were, as Josephus records, marked by wild ferocity and brutality. Josephus' story of his shutting up in the hippodrome the élite of the nation and taking measures to cause them to be murdered directly after his own death, in order that it might not be unaccompanied with mourning[1], may be a slander, but at least illustrates the impression he left of his character in his last days. Thus the history of the massacre of the few babes of Bethlehem and its district is wholly consistent with the man and the occasion. There is no one who could corroborate the evangelist except Josephus, and the silence of Josephus about all that concerns Christianity is so nearly complete[2] that it can hardly be otherwise than intentional. Christianity was an object of hatred and suspicion to the masters of the world, when Josephus was writing[3], and he may well have wished to say as little about it as possible in a work expressly intended to conciliate Gentile readers.

Herod's 'massacre of innocents' is thus an exceedingly credible and natural incident. As to the visit of the Magi—which (we may notice) is introduced into the narrative chiefly as accounting for the threatened

---

Magi and his slaughter of the children of Bethlehem, are quite in keeping with the jealous, irritable, unscrupulous temper of the last " days of Herod the king," as we read them in the pages of Josephus' (*Hist of Jewish Church*, III p 380).

[1] Joseph *Ant.* xvii. 6 5. He describes the king as ' rabid with guilty and innocent alike ', or (c 8 1) ' fierce to all alike, the slave of passion.'

[2] I am assuming that the famous passage (*Ant* xviii. 4 3) about Jesus Christ is at least greatly interpolated

[3] The *Antiquities* was finished about A. D 94, in Domitian's reign On Domitian as a persecutor, see Ramsay, *The Church and the Roman Empire* (Hodder & Stoughton, 1893) p. 259. Josephus would be anxious to dissociate his race from the Christians.

The Virgin Birth of our Lord.

massacre, and consequent flight of Joseph and Mary into Egypt—it has its basis at least in what is natural and well known. The diffusion of Jews in the remoter East, the wide spread of the Jewish Messianic hope[1], the attraction of all sorts of men towards Jewish synagogues—all this makes it not improbable to those who believe in a divine providence that some oriental astrologers should have had their thoughts directed towards Jerusalem, and should have paid a visit there, under the attraction of some celestial phenomenon, to seek a heaven-sent king. It is not improbable because God works upon men by His inspirations through their natural tendencies and occupations[2]—the supernatural, in this as in other cases, operating through the natural.

It was said above that the narrative of Joseph had been worked over by the evangelist in his predominant interest in the fulfilment of prophecy. It is of course maintained that this is less than the truth, and that the prophecies have in fact created the supposed events. so

---

[1] Suetonius' words are well known and often quoted (*Vespas* 4) ' Percrebruerat *oriente toto* vetus et constans opinio, esse in fatis ut eo tempore Iudaea profecti rerum potirentur. Id de imperatore Romano, quantum postea eventu patuit, praedictum Iudaei ad se trahentes rebellarunt.' But it is doubtful whether he has any source of information other than similar passages in Joseph *Bell Jud* vi 5 4 and Tac *Hist* v 13, which attribute such expectations only to the *Jews* (Josephus, the Jew, originated the idea that the prophecy really referred to 'the government of Vespasian'). However, the universal diffusion of the Jews meant the universal diffusion of the Jewish expectations amongst themselves and their more or less attached proselytes.

[2] See St Chrysostom's excellent commentary on the event. God influences men through their national customs and ideas. As the whole Jewish ritual system was only an instance of national Semitic rites taken as they were and made the vehicle of divine leading so now God led the Magi through their astrology. διὰ τῶν συνήθων αὐτοὺς καλεῖ σφόδρα συγκαταβαίνων, κ.τ.λ. (on St. Matt vi 3).

that in particular the Virgin Birth at Bethlehem is a mere reflection of the prophecies of Micah and Isaiah, as represented in the Septuagint version, and that the visit of the Magi with the events following from it is a merely imaginative construction out of materials supplied by the anticipations and incidents of the Old Testament

It must be observed at starting that what we are asked to admit is more than the unconscious modification of some detail of history by adjustment to the language of prophecy. It is quite possible that the introduction of the 'ass' beside the 'colt' in Matt. xxi. 2, the specification of 'thirty pieces of silver' in Matt. xxvi. 15 (cf. xxvii. 3-10), the mingling of 'gall' with wine in Matt. xxvii. 34—details where St. Matthew is unsupported by the other evangelists, may be modifications due to the influence of the language of Zechariah and the Psalmist respectively. But in all these cases the historical event stands substantially the same when the modification is removed. Christ rode into Jerusalem upon the foal, and was betrayed for a sum of money, and was given a drink of wine mingled with myrrh before His crucifixion. In the cases to be discussed in these two chapters the prophecies, if they had any effect on the supposed event, created them altogether. Jesus was in effect born naturally and at Nazareth: there was no visit of Magi or massacre of innocents or flight into Egypt.

Now in general the argument from the influence of prophecy is weakened in proportion as the prophecies in question are such as would not to the pious

The Virgin Birth of our Lord. 33

imagination of a Jew have required fulfilments such as are found for them : in other words, the argument is weakened in proportion as the application of the prophecy is not such as would have suggested itself prior to the event Now there are five prophecies of which the fulfilment is discovered in these two chapters. Of these the last[1], 'He shall be called a Nazarene,' finds its fulfilment in an undoubted event, but as a prophecy cannot be identified with any passage in the Old Testament. The fourth[2] is a passage from Jer xxxi. 15 which describes Rachel, as the mother of Israel, weeping for her children, carried away into captivity to Babylon. It is an historical passage; and while the association of Rachel with Bethlehem, her burial-place[3], naturally suggested its application to the 'massacre of the innocents' —Rachel again weeping over her children—it could hardly by any possibility have *suggested* this latter event. The third[4] is again an historical passage from Hosea xi. 1: 'When Israel was a child then I loved him, and *called my son out of Egypt.* As they called them, so *they* went from them . they sacrificed unto Baalim,' &c. The identification of the Christ with the true Israel no doubt would suggest the *appropriateness* of Christ, like Israel, being delivered from Egypt, when once the event had occurred or when a narrative of it was before the evangelist. But the historical passage cannot in this case either be conceived to have produced the event. Critics are at liberty to say that the evangelist's method of interpreting prophecy is unconvincing. They cannot say he forced the event to the prophecy.

[1] ii 23   [2] ii 17, 18.   [3] Gen. xxxv 15   [4] ii. 15.

On the other hand, there was a prophecy, or set of prophecies, which might have suggested the episode of the Magi, but if it had suggested it, would have suggested it in a different shape. There was a prophecy[1] that 'Gentiles should come to Israel's light, and *kings* to the brightness of his rising,' and another[2] that 'the *kings* of Tarshish and of the isles should bring presents: the *kings* of Sheba and Seba should offer gifts' These prophecies, working in the imagination of later Christendom, did in fact transmute the visit of the Magi into the visit of the three kings. But they could not have produced the event as St Matthew records it, and St. Matthew neither modifies the event to suit them nor refers to the prophecies at all[3].

Such considerations as these must be with us in approaching the first two of the five 'fulfilments' pointed out by St Matthew in these chapters. The second refers us back to a real prophecy of Bethlehem as destined to the glory of producing the heaven-sent ruler of Israel[4]. 'But thou, Bethlehem Ephrathah, which art little to be among the thousands of Judah, out of thee shall one come forth unto me that is to be ruler in Israel.' It does not appear to have originally meant more than that the Messianic king should come of David's line, and so indirectly of David's city. But it

---

[1] Is lx 3   [2] Ps lxxii 10

[3] It should be noticed, as bearing on the date of St Matthew's narrative, that the story of the star, as it appears in Ignatius (c A D 110), *Eph* 19, already shows the influence of mythical exaggeration. It shone astonishingly above all the stars, and the sun and moon and heavenly bodies were attendant upon it Here the accretion manifestly reflects the story of Joseph's dream in Gen xxxvii.

[4] Micah v. 2.

The Virgin Birth of our Lord.

did suggest to the Jews, and apparently before our Lord's time [1], that the Christ was to be himself born at Bethlehem. Did then the prophecy, thus interpreted, produce the event, and was Jesus really born, as Strauss, Renan, Keim, and others affirm, at Nazareth? The suggestion can only be entertained by those who on other grounds have arrived at a low estimate of the historical trustworthiness of the evangelist altogether. The entirely independent narratives of the first and third Gospels agree in placing the birth at Bethlehem, and in St. Luke's gospel this is not connected at all with prophecy. The same argument applies to the first prophecy [2] referred to by St. Matthew (Is. vii 14). As rendered in the lxx version the prophecy ran, 'Behold, the virgin shall conceive,' &c. It does not appear that the Hebrew word need necessarily mean more than 'young woman [3]'. nor does it appear that there was any Jewish expectation that the Christ should be born of a virgin [4]. Did, then, the text as rendered in the Greek suggest the idea? It is impossible to think this if these early narratives are anything better than imaginary productions at all. For again St Luke's and St. Matthew's independent accounts are at one on this point, and if any information from Joseph and Mary underlies them, this is the point on which their information must have centred, and if St Matthew's interest is absorbed in prophecy,

---

[1] See Edersheim, *l c* 1 206, Geikie, *Life and Words of Christ* (Strahan, 1878), 1 148 Cf St John vii 42

[2] St Matt 1. 23

[3] See, among recent Roman Catholic scholars, the Abbé Loisy, *L'Enseignement Biblique* (Paris, 44 Rue d'Assas, 1893), n° 11, p 54

[4] See appended note A.

St. Luke makes no mention of it. Moreover, it may be said generally that the study of the *origines* of the Church will convince any candid student that the truth is rather that the actual events taught the first Christians to read prophecy afresh, than that prophecy induced them to imagine events—at any rate, important events—which did not occur[1].

On the whole, then, (1) the character of St. Matthew's applications of prophecy in these chapters, (2) the fact that he does not modify the account of the Magi to suit obviously applicable prophecies, (3) the agreement with St. Matthew of St Luke, who is without any special interest in prophecy, prevent us from imagining that the Virgin Birth of Jesus at Bethlehem was a romantic and unhistorical idea suggested by the forecasts of the Old Testament. An exact examination of the prophecies and their fulfilment may tend to weaken a certain form of the argument from prophecy, but not the historical truth of the evangelic narrative.

§ 4.

The relation of the two narratives.

What then is the relation of the two narratives? They are indeed obviously independent, but are they incompatible? The present writer is disposed to reply that they are indeed incompatible in certain details as they stand, but that the incompatible elements are

[1] Cf Lightfoot's *Biblical Essays*, p 193

The Virgin Birth of our Lord. 37

explicable quite easily by the use which the evangelists made of the earlier documents upon which they relied.

Thus St. Matthew is apparently ignorant that Joseph and Mary had been at Nazareth before the occasion of their going there from Egypt[1] This is simply explained by the previous residence there not having been alluded to in the document which he used, as it was in that used by St. Luke. On the other hand, St Luke is probably ignorant of the flight into Egypt and supposes that Mary and Joseph returned to Nazareth from Jerusalem immediately after the Presentation[2]. The flight into Egypt was not in his document, and he let the narrative run on as a compiler would who was ignorant of its having occurred[3]. Granted these two points, the narratives are quite compatible with one another—St. Luke i; St. Matt. i. 18–25ᵃ; St. Luke ii. 1–21 [St. Matt i. 25ᵇ]; St. Luke ii. 22–38; St. Matt. ii [St. Luke ii. 39]; St. Luke ii. 40–52, forming a more or less continuous series of pictures.

But hitherto we have left out of consideration the genealogies. That two apparently incompatible genealogies should have been left to stand in the Gospels and create difficulties from the second century downwards, is indeed valuable evidence of the independence of our first and third Gospels, and that they were not modified to suit one another after composition. But what is to be said as to their origin? We should judge that St. Matthew's genealogy was attached to the account of the birth

---

[1] St. Matt. ii 23   [2] St Luke ii 39

[3] St. Luke's account of the interval from the resurrection to the ascension in c xxiv, as compared with Acts i, is suggestive of indifference to verbal accuracy in note of time and place

which supplied him with his material. As already mentioned, we believe it to have been, probably, the work of our Lord's relatives. However unknown to us are the fortunes of David's family after the return from the captivity, it appears that the great Hillel, grandfather of Gamaliel, who belonged to a family of Jewish exiles in Babylon and came to Jerusalem about B.C. 50, was recognized as of David's family, and that appeal was made in vindication of his claim to 'a pedigree found in Jerusalem [1]': it is certain also that the claim of Jesus to be of the royal house was acknowledged at the time and by the later Jews [2]. Under these circumstances it appears probable that the relatives of Jesus constructed for him in the early days of the Church a genealogy from the best sources, written or traditional, which were open to them [3]. Jewish ideas of genealogy were largely *putative* it was thought that a man by marrying his deceased brother's wife could raise up seed unto his brother [4]. It is therefore more than likely that it would have

[1] See Delitzsch, *Jesus and Hillel* (Bagster's trans, 1877) p 139 The statement is based on *Bereschith Rabba*, § 98 Cf. Renan's *Évang* p 60, who refers to Talm. de Jér *Kilaim* IX. 3 (Derenbourg, p 349), from which he infers 'La préoccupation de la race de David est assez vive vers l'an 100' Josephus gives us valuable information as to the keeping of the genealogies of the priests in Jerusalem and in their own families (*Vit* I, *con. Apion.* 1. 7).

[2] See (1) Rom 1 3, St Mark XI 10, Rev XXII 16, Hebr VII 14 πρόδηλον ὅτι (2) Euseb *H E* III 20 for Hegesippus' narrative of our Lord's kinsmen being summoned to satisfy Domitian that though of the house of David they made no dangerous pretensions cf. Renan, *Évang* p 61 (3) The proof which Renan gives (*l c*) that from the beginning of the third century the Jews recognized the royal origin of Jesus (Talm. de Bab *Sanhédrin* 43 a cf Derenbourg, p 349, note 2)

[3] Cf Africanus in Euseb *H E* 1 7 14 εἰς ὅσον ἐξικνοῦντο But I do not pause to discuss the details of the narrative of Africanus

[4] St Matt XXII 24

The Virgin Birth of our Lord.

been held that the espousal of Joseph and Mary constituted Jesus Joseph's son for all the purposes of Jewish reckoning [1]. Luke's genealogy, on the other hand, if we judge from the place where it occurs, appears not to have been attached to the document of the birth [2]. We can make no guess as to its origin. We do not venture to commit ourselves to any existing attempt to conciliate it with St. Matthew's. We only emphasize the fact that the Davidic origin of Jesus was acknowledged, that His family and disciples made honest and independent attempts to draw up the record of His genealogy, and that putative ideas of descent are probably at least in part responsible for the divergence in their results. If indeed it were the fact, as Godet and other modern writers affirm, that in the Talmud Mary is spoken of as the daughter of Heli, it would be natural to identify this Heli with the person who is mentioned as the father of Joseph in St. Luke's genealogy; and to suppose that this genealogy was intended by its unknown compiler as the genealogy of Mary, though it was apparently misunderstood by St. Luke to be the genealogy of Joseph. But in fact the statement, which is originally derived from Lightfoot, is based on a quite untenable translation [2].

---

[1] It is not, I think, possible to argue from the fact that genealogies are traced through Joseph against the original belief in the virgin birth, when these genealogies are in immediate connexion with the account of the virgin birth If the Evangelists who put them there did not think they were incompatible with the virgin birth, it cannot be argued that their original compilers did Cf Loisy, *l c* p 50 '[Les évangélistes] ont évidemment pensé que Joseph avait transmis à Jésus le droit davidique, par cela seul qu'il avait tenu à l'égard de Jésus le rôle de père Ils ont cru qu'une filiation légale et interprétative suffisait pour l'accomplissement des prophéties'

[2] See *Horae Hebraicae* (Oxford, 1859) iii. p 55 The phrase in *Hieros*.

To go on answering objections made to the historical trustworthiness of documents is apt to give an appearance of weakness. People complain, 'There is so much that needs answering. Can a document which gives rise to so many objections be really true?' We return therefore in conclusion to our positive position. The belief in the general trustworthiness of the evangelical records, and in particular the belief in the trustworthy use which St. Luke makes of the documents at his disposal, is well established by the facts. The particular documents of the infancy bear upon them unmistakeable traces—while at the same time undesigned traces—of coming ultimately from Joseph and Mary: the objections made against their historical truth do not really stand, or at least do not stand to any extent which affects the substantial truth of the narrative. in particular the idea that prophecies of the Old Testament created the story that Jesus was born at Bethlehem and born of a virgin will not hold in the light of the use which St. Matthew on the whole makes of prophecy in his first two chapters, nor in the light of the independent testimony which St. Luke affords to these events without exhibiting any interest in prophecy. We conclude then that in all essential features we are justified in taking these narratives for real history.

Chagig fol 77, col 4, is as follows, וחמא מרים ברת עלי בצלים Lightfoot renders *He saw Miriam the daughter of Heli among the shades* (עלי בצלים) But I am assured that the only legitimate translation is *He saw Miriam the daughter of 'Onion-Leaves'* (עֲלֵי בְצָלִים—a nickname of a kind not uncommon in the Talmud), and there is no reason to suppose any reference to our Lord's mother

§ 5.

The tradition of the churches.

Wherever the first and third Gospels were accepted and read in the Christian assemblies, there the Virgin Birth of Jesus would become an accepted fact, like any other incident in the Gospel history. Now the traces of the use of these Gospels go back to the beginning of the second century. We should expect, therefore, that, so far as the literature affords indications, we should find the churches of the second century believing in the Virgin Birth. But something more than this is the case. The earliest churches, in their conflict with the different heresies to which the restless spirit of those days gave rise, make much appeal to *tradition*. The Church has not only documents but oral tradition. This tradition was stereotyped in the varying, but substantially similar, baptismal creeds of east and west. But before it was so stereotyped it was assuming gradually a fixed form. It was the summary of that 'truth' of which the Church was to be the 'pillar and ground [1].' One main function assigned to the apostolic succession of the ministry was that of giving perpetuity to this tradition and preserving it from corruption [2]. It was imparted as rudimentary instruction to every catechumen. Such a 'tradition' is presupposed as imparted and assimilated in every part

---
[1] 1 Tim iii 15.
[2] See Irenaeus, *con Haer* iii 3-4, iv 26 2, Tertullian, *de Praescr.* 32, 36, Hegesippus, ap Eus. *H E* iv. 22

of the New Testament¹. In different books different elements of it are noticed or implied, such as (1) the threefold Name, (2) the chief historical incidents of our Lord's life, (3) instruction in moral duties and in the 'last things,' (4) teaching about the sacraments². Now it is not perhaps too much to argue from St. Luke's preface to his Gospel that the Virgin Birth of Jesus was already part of that oral instruction which had been imparted to Theophilus and to complete which he only needed more secure information³. In any case, what I am now concerned to show is that in the creed-like formulas of the churches the statement of the Virgin Birth had its place from so early a date and along so many different lines of ascent as to force upon us the conclusion that already before the death of the last apostles the Virgin Birth of Christ must have been among the rudiments of the faith in which every Christian was initiated⁴.

[1] See St. Luke 1 4 περὶ ὧν κατηχήθης λόγων Acts 11 42 τῇ διδαχῇ τῶν ἀποστόλων Rom vi 17 εἰς ὃν παρεδόθητε τύπον διδαχῆς 1 Cor xi. 23, xv 1-3 Gal. 1 8, 9 2 Thess iii. 6 ἡ παράδοσις Hebr v. 12 τὰ στοιχεῖα 2 Tim 1 13 ὑποτύπωσιν ὑγιαινόντων λόγων Jude 3 τῇ ἅπαξ παραδοθείσῃ τοῖς ἁγίοις πίστει 2 Pet 1 12 1 John ii 20

[2] See (1) St Matt. xxviii 19, cf Didache, 7 (baptism into 'the Name' implies teaching about it, which is also implied in all that familiarity with the idea of the Father, of the Son, and of the Holy Ghost, which the New Testament takes for granted); (2) Luke 1 1-4, 1 Cor xi 23, xv 3-4, (3) Hebr vi 1-2, 1 Thess iv 1-2, v 2, (4) Hebr vi. 1-6, Rom vi 3, 1 Cor x 15-16, xi 23 ff, cf. Acts ii. 38

[3] St Luke 1 4 'that thou mightest know the certainty concerning the things in which thou wast orally instructed'

[4] It is important to distinguish variations in the words of creeds from variations in the substance of tradition Thus, for example, the creed of the church of Caesarea, as it was presented in the Council of Nicaea (see Socrates, H E 1 8, and Heurtley, de Fide et Symbolo, p 4), and the actual creed of Nicaea itself, state the fact of the Incarnation, but make no specific mention of the *virgin birth*, through which the Incarnation took place πιστεύομεν εἰς ἕνα Κύριον Ἰησοῦν Χριστόν, τὸν Υἱὸν τοῦ Θεοῦ, . . τὸν δι' ἡμᾶς

The Virgin Birth of our Lord. 43

Thus (1) Irenaeus, writing, as he tells us, while Eleutherus was bishop of Rome, i.e. not later than A.D. 190, assures us of the place the Virgin Birth held in the traditions of the whole Church

'The Church,' he says, 'though scattered over the whole world to the ends of the earth, yet having received from the apostles and their disciples the faith

in one God the Father Almighty . . .

and in one Christ Jesus, the Son of God, who was incarnate for our salvation·

and in the Holy Ghost, who by the prophets announced His dispensations and His comings:

and the birth of the Virgin, and the passion, and resurrection from the dead, and the bodily assumption into heaven of the beloved Jesus Christ our Lord, and His appearance from heaven in the glory of the Father . . .

having received, as we said, this preaching and this faith, the Church, though scattered over the whole world, guards it diligently, as inhabiting one house, and believes in accordance with these words as having one soul and the same heart, and with one voice preaches and teaches and hands on these things, as if possessing one mouth For the languages of the world are unlike, but the force of the tradition is [everywhere] one and the same [1].'

τοὺς ἀνθρώπους καὶ διὰ τὴν ἡμετέραν σωτηρίαν κατελθόντα καὶ σαρκωθέντα, ἐνανθρωπήσαντα, παθόντα, κ τ λ This however does not mean any lack of importance attached to the virgin birth Eusebius, the bishop of the church of Caesarea, shows us in his writings that the virgin birth was supposed to be *involved in* any statement of the Incarnation. Thus in *contra Marcellum de Eccl Theol*, after much discussion of the Incarnation in II 1 (Gaisford, p 199), the virgin birth is incidentally mentioned—II 4 (p 205) ὁ ἐν τῇ ἁγίᾳ παρθένῳ γενόμενος, καὶ σαρκωθεὶς καὶ ἐνανθρωπήσας καὶ παθών

[1] *con Haer* 1. 10 1 ἡ μὲν γὰρ ἐκκλησία, καίπερ καθ' ὅλης τῆς οἰκουμένης ἕως περάτων τῆς γῆς διεσπαρμένη, παρὰ δὲ τῶν ἀποστόλων καὶ τῶν ἐκείνων

So he proceeds to specify as agreeing in this faith the churches of Germany, Spain, Gaul, the East, Egypt, Libya, and Italy[1]. In the creed of Tertullian, who represents Rome and Carthage, a little later than Irenaeus, the Virgin Birth holds the same secure and prominent place. 'The rule of faith,' he says, ' is altogether one, single, unalterable; the rule that is of believing in one God Almighty, the maker of the world, and His Son Jesus Christ, born of the Virgin Mary crucified under Pontius Pilate, &c[2]'

The summary of faith which Irenaeus gave belongs, he says, to all the churches, and is preserved by the episcopal successions everywhere. But he lays special stress upon the representative witness of two churches: upon that of the Church of Rome, in which he enumerates the succession of bishops from the time of the foundation of the episcopate by Peter and Paul; and upon that of the Church of Polycarp, Smyrna, with the other churches of Asia For before Irenaeus came to Rome he had been brought up in Asia as the pupil of Polycarp,

μαθητῶν παραλαβοῦσα τὴν εἰς ἕνα θεὸν πατέρα παντοκράτορα πίστιν καὶ εἰς ἕνα Χριστὸν Ἰησοῦν, τὸν υἱὸν τοῦ θεοῦ, τὸν σαρκωθέντα ὑπὲρ τῆς ἡμετέρας σωτηρίας καὶ εἰς πνεῦμα ἅγιον, τὸ διὰ τῶν προφητῶν κεκηρυχὸς τὰς οἰκονομίας. καὶ τὰς ἐλεύσεις, καὶ τὴν ἐκ παρθένου γέννησιν, καὶ τὸ πάθος, καὶ τὴν ἔγερσιν ἐκ νεκρῶν, καὶ τὴν ἔνσαρκον εἰς τοὺς οὐρανοὺς ἀνάληψιν τοῦ ἠγαπημένου Χριστοῦ Ἰησοῦ τοῦ κυρίου ἡμῶν, καὶ τὴν ἐκ τῶν οὐρανῶν ἐν τῇ δόξῃ τοῦ πατρὸς παρουσίαν αὐτοῦ τοῦτο τὸ κήρυγμα παρειληφυῖα καὶ ταύτην τὴν πίστιν, ὡς προέφαμεν, ἡ ἐκκλησία, καίπερ ἐν ὅλῳ τῷ κόσμῳ διεσπαρμένη, ἐπιμελῶς φυλάσσει, ὡς ἕνα οἶκον οἰκοῦσα καὶ ὁμοίως πιστεύει τούτοις, ὡς μίαν ψυχὴν καὶ τὴν αὐτὴν ἔχουσα καρδίαν, καὶ συμφώνως ταῦτα κηρύσσει καὶ διδάσκει καὶ παραδίδωσιν, ὡς ἓν στόμα κεκτημένη καὶ γὰρ αἱ κατὰ τὸν κόσμον διάλεκτοι ἀνόμοιοι, ἀλλὰ ἡ δύναμις τῆς παραδόσεως μία καὶ ἡ αὐτή

[1] *con Haer* 1 10. 2 Cf. III. 4. 2, where this is repeated in substance, and the virgin birth still appears among the rudiments In IV 33. 7, a shorter form is given, where only the Incarnation is actually specified

[2] See *de Virg. Veland* 1 (written about A D 210).

The Virgin Birth of our Lord. 45

who had himself belonged to the circle of the last of the apostles. So that his testimony has value both for the range which it covers and for the source out of which it springs. We have evidence however of the truth of what he says from earlier witnesses.

(2) Justin Martyr passed before Bar-cochba's revolt (A. D. 132–6) from his Samaritan home in Palestine to Ephesus, and from Ephesus to Rome His summaries of Christian belief, which he gives in his *Apologies* (c. 150) and *Dialogue*, have sometimes a creed-like ring: and in these creed-like summaries the Virgin Birth holds the same conspicuous place as in those of Irenaeus 'For in the name of this very person,' he says to Trypho the Jew, 'the Son of God, and first begotten of all creation, and born of a virgin and made passible man, and crucified under Pontius Pilate by your people, and dead, and risen from the dead, and ascended into heaven, every demon when exorcised is conquered and subdued [1].'

---

[1] *Dial* 85 κατὰ γὰρ τοῦ ὀνόματος αὐτοῦ τούτου τοῦ υἱοῦ τοῦ θεοῦ καὶ πρωτοτόκου πάσης κτίσεως, καὶ διὰ παρθένου γεννηθέντος καὶ παθητοῦ γενομένου ἀνθρώπου, καὶ σταυρωθέντος ἐπὶ Ποντίου Πιλάτου ὑπὸ τοῦ λαοῦ ὑμῶν καὶ ἀποθανόντος, καὶ ἀναστάντος ἐκ νεκρῶν καὶ ἀναβάντος εἰς τὸν οὐρανόν, πᾶν δαιμόνιον ἐξορκιζόμενον νικᾶται καὶ ὑποτάσσεται Here we have, no doubt, a reflection of the *formula of exorcism*, cf Origen *c Cels* 1 6 οὐ γὰρ κατακλήσεσιν ἰσχύειν δοκοῦσιν ἀλλὰ τῷ ὀνόματι Ἰησοῦ μετὰ τῆς ἀπαγγελίας τῶν περὶ αὐτὸν ἱστοριῶν But the formula of exorcism is not likely to differ in the facts recited from the creed of baptism Other summaries in Justin are *Apol* 46 διὰ παρθένου ἄνθρωπος ἀπεκυήθη καὶ Ἰησοῦς ἐπωνομάσθη καὶ σταυρωθεὶς ἀποθανὼν ἀνέστη καὶ ἀνελήλυθεν εἰς οὐρανόν *Apol* 31 γεννώμενον διὰ παρθένου καὶ ἀνδρούμενον καὶ θεραπεύοντα πᾶσαν νόσον καὶ φθονούμενον καὶ ἀγνοούμενον καὶ σταυρούμενον . . καὶ ἀποθνήσκοντα καὶ ἀναγειρόμενον καὶ εἰς οὐρανοὺς ἀνερχόμενον (this is a summary of the prophecies about Christ) In all the above quotations virgin birth, incarnation, crucifixion, death, resurrection, ascension, are the chief points of belief about Christ.

(3) Still earlier, Ignatius, who must have become bishop in Antioch by the very beginning of the second century, as he passes through the churches of Asia on his way to his martyrdom, about A D. 110, gives the same witness as Justin. 'The virginity of Mary and her childbearing and in like manner the death of the Lord,' that is, the atoning value of the death, are 'three mysteries of loud proclamation which were wrought in the silence of God.' That is to say, hidden as were the original transactions, they have become part of the loudly proclaimed message of the Church[1].

(4) The Christian philosopher Aristides of Athens is not so widely representative a man as those hitherto mentioned, but he and Quadratus are the earliest Christian apologists. And in his recently recovered *Apology*[2] the Virgin Birth is mentioned, and in such a manner as to

[1] Ign *Eph* 19 ἡ παρθενία Μαρίας καὶ ὁ τοκετὸς αὐτῆς, ὁμοίως καὶ ὁ θάνατος τοῦ κυρίου τρία μυστήρια κραυγῆς ἅτινα ἐν ἡσυχίᾳ θεοῦ ἐπράχθη cf cc 7, 18 *Smyrn* 1 γεγεννημένον ἀληθῶς ἐκ παρθένου, βεβαπτισμένον ὑπὸ Ἰωάννου ἀληθῶς ἐπὶ Ποντίου Πιλάτου καὶ Ἡρώδου τετράρχου καθηλωμένον ὑπὲρ ἡμῶν ἐν σαρκί .. ἵνα διὰ τῆς ἀναστάσεως, κτλ *Trall* 9 Ἰησοῦ Χριστοῦ τοῦ ἐκ γένους Δαυείδ, τοῦ ἐκ Μαρίας, ὃς ἀληθῶς ἐγεννήθη, ἔφαγέν τε καὶ ἔπιεν, ἀληθῶς ἐδιώχθη ἐπὶ Ποντίου Πιλάτου, ἀληθῶς ἐσταυρώθη καὶ ἀπέθανεν .. ἀληθῶς ἠγέρθη The birth of Mary and the passion and the resurrection are already in Ignatius the chief *moments* of the incarnate life.

[2] The date is c. 126, or perhaps 140 See *Texts and Studies* (Cambridge, 1891) vol 1 no 1, pp 6 ff. The editor of the *Apology*, Mr Rendel Harris, says (p. 25) 'Everything that we know of the dogmatics of the early part of the second century agrees with the belief that at that period the virginity of Mary was a part of the formulated Christian belief We restore the fragments of Aristides' creed, then, as follows —

We believe in one God, Almighty,	He was pierced by the Jews:
Maker of heaven and earth ·	He died and was buried ·
And in Jesus Christ His Son,	The third day He rose again .
. . . .	He ascended into heaven,
Born of the Virgin Mary ·	
. . . .	He is about to come to judge'

The Virgin Birth of our Lord.

suggest that it had a place in the creed of the Church of his day. 'The Christians,' he says. 'reckon the beginning of their religion from Jesus Christ, who is named the Son of God Most High . and it is said that God came down from heaven, and from a Hebrew virgin took and clad Himself with flesh . . . He was pierced by the Jews, and He died and was buried; and they say that after three days He rose and ascended to heaven.'

(5) The Church of Alexandria has distinctive characteristics and a more or less separate history. It is therefore important to notice that in respect of the emphatic belief in the Virgin Birth it did not differ from other churches. When Origen (c A.D. 230) states in summary 'the teaching of the Church which has been handed down from the apostles in the order of succession and continues in the churches to the present time,' he specifies that Jesus Christ 'was born of a virgin and of the Holy Spirit, that He was truly born, did truly suffer and truly die, did truly rise from the dead and after His resurrection was taken up ' · and when arguing with Celsus the Platonist, he exclaims 'Who has not heard of Jesus' virgin birth, of the crucified, of His resurrection, of which so many are convinced, and the announcement of judgement to come?[1]' So the earlier Clement (c. 190–200) describes 'the whole dispensation' thus: 'When one says that the Son of God who made the universe took flesh and was conceived in the womb of a virgin . . . and suffered and rose again[2].'

(6) Besides the testimonies to the place the Virgin

---

[1] *de Princip.* pref quoted below, p 108, and *con. Cels* 1. 7.
[2] Clem. *Strom.* vi 15 127.

Birth held in the creeds which were taking shape in the second century, we may mention that it is referred to in the *Testament of the Twelve Patriarchs*[1]. and that if, as Origen tells us, the *Gospel of Peter* affirmed that 'the brethren of the Lord' were the sons of Joseph by a former wife, that docetic production of the early part of the second century recognized not only the virginity, but the perpetual virginity, of Mary[2].

We have evidence then that the Virgin Birth held a prominent place in the second-century tradition or creed of the churches of Rome[3], Greece[4], Africa[5], Asia[6], Syria and Palestine[7], Alexandria[8]. Such a consensus in the second century, reaching back to its beginning,

---

[1] *Test Joseph* 19 ἐκ τοῦ Ἰούδα ἐγεννήθη παρθένος καὶ ἐξ αὐτῆς προῆλθεν ἀμνὸς ἄμωμος. These *Testaments* have been commonly quoted as the work of a 'Nazarene' Jewish Christian written in the earlier part of the second century, probably before Bar-cochba's revolt (A D. 132). But Mr Conybeare has discovered an Armenian ms. in which some of the manifestly Christian allusions disappear. See *Jewish Quarterly Review*, April 1893, p. 375 The particular passage cited above appears in a longer but less plainly Christian form, p. 390. This and other evidence makes for the theory that it was originally a purely Jewish work gradually interpolated with Christian passages see Dr. Kohler, *l c* p 401 (If we cannot however quote this work as evidence for Jewish Christian belief, we can get behind it: for the documents of the birth in Matthew and Luke unmistakeably came from *Jewish* circles)

[2] Origen, *in Matt* x 17 τοὺς δὲ ἀδελφοὺς Ἰησοῦ φασί τινες εἶναι, ἐκ παραδόσεως ὁρμώμενοι τοῦ ἐπιγεγραμμένου κατὰ Πέτρον εὐαγγελίου ἢ τῆς βίβλου Ἰακώβου, υἱοὺς Ἰωσὴφ ἐκ προτέρας γυναικὸς συνῳκηκυίας αὐτῷ πρὸ τῆς Μαρίας As is well known, a fragment from the end of the Gospel has recently been discovered For the above argument cf *Ch Quart Rev.* Jan 1893, p 480. Dr. Taylor finds reference to the virgin birth in the *Shepherd* of Hermas . see *Hermas and the Four Gospels* (Cambridge, 1892), pp 29–32

[3] Irenaeus. [4] Aristides. [5] Tertullian
[6] Irenaeus, Justin, and Ignatius.
[7] Ignatius, Justin, documents for first and third Gospels
[8] Clement and Origen

The Virgin Birth of our Lord.

among very independent churches, seems to us, apart from any question of the Gospels, to prove for the belief an apostolic origin. It could not have taken such an undisputed and universal position unless it had really had the countenance of the apostolic founders of churches—of Peter and Paul and John, of James and the Lord's 'brethren.' The argument of Tertullian and Irenaeus from the identity of distinct traditions to their apostolic origin has within certain limits conclusive force.

For there is a *consensus* of traditions. Opponents of the Virgin Birth appear, but it must be admitted that they are innovating upon earlier tradition or retrograding from it, and that they are opponents also of the principle of the Incarnation. There are no believers in the Incarnation discoverable, who are not also believers in the Virgin Birth: while on the other hand, it must be said that the teaching of the Virgin Birth proceeded out of that thoroughly Jewish section of the early Christian Church in which the belief in the Incarnation was not clearly developed out of the belief in Jesus as the Messiah.

(1) The first Christian who is known to have denied the Virgin Birth is Cerinthus, whom a credible tradition makes a contemporary of St John. Among much that is legendary in his story, certain facts emerge as very probably true[1]. He was a Jew, 'trained in the teaching of the Egyptians,' i.e. presumably in Alexandria His teaching in some respects was characteristically Jewish, in particular in its chiliastic eschatology and, apparently, in its insistence upon the permanent obligation of the Jewish ceremonial law, at least in parts. But his

[1] See *Dict of Chr. Biog*, art CERINTHUS.

Judaism was tinged with that oriental horror of the material world which he would have learnt from the great Alexandrian Jew Philo, and which was one main characteristic of the various gnostic sects. The 'gnostic' tendency led him to attribute the creation of the world to a lower power than the Supreme God, and to draw a distinction between Jesus the material man and the 'spiritual' Christ. He declared that Jesus was not born of a virgin but was the son of Joseph and Mary, after the ordinary manner, only as he was pre-eminent beyond all other men in moral excellence, so after his baptism the Christ in the form of a dove descended upon him from the supreme region to enable him to reveal the unknown Father and to work miracles: but finally left him again before the passion, so that the man Jesus suffered and rose again, but the Christ remained spiritual and impassible[1]. This is a doctrine which has remarkable affinity with the sort of gnostic docetism which appears also in the *Gospel of Peter*, though that document is intensely anti-Jewish, and appears to have accepted the Virgin Birth[2]. We need not dwell long upon it. Whatever its importance for the history of the Church, it is wholly alien from

---

[1] Iren *con Haer* 1. 26. 1 'Iesum autem subiecit non ex virgine natum (impossibile enim hoc ei visum est), fuisse autem eum Ioseph et Mariae filium similiter ut reliqui omnes homines, et plus potuisse iustitia et prudentia et sapientia prae omnibus. Et post baptismum descendisse in eum ab ea principalitate, quae est super omnia, Christum figura columbae, et tunc annuntiasse incognitum Patrem et virtutes perfecisse: in fine autem revolasse iterum Christum de Iesu et Iesum passum esse et resurrexisse, Christum autem impassibilem perseverasse, exsistentem spiritualem.'

[2] See toward the beginning of the recovered fragment, *The Gospel according to Peter*, a lecture by J A. Robinson (Camb. 1892) pp. 20 f.

The Virgin Birth of our Lord. 51

the Christianity of James or Peter, Paul or John, Matthew or Luke. To them there is no antagonism, as there is none in the canonical Old Testament, between God and the material world, and no objection, therefore, arising from such an idea to belief in the incarnation and the passion of the Son of God. The separation between the higher impassible person Christ and the lower Jesus is alien to them. Of Cerinthus then it is emphatically true that he does not represent earlier tradition, and that his rejection of the Virgin Birth arises from a rejection of the principle of the Incarnation.

(2) Justin Martyr, in argument with the Jew Trypho, tells him of the existence of a considerable body of Christians (men 'belonging to our race') who denied the Incarnation and the Virgin Birth, but still believed Christ to be the Messiah. They are not the majority, for the majority prefer to be guided by the teaching of the prophets and of Christ. But they exist, and Justin is ready to urge Trypho and other Jews, if they cannot accept the idea of the Incarnation and Virgin Birth, at least to come as far as these persons and to believe that Jesus is the Messiah [1].

The Christians here alluded to are no doubt the

[1] Justin. *Dial. c. Tryph.* 48 οὐκ ἀπόλλυται τὸ τοῦτον εἶναι Χριστὸν τοῦ θεοῦ, ἐὰν ἀποδεῖξαι μὴ δύνωμαι ὅτι καὶ προυπῆρχεν υἱὸς τοῦ ποιητοῦ τῶν ὅλων, θεὸς ὤν, καὶ γεγέννηται ἄνθρωπος διὰ τῆς παρθένου .. καὶ γὰρ εἰσί τινες, ὦ φίλοι, ἔλεγον, ἀπὸ τοῦ ἡμετέρου γένους ὁμολογοῦντες αὐτὸν Χριστὸν εἶναι, ἄνθρωπον δὲ ἐξ ἀνθρώπων γενόμενον ἀποφαινόμενοι οἷς οὐ συντίθεμαι, οὐδ' ἂν πλεῖστοι ταὐτά μοι δοξάσαντες εἴποιεν ἐπειδὴ οὐκ ἀνθρωπείοις διδάγμασι κεκελεύσμεθα ὑπ' αὐτοῦ τοῦ Χριστοῦ πείθεσθαι, ἀλλὰ τοῖς διὰ τῶν μακαρίων προφητῶν κηρυχθεῖσι καὶ δι' αὐτοῦ διδαχθεῖσι. In c. 49 he gives us to understand that these (Ebionite) Christians believed Jesus to have been 'anointed (at His baptism) in accordance with divine selection, and thus to have become Christ.'

'Ebionites,' as they are called by Irenaeus and later writers. Two things are worth notice in this passage of Justin. First that his willingness to call the Ebionites Christians indicates that the line of demarcation between orthodoxy and heresy was not at that time, at least in his Palestinian home, as sharply drawn as it was in the Church at large before the end of the second century[1]. Palestinian Ebionism in fact probably represents a gradual 'reversion to type' or deterioration from the original apostolic standpoint towards pre-Christian Judaism. There was no originator of the heresy such as the 'Ebion' whom the Fathers imagined Secondly, we should notice the rejection of the Virgin Birth coincided in this case, as in that of the Cerinthians, with a rejection of the principle of the Incarnation.

It is of course often maintained that Ebionism—i.e the doctrine that Christ was naturally born and was a mere man to whom the Divine Spirit united Himself at His baptism, anointing Him to be the Christ—is the original Jewish Christianity. To this we reply that there is no Christianity older than the Jewish Christianity of the documents used by St. Luke in the first two chapters of his Gospel and the opening chapters of the Acts. What appears to be the case, to judge from the early history of the Acts, is that all the stress at the beginning of the apostolic preaching was laid on the Messiahship

---

[1] See Stanton, *Jewish and Christian Messiah*, p. 167. I am concerned here only with the older 'Pharisaic Ebionism' The 'Gnostic Ebionism' was a later formation, and, in part at least, admitted the miraculous birth. See Hippolytus, *Philosoph* ix 14; Origen, *c. Cels* v. 61, and cf *Dict. of Chr Biog*, s v EBIONISM. The 'Nazarenes' are also called Ebionites (Orig. *c. Cels*. ii. 1, v. 61), but they admitted the miraculous birth

of Jesus, as vindicated in His resurrection from the dead and His glorification in heaven, whence He should come again to judge the quick and the dead. Many Jews no doubt became Christians confessing simply in this sense that 'Jesus was Lord.' They had no theology of His person of a distinctive sort. It is this sort of Judaism, intensely conservative and tending to reaction, with which St. Paul is confronted. His anti-judaistic epistles are an attempt to persuade its adherents that they must recognize more fully the fresh departure involved in Christianity, or else go backwards and prove false to Christ. In his earlier epistles the point of controversy is not the person of Christ, but the basis of justification. But in 'the epistles of the first captivity' it is the person of Christ which is his starting-point for exhibiting the inadequacy of Judaism. Similarly in the Epistle to the Hebrews we have an apostolic writer striving to lift Judaizing Christians out of an inadequate and reactionary position into a fuller conception of the person of Christ. More and more the decision whether 'Judaizers' would go forward into a full Christianity or slide backward out of the Christian Church turns on their conception of the person of Christ. In the document called the *Didache* we have a specimen of an inadequate, indecisive Jewish Christianity. It has indeed broken with legalism and circumcision—as a result in part of the destruction of Jerusalem and the Temple—but it has got no distinctive Christian theology beyond the barren recitation of the formula of baptism[1]. Out of such inadequate

---

[1] See my *Church and the Ministry* (Longmans), app note L.

Christianity, the Ebionites of Justin's experience had their origin. We have it on the authority of Hegesippus, who certainly was a Catholic Christian [1], that the Church (of Jerusalem and Palestine) 'continued a pure and uncorrupt virgin'—i.e. undefiled by *open* heresy—till the time of the martyrdom of Simeon, at the beginning of the second century [2]. This would naturally mean that about this time there arose the conscious antagonism of Ebionism to Catholic Christianity. Ebionism may thus be regarded as a real inheritor of the inadequate Judaism of St. Paul's day, but it is a falling away from the Christian positions, which were not only held by St. Paul and St. John in his Gospel and Epistles, but belong also to the Apocalypse, to St. Peter's Epistle, and are involved in the language of St. James about Christ. The full Messianic belief as it appears in the early speeches of the Acts was in fact found incompatible with anything short of the doctrine of the Incarnation [4].

[1] See *Dict of Chr. Biog*, s. v.

[2] ap. Eus *H E*. III 32. Hitherto the heretical tendencies had been secret, ἐν ἀδήλῳ που σκοτίως φωλευόντων.

[3] The Apocalypse involves the full belief in the Incarnation see the worship paid to Christ, v 11–14, and compare xix 10, xxii 9, see also i. 8, 17, xxi. 6, xxii 13 St Peter's first Epistle involves the doctrine of the Incarnation, i e the pre-existence of Christ, see i. 11, for His identity with 'the Lord' of the Old Testament, see iii 14 St. James identifies Christ's Lordship with that of God, especially in v. 7–11, 15, and cf ii. 1

[4] Mr Simcox, *Early Church History*, pp 296 f, gives an excellent account of the origin of Ebionism

§ 6.
The theory of legend.

But once more—and for the last time—it is suggested that the miraculous history of the nativity of Jesus Christ, with its accompanying incidents, is to be accounted for by a very general tendency to decorate the cradles of heroes with legendary stories, and especially with anticipations of future greatness   Thus of our Lord's human contemporary Augustus (B C. 63-A. D. 14) it is recorded by Suetonius[1] (c. A D 120) on the authority of Julius Marathus, the Emperor's freedman, that a few months before he was born a prodigy at Rome was publicly recognized as intimating that 'nature was producing a king for the Roman people'; that the Senate in a panic decreed that no child of that year should be brought up, but that those among the senators who had wives with child took care that the decree should not be published   Further he relates, on the authority of the *Theologumena* of Asclepiades of Mende, that Atia, whose second child was Augustus, had been visited, while she was sleeping with other matrons in the temple of Apollo, by a serpent which had left his mark on her person, from which it was concluded that Apollo, in the guise of the serpent, had been the father of Augustus.

---
[1] Suet *Aug.* c 94   Renan (*Évang.* p 194) thinks this story in part accounts for the narrative of the massacre of the innocents   see also Estlin Carpenter, *Synoptic Gospels*, [Unitarian] Sunday School Association, 1890, p 154   On Mr. Conybeare's restatement of the legend theory see app note A.

Again, the earlier narrative of the Buddha [1] relates how 'the knowledge of his birth was made known by rejoicing deities to a hermit named Asita, who thereon repaired to Suddhodana's palace, saw the child in his glory surrounded by deities, &c., and announced to the Sakyans that the child was to be a Buddha [2].'

This story of the Buddha was possibly, and those of Augustus were certainly, current in the generation which followed the death of the persons to whom they relate. And it is not at all disputed that legends might have gathered rapidly around the infancy of Jesus Christ. Nay, more : it is a fact that such legends did actually gather round both His infancy and that of His mother. The apocryphal gospels narrate the details of the infancy of Mary, and they tell also how, when Mary was to bring forth her child, Joseph went out to fetch a midwife and saw the birds stopping in mid-air and every living thing struck motionless, how after the flight into Egypt the idols of Egypt recognized the child as the true God; how His swaddling-clothes worked miracles; how He made clay birds to fly, turned boys into kids, taught His teachers, disputed on astronomy and metaphysics, and worked all manner of miracles. These stories are exactly of the same literary quality as the legends of Augustus and the Buddha, though it would seem as if the higher temper of the Church restrained for

---

[1] Referred to in this connexion by Estlin Carpenter (*l c*) as analogous to St Luke ii 25 ff

[2] Copleston, *Buddhism* (Longmans, 1892) p. 34 Of the visit of Asita, Copleston says (p 36) It 'is not mentioned by Prof Oldenberg among the points contained in the oldest tradition, but whatever be the date of the Sutta which contains it, it certainly belongs to the older cycle of traditions'

a while the action of the vulgar imagination. But there is all the difference in the world between these silly tales and the narrative of the canonical Gospels with its marked reserves and spaces of silence. In the narrative of St. Luke the holy Child in the temple is only represented as impressing the doctors with the intelligence of a perfect boy, not with a vulgar and miraculous omniscience.

The fact that there exists a tendency to decorate with legend the infancy of heroes can in itself be no argument against our having a real history of certain rare events attendant upon the birth and childhood of Jesus The tendency itself only points to the general recognition of a truth—the truth that a hero or religious leader is in a special sense God-sent. In the case of our Lord two considerations in particular give a special credibility, apart from the question of the evidence for the narratives containing them, to the miraculous circumstances alleged to have attended His birth. For in the first place, His subsequent life was miraculous and His mode of exit from it[1]; and beyond all question this fact conditions the evidence as to His nativity. In the second place, the providential circumstances which attended His nativity are part of a much larger set of phenomena—the phenomena of prophecy. And reasonable criticism, if it has more or less modified our view of these phenomena, has not by any means destroyed their force[2]. If then the advent of our Lord was providentially prepared for by

---

[1] The present argument is not (see above p. 5) with those who deny the miracles of Christ and His resurrection.
[2] Cf *Lux Mundi* (Murray), small ed pp 253-4

forecasts of inspired men, extending over a long period of time—if there was certainly this supernatural preparation for His advent—this fact gives greater probability to the prophecies of Zacharias, Simeon, and Anna, which again receive confirmation from the later, but not less prophetic, testimony of John the Baptist, one of the best accredited elements in the Gospel history.

Under these circumstances we cannot but feel that, in all reason, the resemblances between the birth-stories of Jesus and those of the Buddha and other religious heroes must have been very much closer than in fact they are to justify the idea that they are simply similar growths. In fact in the older Buddha legend the nearest approach to resemblance lies in the visit and prognostication of Asita, as compared with the prophecies of Simeon. And of this visit of Asita Bishop Copleston remarks, 'It takes its particular shape from the visit of the astrologer —which is still almost universal among the Sinhalese—to prepare the horoscope of a new-born child[1].'

In the later and developed legend, which is given in one form in Prof. Rhys Davids' *Buddhist Birth Stories*[2],

[1] *Buddhism*, pp 35-6

[2] In Trubner's Oriental Series, 1880, vol xvi pp 58 ff. Another form of legend is translated in Beal's *Romantic Legend of Sâkya Buddha* (Trubner, 1875). Jerome appears to be speaking inaccurately when he says (*adv Jovin* 1. 42, ed Vallarsi II p 309) that it is handed down as a tradition 'among the Gymnosophists of India that Buddha, the founder of their system, was brought forth by a *virgin* from her side.' One later legend was that (see Beal's *Romantic Legend*, pp. 36 ff) 'At this time when Bôdhisatwa was about to descend and in a spiritual manner enter the womb of Queen Mâya [the mother of the Buddha], then that Mâya on that very night addressed Suddhôdana Râja, and said, "Mahârâja! I wish from the present night to undertake the eight special rules of self-discipline, to wit not to kill anything that lives, . to have no sexual pleasures, &c." To this her husband consents, and the Buddha "descended from Tusita to sojourn on earth,

The Virgin Birth of our Lord.

what strikes the present writer, as he reads it at length, is the profound contrast which it presents to the narratives of our Lord's birth and infancy; the points of resemblance seem as few as are consistent with the fact that, according to the later Buddhist belief, a quasi-divine Bodisat was becoming a Buddha by a human birth for the salvation of mankind. And it must be remarked that only by reading the legend itself at length can anything like a right impression be obtained. Such selected and adapted stories as are versified in Sir Edwin Arnold's *Light of Asia*, or even such a summary as Professor Rhys Davids gives in his *Hibbert Lectures*[1], give an impression thoroughly misleading.

For clearness sake I restate this argument as follows.

(1) The tendency to invest the birth of heroes with legendary stories and prognostications of future greatness proves in itself neither more nor less than a universal human tendency to believe in a special divinity attaching to specially great and good men, and therefore a special likelihood of divine intervention to signalize their birth

and entered on the right side of Queen Māyā and there rested in perfect quiet" At once a bright light shone on the whole universe, every kind of physical portent occurs, while Māyā in the midst of her sleep dreamed that a white elephant, with six tusks, &c , entered her side In the morning again she addressed her husband, and said, after telling her dream, " From this time forth *I will no more partake of any sensual pleasure* "' Then after ten months' gestation she gave birth to the Buddha According to this account it is suggested indeed that the conception of the Buddha was without the intervention of the father, but his mother was not a virgin. Cf on the subject, Rhys Davids' *Buddhism* (S P C K) pp 183-4. This legend of course is quite without historical value On Buddhist books, see Copleston, *op cit* p 23; Rhys Davids, *op. cit* pp 11 ff

[1] *Hibbert Lectures* (Williams & Norgate, 1881) p 148.

This tendency is in itself rooted in a great truth, and can at least afford no argument in general against such special divine manifestations having at some time or times occurred.

(2) It could only afford an argument against such divine manifestations in the particular case of the birth of Jesus Christ if the supposed manifestations in this case were of a markedly generic type, i.e. bore very much closer resemblances than in fact they do to those which are pretended in other cases.

(3) In fact in the case of our Lord 'the distinction between history and legend could not be better marked than by the reserve of the canonical and the vulgar tattle of the apocryphal Gospels [1].'

(4) Moreover the particular phenomena, prophetic or miraculous, attendant on our Lord's birth cannot be separated from the subsequent miracles of the life and resurrection and the whole phenomenon of prophecy from Micah and Isaiah down to John the Baptist.

We conclude therefore that we may simply pay attention to the positive evidence which indicates that the histories of the nativity are trustworthy [2].

But setting aside supposed heathen parallels, it is more opportune to ask whether the circumstances of our Lord's birth can be regarded as mere repetitions of Old Testament incidents. Is the story of the birth of John the Baptist a mere repetition of that of Samuel, and

---

[1] Dr A M. Fairbairn, *Studies in the Life of Christ* (Hodder & Stoughton, 1881) p 31

[2] I have assumed in this discussion that the Christian story was not influenced by the Buddhist—which is certain—and also that the Buddhist stories are not reflections of the Christian

The Virgin Birth of our Lord.

the perils of the Christ of the perils of Moses[1]? No, we reply, unless there is *no* similarity in historical incidents and *no* similarity in the methods of God. But for our present purpose we only need to insist that the Old Testament afforded no analogy for the circumstances of our Lord's birth. The perils of Moses resemble those of the infant Christ, but very remotely, and there is no analogy in the Old Testament for the Virgin Birth.

It has however been alleged[2] that the language of Philo, 'whose influence may be traced in almost every page of the fourth Gospel,' suggests in the case of the Old Testament mothers of saints a sort of 'miraculous conception' without the intervention of a man, which may have afforded a basis for the attribution of a miraculous conception to Mary. For instance ' Moses,' says Philo, 'introduces Sarah as pregnant *when alone* and as *being visited by God.*'

To this suggestion the answer is twofold. (1) The language of Philo is characteristic and peculiar. He calls attention[3] to the supposed fact that in the case of Old Testament saints—Abraham, Isaac, Jacob, Moses—no mention is made of their 'knowing' their wives. This it is explained is because the woman symbolizes the senses from which the lovers of wisdom must keep

---

[1] Renan, *Évang.* pp 189-91 'La légende de Samuel engendra celle de Jean-Baptiste. . . . Quant aux dangers dont on supposait que fut entourée l'enfance de Jésus, c'était là une imitation de l'enfance de Moïse, qu'un roi aussi voulut faire mourir, et qui fut obligé de se sauver à l'étranger'

[2] *The Kernel and the Husk*, pp. 270 ff This argument has been recently repeated by Mr. Conybeare in the *Academy* in connexion with the question raised by the Codex Sinaiticus, on which see appended note B.

[3] See esp. *de Cherub.* pp. 115-6, and cf. the account of Bethuel in *de Profugis*, p. 457.

themselves aloof. Those who are called their wives, such as Sarah, Rebecca, Leah, Zipporah, were in name women, but in fact virtues. Such virtues can conceive seed 'only *from* God,' though—as God needs nothing for Himself--they conceive seed *to* the men who are their lovers. It is for this reason that Holy Scripture uses such modes of speech as indicate that these women, i e. virtues, conceive *for* their husbands indeed but *from* God. Thus (Gen. xxi. 1) Sarah is introduced as pregnant when God visits her alone. Of Leah it is said (xxix. 31) that God 'opened her womb,' which is the work of the man Rebecca (xxv. 21) conceived divinely in answer to Isaac's prayer. Again ' apart from supplication and prayer Moses having taken to wife the winged and lofty virtue Zipporah found her with child of no mortal[1].' The meaning of this mystical language of his Philo subsequently guards. Men, he says, make virgins into wives. God, by spiritual relationship with souls, makes wives into virgins. 'The scripture (Jer. iii. 4. lxx) is careful to describe God as the husband not of a virgin but of virginity.' Now all this argument, which is quite in the mystical gnosticizing manner of Philo, is wholly alien to the spirit both of the Old Testament and of the New. We notice, for example, that when St. Paul is speaking in the case of Isaac of a 'birth after the spirit[2],' he shows no tendency to pass like Philo to the idea of 'virginity,' or to shrink from associating divine action with the language descriptive of the ordinary physical process of generation. Further

---

[1] This seems built on no words in the biblical account
[2] Gal. iv. 22, 29.

The Virgin Birth of our Lord. 63

there is no evidence justifying the belief that such a mode of thought as is found in Philo existed in the Palestinian Judaism out of which the narratives of the nativity have their origin

(2) Setting aside the question whether Philo did or did not influence the fourth Gospel, it may be taken for certain he did not influence the language of the authorities upon which St. Matthew and St. Luke depend[1]. On the whole we may say that there is no connexion at all probable between the thoughts and language of the narratives of the nativity and the speculations of Philo about spiritual virginity

§ 7.

The connexion of doctrine and fact.

What has been hitherto attempted is both to vindicate the historical character of the records of our Lord's miraculous birth at Bethlehem and also to show that in the earliest tradition of the Christian churches, as far as we can trace it, the belief in the Virgin Birth is found as a constant accompaniment of the confession of His Incarnation. What we have finally to do is to show cause why we should regard the belief in the Virgin Birth as, in fact, inseparable from belief in the

---

[1] The author of *The Kernel and the Husk* assumes that the idea of the virginity of Mary was of *Gentile* origin, which is contrary to the evidence The documents of the nativity are intensely Jewish.

Incarnation and, even more from belief in the sinless Second Adam.

For beyond a question, our opinion as to the inseparability of the supposed fact from the Christian idea will affect our estimate of the evidence. The historical evidence for our Lord's birth of a virgin is in itself strong and cogent. But it is not such as to compel belief. There are ways to dissolve its force. To produce belief there is needed—in this as in almost all other questions of historical fact—besides cogent evidence, also a perception of the meaning and naturalness, under the circumstances, of the event to which evidence is borne. To clinch the historical evidence for our Lord's virgin birth there is needed the sense, that being what He was, His human birth could hardly have been otherwise than is implied in the virginity of His mother.

The logic of the matter may be represented on the ground of the Incarnation. Granted that the eternal Son of God did at a certain moment of time take flesh by a real incarnation in the womb of Mary,—granted that He was born as man, without change of personality or addition of another personality, but simply by the assumption of a new nature and by an entrance into new conditions of life and experience—granted in this sense the incarnation of the Son of God in the womb of Mary, can we conceive it to have taken place by the ordinary process of generation? Do not we inevitably associate with the ordinary process of generation the production of a new personality? Must not the denial of the Virgin Birth involve the position that Jesus was simply a new human person in whatever specially

The Virgin Birth of our Lord.

intimate relations with God? This seems to the present writer to be very probably the case, but at the same time to be a question very difficult to argue. But the argument becomes almost irresistible when the question is removed from the idea of incarnation strictly considered, to the associated idea of the sinless humanity, the humanity of a 'Second Adam'

Jesus Christ was a new departure in human life. Philosophers of different ages, from Plato to Carlyle, have been found scoffing at contemporary reformers, on the ground that their proposed reforms did not, could not, go deep enough to get at the root of the evils of human society. What is wanted to remedy these evils is a fresh departure—in some sense, a new birth, or regeneration of humanity[1]. So moral philosophers have reasoned: but it has been a matter of words. Jesus Christ alone has, in any adequate sense, translated this logical demand into actual reality. In Him we really find a 'Second Adam,' a new manhood. He appears among men in all the fulness of human faculties, sympathies, capacities of action and suffering; He was in all points such as we are *except sin*. But what an exception! As Jesus moves among the men of His day, as His historical presentation renews His image for each generation, by how great a gulf is He separated in His sinlessness, His perfection, from other men. He is very man, but new man. And with this quality of His person coincides His method. He will not take other men as He finds them and make the best

[1] See Carlyle, *Past and Present*, bk 1 ch 4 'Morrison's pill', Plato, *Republic*—the argument of the whole work, especially bk. iv pp 425-6

of them. He demands of them the acceptance of a new birth, the fundamental reconstruction of their moral being on a new basis, and that basis Himself. 'Except a man be born anew he cannot see the kingdom of God' 'Except ye turn'—with a radical conversion of the moral tendency of your being—'except ye turn and become as little children, ye shall in no wise enter into the kingdom of heaven[1]' Christ demands, then, a fundamental moral reconstruction of humanity, and He makes it possible because He offers to men a new life. He offers to reproduce in each man who will believe in Him and yield himself to Him, the quality of His own life by the bestowal of His own Spirit. Himself the New Man, He can make all men new. But granted that in this fundamental sense Christ Jesus is a new moral creation, is it possible that this new moral creation can have involved anything short of a new physical creative act? Does not all we know of physical heredity, all we know of the relation of spirit and body, lead us to believe that the miracle of a new moral creation must mean the miracle of a new physical creation? If the moral character was new, must not the stuff of the humanity have been new too? Must not the physical generation of the Second Adam have been such as to involve at once His community with our nature and His exemption from it? I am not laying all the stress on this sort of logic. I would, here and elsewhere, keep *a priori* arguments in their place. But this logic seems to me at least strong enough to clinch the historical argument or even to condition the

[1] St John iii 3, St Matt xviii 3

historical discussion by an antecedent expectation that the birth of the Second Adam must have been physically as well as morally miraculous.

I have come to the end of the task which I set myself at the beginning of this discussion. Something I trust has been done to show on the one hand the weakness of the objections brought against the historical character of the narratives of the nativity and on the other hand the strength of the positive ground on which they stand. We cannot be accused of an uncritical, unhistorical disposition in accepting the Virgin Birth of Jesus Christ as a fact of history. Throughout this discussion I have, for obvious reasons, avoided resting anything on the question of authority. But considering the position which the Virgin Birth holds in the creeds, it cannot be denied that the authority of the Christian Church is committed to it as a fact, beyond recall. To admit that its historical position is really doubtful would be to strike a mortal blow at the authority of the Christian Church as a guide to religious truth in any real sense Such a result is in itself an argument against the truth of any position which would tend to produce it; for it is very difficult to scrutinize narrowly those articles of the Christian faith which have really been believed and taught in the Church *semper, ubique, ab omnibus*, without being struck with the conviction that a divine providence has been guarding the Church in her production of such definitions or formal declarations of her faith as can really be called catholic—guarding her from asserting anything which can reasonably be called unwarranted or superstitious; and such a conviction does in itself create a presumption against any conclusion which would invalidate any single article of the original creed

DISSERTATION II

THE CONSCIOUSNESS OF OUR LORD IN HIS MORTAL LIFE

THE subject of the following discussion is our Lord's consciousness during the period of His human and mortal life In the first part (I) what appears to be the view of the New Testament writers will be provisionally stated with the evidence upon which it rests. In the second part (II) the teaching of the Church on the subject will be exhibited at times in outline, at other times more fully, and its relation will appear to the provisional conclusion already reached. In the third part (III) the conclusion will be restated, its relation to Church authority examined and its rationality vindicated.

Any writer who cares for Catholic sentiment and traditional reverence—nay more, any writer who realizes in any degree the limits which are set to human thought —must approach this subject with great unwillingness. But there is so much in the New Testament directly bearing upon it that if the character in the Gospel is to be a real object of contemplation, for the intellect as well as for the heart, it can hardly be avoided. That the actual evidence has been in fact so little considered has led to serious dangers in the way of unscriptural theorizing. So that it appears to the present writer that to refuse to consider the subject, in full view of the New Testament language about it, would be a false reverence, or what Hilary of Poitiers calls an 'irreligious solicitude for God [1].'

But if so anxious a subject has to be approached at all, one may be pardoned for dwelling a little by way of preface on the place which it holds with reference to the creed of Christians, and on the temper in which it ought to be approached.

First, then, this is not a question which ought to be encountered on the road towards orthodoxy. Its logical place is, I venture to think, that in which I have tried, summarily, to treat it in the *Bampton Lectures* of 1891, i.e. after faith in the Incarnation has been established. It requires only a little thought to see that the belief that God is incarnate in Jesus Christ does not carry with it to any tolerably cautious mind one certain and necessary conclusion, *a priori*, as to the question of the consciousness of the incarnate person. And conversely the utterances in the Gospels which must determine our conclusion on this mysterious subject will not be found to touch those moral and theological claims, those spiritual and physical powers of Jesus Christ, which justify, or rather postulate, the belief in the Incarnation. It is hoped that these assertions will be justified in the course of our discussion to the minds of any who feel doubtful about them at starting. For the present they

---

[1] *de Trin.* iv 6 'O stultos atque impios metus, et irreligiosam de Deo sollicitudinem!' The exclamation has reference to the fear professed by the Arians lest by confessing the eternity of Christ they should do violence to His nature as Son.

The Consciousness of our Lord.

are assumed. And in accordance with this assumption the truth of the Incarnation is, in this essay, taken for granted, and, though no special view is put forward as to the nature of inspiration, the language of our Lord in the Gospels about Himself is taken to be historically true.

Secondly, the question of our Lord's consciousness is not—*granted His infallibility as a teacher*—one which ought to harass the ordinary life of faith. Thousands of pious Christians have believed that the eternal 'Son of God for us men and for our salvation came down from heaven and was incarnate, and was made man, and was crucified, and rose again,' and on the basis of this faith have read their Gospels and taken the real human experience and sympathy of our Lord for truth in simple trust, without any inquiries into the condition of our Lord's consciousnesss seriously arising. And this is quite right. People who do not feel bound to embark upon the difficulties of mental philosophy as regards men in general, still less as regards God, have no cause to be disturbed in regard to similar problems in relation to the person of Him who is both God and man. And when the questions are reached, if we realize the difficulty of understanding the human mind and the certain incomprehensibility of that which is divine, we shall not even imagine that the problems here raised can be fully sounded or solved. We shall bow in awful reverence before the deep things of God, but we shall, none the less, in this as in other departments of inquiry, seek to go as far as we can, and at least to be true to all the facts which are, and can be brought to be, at our disposal. Nor shall we be surprised if more accurate investigations require in us some change of mind, not in the region of our central faith, but in its more outlying districts. For myself as an author I would only ask to be read carefully by those who wish to criticize me, so that, as far as it is given me to express my meaning plainly, I may be judged for what I have said and not for what I have not. Throughout this discussion I shall be so frequently citing authorities that I may be forgiven for citing, as a conclusion to these few words of preface, some passages from the father already referred to, Hilary of Poitiers—passages which admirably express the temper of mind required in approaching either the doctrine of the Holy Trinity, which was Hilary's subject, or our Lord's consciousness as man, which is what lies before us.

(1) *That such inquiries are not necessary for faith*

De Trin. x. 70 'Non per difficiles nos Deus ad beatam vitam quaestiones vocat, nec multiplici eloquentis facundiae genere sollicitat In absoluto nobis ac facili est aeternitas, Iesum et suscitatum a mortuis per Deum credere et ipsum esse dominum confiteri. Nemo itaque ea quae ob ignorationem nostram dicta sunt ad occasionem irreligiositatis usurpet.'

(2) *As regards the incomprehensibility of God and that we can know Him only through His own disclosure of Himself.*

'Perfecta scientia est sic Deum scire ut licet non ignorabilem tamen inenarrabilem scias' (ii. 7).

'Animus humanus, nisi per fidem donum Spiritus hauserit, habebit quidem naturam Deum intelligendi sed lumen scientiae non habebit' (ii. 34).

'Nec enim concipiunt imperfecta perfectum, neque quod ex alio subsistit absolute vel auctoris sui potest intelligentiam obtinere vel propriam' (iii. 24).

'Neque enim nobis ea natura est ut se in caelestem cognitionem suis viribus efferat. A Deo discendum est quod de Deo intelligendum sit, quia non nisi se auctore cognoscitur . . . Loquendum ergo non aliter de Deo est quam ut ipse ad intelligentiam nostram de se locutus est' (v. 21).

(3) *As regards the readiness to change our minds and to advance to more accurate knowledge of divine things.*

'Et si forte humanae conditionis errore praesumptum aliquid sensu tenebimus, profectum intelligentiae per revelationis gratiam non recusemus. Ne intellexisse aliquid semel suo sensu ad id valeat ut pudeat rectius aliquid demutando sentire' (xi 24).

(4) *The author's request for fair-minded readers.*

'Optimus lector est qui dictorum intelligentiam exspectet ex dictis potius quam imponat, et retulerit magis quam attulerit, neque cogat id videri dictis continei i quod ante lectionem praesumpserit intelligendum' (i. 18).

I.

THE VIEW OF OUR LORD'S CONSCIOUSNESS DURING HIS HUMAN AND MORTAL LIFE WHICH IS PRESENTED IN THE NEW TESTAMENT.

It should be explained at the beginning of this part of our inquiry that the question whether the views of all the New Testament writers as to our Lord's person and consciousness are in substantial agreement or not, is not here directly argued. It is plain that there is independence among them, differences of point of view and different stages of theological development. Thus, in the speeches of the early part of the Acts, our Lord is simply regarded as the Messiah; in other parts of the New Testament the view of His authority as Messianic seems to be merged into the view of it as strictly divine: He is 'the Lord' or 'the Son of God.' In St. Paul and St. John the divine sonship of Jesus Christ appears as the central point of a definite Christian theology: and it must be noted that St. Paul and St. John plainly regard their theology not as the result of their own speculation, but, in the strictest sense, as revealed truth[1]. In each of the Gospels both views of our Lord's person exist, and closer examination contradicts the still current opinion that in the synoptists He

[1] Cf Sanday, *Bampton Lectures*, p. 353 'It [the inspiration of the apostles] is more sustained than the inspiration of the prophets in the Old Testament, it extends not merely to single truths revealed for a special object, but to a body of connected truths, a system of theology.'

appears as the Messiah, the Son of Man, in the fourth Gospel as the incarnate Word of God The divine sonship proper emerges out of the Messianic claim in the common synoptic tradition and the Messianic character is prominent in St. John. But still there is a difference in the point of view, and the strictly divine nature of Jesus is more emphatic in the fourth Gospel than in the other three. Thus there exist among the writers of the New Testament differences in point of view as regards the person of Christ and distinct stages of doctrinal development. But that these differences are not discrepancies may be best shown by the fact that they admit of being brought together in one comprehensive theory without violence to any.

§ 1.

The evidence of the Gospels[1].

The conditions of our Lord's early childhood are veiled from us. Nothing is told us about His education, nor are we given any glimpse of Him at the period when men learn most from those outside them, but He grew so truly as a human child that Joseph and His mother had not been led to expect from Him conduct incompatible with childhood, when they took Him up with them to the temple in His thirteenth year. This must mean that He was taught as the young are taught;

[1] What follows is largely, but not altogether, repeated from my *Bampton Lectures*, pp. 145 ff.

and in the temple courts He impressed the doctors as a child of marvellous insight and intelligence. Not but what, even then, there was present to Him the consciousness of His unique sonship: 'Wist ye not,' He said to His parents, 'that I must be about my Father's business [1]?' but that consciousness of divine sonship did not, we are led to suppose, interfere with His properly human growth 'The child grew and waxed strong,' says St Luke, 'becoming full of wisdom, and the favour of God was upon him.' Again, 'Jesus advanced in wisdom and stature, and in favour with God and men [2],' —the phrase being borrowed from the record of Samuel's childhood, with the specifications added, 'in wisdom and stature.' There was a real growth in mental apprehension and spiritual capacity, as in bodily stature.

The divine sonship is impressively asserted at the baptism of Jesus by John in the river Jordan [3]. The pre-eminent dignity of the person of Jesus appears indeed nowhere in the Gospels more strikingly than in His

---

[1] St Luke ii 49 ἐν τοῖς τοῦ πατρός μου, 'among my Father's matters,' or, perhaps, 'in my Father's house' (as R V) The expression ' my Father' appears to involve, in some measure, a repudiation of Mary's phrase 'thy father,' as applied to Joseph (ver 48) I think it is plain that our Lord claims a certain unique sonship, but was the consciousness of this derived from meditation on such phrases in the O T as ' He shall call me, Thou art my father' (Ps lxxxix 26), the child Jesus being already conscious of His Messianic mission as Son of David' or was it the absolute consciousness of divine sonship? To answer this question requires, perhaps, more knowledge than we possess But it is plain that to our Lord's mind during His ministry the office of the Messiah, including as it did the office of universal and ultimate Judge, was inseparable from proper divine sonship The Christ was also the Son of God cf above, p 17, n 8, for a very brief discussion of the relation of the *Messianic* to the *divine* claims of our Lord

[2] St Luke ii 40, 52, cf 1 Sam ii 26   [3] St Mark i. 11.

The Consciousness of our Lord.

relation to John the Baptist, as described in all the Gospels, and that this pre-eminent dignity carried with it throughout our Lord's ministerial life a consciousness of properly divine sonship, it is not possible for any one to doubt who accepts, even generally, the historical character of the synoptic Gospels and of St John's. If His eternal pre-existence is plainly asserted by Him only in St. John, yet this is not separable from the essential sonship asserted in the synoptists [1]. But this consciousness of divine sonship is represented as co-existing with a really human development of life. He receives as man the unction of the Holy Ghost; He was led as man 'of the Spirit into the wilderness,' and hungered, and was subjected as man to real temptations of Satan, such as made their appeal to properly human faculties and were met by the free employment of human will. He was 'in all points tempted like as we are, apart from sin [2].' When He goes out to exercise His ministry, He bases His authority on the unction of the Spirit according to Isaiah's prophecy. 'The Spirit of the Lord is upon me,' He reads, 'because he anointed me to preach [3].' 'God,' comments St. Peter, 'anointed Jesus of Nazareth with the Holy Ghost and with power who went about doing good, and healing all that were oppressed of the devil; for God was with him [4].' Thus if His miraculous power appears as the appropriate endowment of His person, it

---

[1] The essential sonship is in the synoptic Gospels expressed in such passages as St Matt xi 27, St Mark xii 6, 37, xiii 32, xiv. 62, and the parallel passages

[2] Hebr iv 15 On the temptations 'apart from sin,' see *Bampton Lectures*, pp 221-222

[3] St. Luke iv 18   [4] Acts x 38

was still a gift of God to Him as man. 'The power of the Lord was with him to heal,' says the evangelist: 'by the Spirit of God,' He Himself declared, He cast out devils[1] and St. John, in recording the words of Jesus before the raising of Lazarus, would teach us to see, at least in some of His miracles, what is suggested also elsewhere by our Lord's gestures, a power dependent on the exercise of prayer. 'Father, I thank thee that thou didst hear me[2].'

Once more, to come more closely to our proper subject, while as very Son Jesus knows the Father as He is known of Him and reveals Him to whom He will, He does not appear to teach out of an absolute divine omniscience, but rather as conditioned by human nature. It is surely beyond question that our Lord is represented in the Gospels as an infallible no less than as a sinless[3] teacher. He challenges criticism. He speaks in the tone of authority only justifiable to one who taught with absolute certainty 'the word of God.' 'Heaven and earth,' He said, 'shall pass away, but my words shall not pass away[4].' But infallibility is not omniscience. Again it is beyond question that our Lord's consciousness, not only towards God but towards the world, was extraordinary. Thus He frequently exhibits a supernatural knowledge, insight, and foresight. He saw Nathanael under the fig-tree, and knew the incident in the life of the Samaritan woman, and told Peter how he would find the piece of money in the

---

[1] St. Luke v. 17, St. Matt xii 28

[2] St John xi 41, St. Matt. xiv 19; St Mark vii 34. cf v 19.

[3] On our Lord's sinlessness and impeccability, see *B L* pp. 165 ff, also p. 153

[4] St Matt. xxiv. 35.

fish's mouth, and the disciples how they would find the colt tied up in the village and the man bearing a pitcher of water to take them to the upper chamber. He discerned 'from the beginning' the heart of Judas[1], and prophesied the denial of Peter, and had in view His own passion, death, and resurrection the third day. But all such supernatural illumination is, if of higher quality, yet analogous to that vouchsafed to prophets and apostles[2]. It is not necessarily divine consciousness. It suggests in itself no more than the remark of the woman of Samaria, 'I perceive that thou art a prophet[3].' And it coincides in the case of our Lord with apparent limitations of knowledge. The evidence for this we may group under four heads.

(1) There are constantly attributed to our Lord human experiences which seem inconsistent with practical omniscience. Thus He expresses surprise at the conduct of His parents, and the unbelief of men, and the barrenness of the fig-tree, and the slowness of His disciples faith[4]. He expresses surprise on many occasions, and therefore, we must believe, really felt it, and on other occasions He asks for information and receives it, as when He came down from the Mount of Trans-

---

[1] St John vi 64. The words 'from the beginning' apply undoubtedly to the early days of His ministry, when He first began to gather around Him a circle of personal disciples. Cf xv 27, xvi 4; Acts i. 21, 22

[2] 2 Kings vi 12 'Elisha, the prophet that is in Israel, telleth the king of Israel the words that thou speakest in thy bedchamber.' Cf v 26 'Went not mine heart with thee?' Acts v 3, 4 (St Peter discerning the sin of Ananias), xxi 11-14 (the foreknowledge of St. Paul's fate)

[3] St John iv. 19 Cf. St Luke vii 39 'This man, *if he were a prophet*, would have perceived who and what manner of woman this is which toucheth him, that she is a sinner.'

[4] St Luke ii 49, St Mark vi 6, xi 13, iv 40, vii. 18, viii. 21, xiv. 37.

figuration and was presented with the child which the disciples had failed to cure, He asked the father, like any physician, 'How long time is it since this hath come unto him?' and when He is on His way to heal Lazarus, He asks 'Where have ye laid him[1]?' It is of course a common form of human speech for men to ask questions in order to draw out the feelings of others or to reproach them, without any implication of ignorance on their own part. Thus some of our Lord's questions are not asked for the sake of information[2] — and this is apparently true of all those asked after the resurrection[3]—but there are a number on the other hand of which this is not at all a natural explanation. They represent a natural need of information It is in agreement with this that, as St Luke especially teaches us[4], He lived in the constant exercise of prayer to God, which is the characteristic utterance of human faith and trust, that human faith and trust of which the Epistle to the Hebrews sees in Jesus the supreme example[5].

This reality of human faith becomes more obvious as the anxieties and terrors of the passion close in upon Him. He shows us then the spectacle of true man, weighted with a crushing burden, the dread of a cata-

---

[1] St Mark ix 21, cf vi 38, viii 5, St Luke viii 30, St John xi 34

[2] e g St Matt xvi 8-11, and esp. St John vi. 6 'This he said to prove him, for he himself knew what he would do'

[3] St Luke xxiv. 17, 19, 41 ; St John xx 15, 29 (R. V. margin), xxi. 5, 15-17.

[4] St. Luke iii 21, v 16, vi 12, ix 18, 28, xxii 32, 42, x 21.

[5] Hebr ii 13 'I will put my trust in him', xii. 2 'the captain of our faith,' i e leader in the life of faith, see Westcott *in loc.*

strophe awful and unfathomed No doubt it is implied that the burden was voluntarily accepted [1], but accepted it was in all its human reality. It was only because the future was not clear that He could pray: 'O my Father, if it be possible, let this cup pass away from me [2].' Boldly simple is the language of the inspired commentator on this scene of the agony: 'Christ,' he says, 'in the days of his flesh, having offered up prayers and supplications with strong crying and tears unto him that was able to save him from death, and having been heard for his godly fear, though he was a son, yet learned obedience by the things which he suffered [3].' No language less than this would correspond with the historical narrative, but it is language which implies very strongly the exercise of human faith in our Lord's case; nor is it possible that He could have cried with real meaning upon the cross, 'My God, my God, why hast thou forsaken me?' unless He had really entered into the experience which originally prompted that cry of the psalmist, into the trial of the soul from whom God hides His face, the trial of the righteous man, as far as his own perception goes, forsaken.

(2) Though our Lord knew so well, and told so plainly, the moral conditions of the great judgement to come, and discerned so clearly its particular application in the destruction of Jerusalem, yet He expressly declared, as St. Matthew as well as St. Mark assures us, that of the day and the hour of His second coming no one knew except the Father, 'not even the angels of heaven,

---

[1] St. John xii 27, x. 11, St Matt xxvi. 53, 54
[2] St Matt xxvi 39.   [3] Hebr. v 7, 8.

neither the Son¹'; and we cannot hold this declaration apart from the other indications that are given us of a limited human consciousness. It may fairly be contrasted with the phrase used to the apostles after the resurrection², 'It is not *for you to know* times or seasons, which the Father hath set within his own authority.' More than this · no one can study attentively the eschatological discourses of our Lord in the various accounts given us of them, without reaching the conviction that they are strictly of the *prophetic* quality and exhibit the limitations proper to prophecy—that is to say, they announce the moral and spiritual conditions of the judgement to come on the Jewish nation and on the world at large, but they cannot be rightly described as history written beforehand by the hand of omniscience. It is therefore quite misleading to argue, as many orthodox persons have argued in ancient and modern times, that one who knew so much as these discourses disclose must have also known (in fact) the day and hour of the end.

(3) A similar impression is left on our mind by the Gospel of St. John. Unmistakeably is our Lord there put before us as the eternal Son of the Father incarnate,

---

[1] St. Matt xxiv 36 [R V. This reading will, I suppose, stand preferred in spite of the fact that the new Sinaitic palimpsest omits the words 'neither the Son'], St Mark xiii 32 It has been suggested that ignorance is here predicted of 'the Son,' used absolutely, not of the incarnate Son in the period of His humiliation merely This seems to me a greatly overstrained argument The Son was speaking of Himself as He then was.

[2] Acts i 7 (R. V.) After the resurrection our Lord speaks of the day of the end as reserved in 'the Father's power' But He does not any longer suggest that He is ignorant of the day, and He seems to speak of Himself as not only foreseeing but controlling the time of St John's death in a manner unlike to that in which He spoke in His mortal life (St John xxi. 22).

The Consciousness of our Lord.

and unmistakeably is the inner, essential unity of the Son and the Father and their continual abiding one in the other there insisted upon [1], but it also appears that the Son of the Father is living and teaching under restrained human conditions He has 'come down' from the heaven where He 'was before' with the Father, He has been 'sanctified and sent into the world,' He has 'come out from God,' He 'has left the glory [2].' Thus He 'speaks the words of God' indeed infallibly, but it is, as St. John tells us, because God 'giveth not the Spirit by measure [3],' that is, because of the complete endowment of His manhood. He Himself says that He accomplishes 'what the Father taught him' · that He can do only 'what he sees the Father doing': that the Father makes to Him a progressive revelation, 'he shall show him greater works than these'. that the Father 'hath given him commandment what he should say and what he should speak': that the Father 'hath given

---

[1] x 30, xvii. 21, 22

[2] vi 62, x 36, xiii 3, xvi 27, xvii 5. In iii 13 the words ὁ ὢν ἐν τῷ οὐρανῷ—'which is in heaven'—are very doubtful, see Westcott *in loc* 'Heaven' and 'glory' are apparently what He had abandoned. 'God,' that is 'the Father,' is still with Him · and therefore 'glory' of a different sort which He can communicate to His disciples (xvii. 22, cf i 14) [In the recently discovered Sinaitic palimpsest the Syriac translates 'the Son of Man which is from heaven.']

[3] iii. 34 ὃν γὰρ ἀπέστειλεν ὁ θεὸς τὰ ῥήματα τοῦ θεοῦ λαλεῖ, οὐ γὰρ ἐκ μέτρου δίδωσιν τὸ πνεῦμα. The words may be translated, '*the Spirit giveth not* [to Him] *by measure*', hardly, I think, '*he* [the Son] *giveth not the Spirit by measure*' The unmeasured, full, gift bestowed upon the Son is put in contrast to the measured partial gift which in Rabbinic belief was bestowed upon prophets, and in Christian belief upon members of the Church (1 Cor. xii 11); cf. Alford *in loc*. What the exact content of the full human endowment would have been we cannot say *a priori* But it was a human endowment, an endowment of our Lord as man, and suggests therefore properly human limitations

him' the divine 'name,' that is, the positive revelation of Himself, to communicate to the apostles: that He has made known to them 'all things that he had heard of the Father' or 'the words which the Father had given him[1].' The idea is thus decidedly suggested of a message of definite content made over to our Lord to impart. Now, even though we bear in mind to the fullest extent the eternal subordination and receptivity of the Son, it still remains plain that words such as have been quoted express Him as receiving and speaking under the limitations of a properly human state

We must also notice that our Lord repeatedly speaks of that inner leading by which the divine love draws human souls and prepares them to welcome the Christ, as not His own but the Father's: He speaks of it as belonging to the *Father*, as distinguished from *Himself*. 'All that which the Father giveth me, shall come to me; and him that cometh to me I will in no wise cast out.' 'No man can come to me, except the Father which sent me draw him. and I will raise him up in the last day. It is written in the prophets, And they shall all be taught of God. Every one that hath heard from the Father, and hath learned, cometh unto me[2].' Now of course this inner leading belongs to the eternal Word (and to the Spirit) as much as to the Father. But our Lord's mode of speech leads us to think of Him, under the conditions under which He spoke, as not inwardly inspiring human souls, but dealing with them only in the spiritual relationship

---

[1] viii 28, v. 19, 20, xii. 49, xvii. 11, 8, xv. 15
[2] vi 37, 39, 44-45, cf x 29, xvii 6, 9, 24

which belongs to humanity. I do not say more than 'leads us to think of Him,' because the full metaphysical reality may not admit of expression in human words. But the tendency of what is said must be admitted.

(4) Lastly, there is the argument from silence, coincident with these indications. Our Lord exhibits insight and foresight of prophetic quality He exhibits towards all facts of physical nature the receptiveness of a perfect sonship, so that, for example, the laws of natural waste and growth are pointed out by Him with consummate accuracy in the parable of the sower. But He never enlarges our stock of natural knowledge, physical or historical, out of the divine omniscience.

The recognition of these phenomena of our Lord's life leads us to the conclusion that up to the time of His death He lived and taught, He thought and was inspired and was tempted, as true and proper man, under the limitations of consciousness which alone make possible a really human experience. Of this part of our heritage we must not allow ourselves to be robbed, by being 'wise above that which is written.'

At the same time it must be remembered that this idea of the meaning of the Incarnation is suggested by the Gospel narrative concurrently with the truth of our Lord's divinity, which is here not proved but assumed. The facts which continually suggest that He is more than man, that He is in a unique sense Son of God[1], and those which suggest that He is living and speaking under conditions of human limitation, are indissolubly

---

[1] Summarized in *B L* i and iii

intermingled with one another. One impression is given by the Gospels, taken together, of a real entrance of the eternal Son of God into our manhood and into the limited conditions of consciousness necessary to a really human state. This view alone can interpret and hold together all the phenomena, and this view does hold them all together and does enable us to read the Gospels without doing violence to any element in the many-sided but consistent picture which they present.

§ 2.

The language of St. Paul.

This idea of the meaning of the Incarnation derived from the Gospels, *while it has no single certain passage of the New Testament against it*, is on the other hand at least strongly reinforced by the language already quoted of the Epistle to the Hebrews[1], and also by St. Paul's language in two remarkable passages of his epistles. In a passage of the Epistle to the Philippians he is holding up our Lord in His incarnation as an example of humility, and this leads him to give, as we may say, a certain theory of it. He describes it as a self-emptying[2]. Christ Jesus pre-existed, he declares, in the *form*

---

[1] Hebr v. 7, 8.

[2] Phil ıı 5-11 τοῦτο φρονεῖτε ἐν ὑμῖν ὃ καὶ ἐν Χριστῷ Ἰησοῦ, ὃς ἐν μορφῇ θεοῦ ὑπάρχων, οὐχ ἁρπαγμὸν ἡγήσατο τὸ εἶναι ἴσα θεῷ, ἀλλὰ ἑαυτὸν ἐκένωσεν, μορφὴν δούλου λαβών, ἐν ὁμοιώματι ἀνθρώπων γενόμενος καὶ σχήματι εὑρεθεὶς ὡς ἄνθρωπος ἐταπείνωσεν ἑαυτὸν γενόμενος ὑπήκοος μέχρι θανάτου, θανάτου δὲ σταυροῦ. See Lightfoot *in loc.*

of God. The word 'form' transferred from physical shape to spiritual type, describes—as St. Paul uses it, alone or in composition, with uniform accuracy—the permanent characteristics of a thing Jesus Christ then, in His pre-existent state, was living in the permanent characteristics of the life of God In such a life it was His right to remain. It belonged to Him. But He regarded not His prerogatives, as a man regards a prize he must clutch at. For love of us He abjured the prerogatives of equality with God. By an act of deliberate self-abnegation, He so emptied Himself as to assume the permanent characteristics of the human or servile life: He took the *form* of a servant. Not only so, but He was made in outward appearance like other men and was found in fashion as a man, that is, in the transitory quality of our mortality. The 'form,' the 'likeness,' the 'fashion' of manhood, He took them all. Thus, remaining in unchanged personality, He is exhibited as (to use Dr. Westcott's words[1]) 'laying aside the mode of divine existence' (τὸ εἶναι ἴσα θεῷ) in order to assume the human.

Again, St Paul describes the Incarnation as a 'self-beggary[2].' The metaphor suggests a man of wealth

---

[1] In the *Speaker's Commentary*, on St John 1 14 The question has been asked, Does St Paul imply that Jesus Christ abandoned the μορφὴ θεοῦ? I think all we can certainly say is that He is conceived to have emptied Himself of the divine mode of existence (μορφή), so far as was involved in His really entering upon the human mode of existence (μορφή) St Paul does not use his terms with the exactness of a professional logician or scholastic On the subject, and on the passage generally, see Bruce, *Humiliation of Christ* (Clark, 1876) lect 1.

[2] 2 Cor viii 9 γινώσκετε γὰρ τὴν χάριν τοῦ κυρίου ἡμῶν Ἰησοῦ [Χριστοῦ], ὅτι δι' ὑμᾶς ἐπτώχευσεν πλούσιος ὤν, ἵνα ὑμεῖς τῇ ἐκείνου πτωχείᾳ πλουτήσητε.

who deliberately abandons the prerogatives of possession to enter upon the experience of poverty, not because he thinks it a better state, but in order to help others up through real fellowship with their experience to a life of weal. 'Ye know the grace of our Lord Jesus Christ, that, though he was rich, yet for your sakes he beggared himself, that ye through his poverty might become rich' This is how St. Paul interprets our Lord's coming down from heaven, and it is manifest that it expresses something very much more than the mere addition of a manhood to His Godhead. In a certain aspect indeed the Incarnation is the folding round the Godhead of the veil of the humanity, to hide its glory, but it is much more than this. It is a ceasing to exercise, at least in a certain sphere, and *so far as human thought can attain*, some natural prerogatives of the divine existence; it is a coming to exist for love of us under conditions of being not natural to Godhead. For our sakes the Son of God abandoned His own divine prerogatives in God in order to win and merit, as man, by gradual and painful effort, a glory which, by right, might have been His all along, the glory which He had with the Father before the world was. And that glory in fact He received as the reward of His human obedience: because of the obedience of His mortal life God, says St. Paul, 'highly exalted him, and gave unto him the name which is above every name—the divine name.' So that ' In him (i.e. in the exalted Christ) dwelleth all the fulness of the Godhead bodily,' in him ' are all the treasures of wisdom and knowledge hidden [1].'

[1] Phil. ii 9, Col. ii 3, 9. These phrases are used of Christ in glory.

§ 3.

An absolute κένωσις not affirmed in the New Testament.

The view here expressed leaves a great deal unexplained, and specially the relation of the Incarnation to the eternal and cosmic functions of the Word. The Word or Son in the Incarnation comes forth from the Father, comes down from heaven. The Father, on His side, is represented as 'sending' Him and 'giving Him up[1].' There is no text, certain enough to be quoted—'the Son of Man which is in heaven' being, as has been mentioned, highly uncertain on critical grounds—which directly suggests that the incarnate Person during the period of His humiliation was still none the less *in heaven*, i.e. in the fulfilment of His divine functions. On the other hand the theology of St. John, St. Paul and the Epistle to the Hebrews leads us to believe that the Word belongs to the eternal life of God, and is also the sustaining principle of all creation —' in whom all things consist,' who 'bears along all things by the utterance of his power[2].' In the first of these passages St. Paul is contemplating the Son of God as holding an eternal place in the life of God as His image or self-expression, and a fundamental and permanent relation to all created things, not to men or to

---

[1] St John iii 16 ἔδωκεν, Rom viii. 32 παρέδωκεν, St. John xx 20, 1 St John iv 9 ἀπέσταλκεν.
[2] Col 1. 17 τὰ πάντα ἐν αὐτῷ συνέστηκεν, Hebr 1. 3 φέρων τὰ πάντα τῷ ῥήματι τῆς δυνάμεως αὐτοῦ

this world only, but also to all unseen intelligences and beings whatsoever. In Him they had their origin; toward Him they tend; in Him they permanently subsist. 'He is the principle of cohesion in the universe. He impresses upon creation that unity and solidarity which makes it a cosmos instead of a chaos[1].' St Paul goes on to suggest how this fundamental relation of the Son to the universe as its creator, its immanent principle of life and order. and its goal or end, is reproduced in His relation to the new creation, the Church. But the language which he uses of the relation of the Son to nature is such as to make it almost impossible to imagine that St Paul conceived it to be *interrupted* by the Incarnation. The Incarnation is an episode in it, or rather its consummation and completion. How much St. Paul reflected upon the relation of the 'self-emptying' of the Son which he postulates in other epistles to this permanent cosmic function which he here describes, we cannot say. But he must at least have been prepared to postulate the first with all reality, and still to maintain the permanence of the second. Again, in the passage just quoted from the prologue of the Epistle to the Hebrews, the Son's function of 'bearing along all things by the utterance of his power' appears to be conceived of as continuous and not affected by that purging of our sins and subsequent sitting down on the right hand of the divine majesty, for the realization of which the author of the epistle postulates His entrance into all sinless human experience and infirmity. This writer also must have believed the self-emptying in the one sphere

[1] Lightfoot *in loc*

The Consciousness of our Lord.

to have been compatible with the cosmic function in another sphere. Nor has the thought of the Church found the abandonment of the cosmic position even a conceivable hypothesis Thus, if we are asked the question—Can the functions of the Son in the Godhead and in the universe have been suspended by the Incarnation? we cannot but answer, with the theologians of the Church from Irenaeus to Dr. Westcott, that it is to us inconceivable[1]. Nor can we dissociate the fulfilment of these functions from the exercise of omniscience. We must suppose, then, that in some manner the humiliation and the self-limitation of the incarnate state was compatible with the continued exercise of divine and cosmic functions in another sphere. But although we cannot but suppose and believe this, we must remember that the language of the New Testament is much more full and clear on the fact of the human limitations than on the permanence of the cosmic functions; and that our capacities for speculation about God, beyond what is disclosed in experience and revelation, are exceedingly limited. If Scripture represents the divine intention, then we should conclude that it is the divine intention that we should meditate on the reality of the self-humiliation of the Son which is revealed to us and pressed upon our notice; and if we can but very dimly hold this together with the unchangeable exercise of His divine functions in the life of God and in the universe, we shall surely not be surprised for beyond all question we 'know in part,' we see 'as in a mirror,' we understand 'as in a riddle' the mysteries of God.

[1] See below, pp 98 ff

§ 4.

Provisional conclusion.

Our examination of the New Testament language—especially of the narrative of the Gospels and of the theology of St. Paul and St. John—would so far appear to justify a conclusion which may be stated in two ways.

(1) The Incarnation of the Son of God was no mere addition of a manhood to His Godhead: it was no mere wrapping around the divine glory of a human nature to veil it and make it tolerable to mortal eyes. It was more than this. The Son of God, without ceasing to be God, the Son of the Father, and without ceasing to be conscious of His divine relation as Son to the Father, yet, in assuming human nature, so truly entered into it as really to grow and live as Son of Man under properly human conditions, that is to say also under properly human limitations. Thus, if we are to express this in human language, we are forced to assert that within the *sphere* and *period* of His incarnate and mortal life, He did, and as it would appear did habitually—doubtless by the voluntary action of His own self-limiting and self-restraining love[1]—cease from the exercise of those divine functions and powers, including the divine omniscience, which

[1] St. John x. 18.

The Consciousness of our Lord.

would have been incompatible with a truly human experience.

(2) Jesus Christ, the Son of God incarnate, was and is, at every moment and in every act, both God and man, personally God made man; He is as truly God at His birth or death as now in His glory, and as truly man now in His glory as formerly in His human birth and mortal life, but the relation of the Godhead and the manhood is not the same throughout. Now in His glory we must conceive that the manhood subsists under conditions of Godhead, 'the glory of God' but formerly during His mortal life and within its sphere, the Godhead was energizing under conditions and limitations of manhood. The Son of God really became and lived as Son of Man.

This provisional conclusion may be further defined by contrasting it, broadly, with other well-known views, before we go on to examine it in the light of the historical development of theology.

It is opposed, then, on the one side, to the view, which I must call the *a priori*, dogmatical and unhistorical view that Christ's human mind was from the first moment of the Incarnation and continuously flooded with complete knowledge and with the glory of the beatific vision, so that He never could really grow in knowledge or be ignorant of anything, or be personally in any perplexity or doubt[1]. It is opposed, on the other hand, to the *a priori*, humanitarian and also unhistorical view that the Son in becoming man ceased to be conscious of His own eternal sonship, and became, not

---
[1] On which see further II. § 8.

merely a human, but a fallible and peccable teacher. This view is unhistorical equally with the other. That the consciousness and claim of Christ is represented in the Gospels as properly divine, the claim of the Son of God, does not admit of reasonable doubt: and again His words as a whole, with the claims they involve and the tone impressed upon them, will not allow us to think of Him as liable to sin or liable to mislead[1]. He never, as He is represented to us in the Gospels, fears sin or hints at His inadequacy to the tremendous mission which He bore. He challenges criticism. He speaks as the invincible emancipator of man, the deliverer who stands in no relation to sin but as the discerner, the conqueror, the judge of it in all its forms and to the end of time[2]. In the same way, whenever and whomsoever He teaches, it is in the tone which could only be morally justifiable in the case of one who taught infallibly 'the word of God' 'Heaven and earth,' He said, 'shall pass away, but my words shall not pass away[3].' 'Lo,' said the apostles, amazed at the calm authority of His tone, 'now know we that thou knowest all things and needest not that any man should ask thee; by this we believe that thou camest forth from God[4].'

Both these views then appear to be equally contra-

---

[1] See above, p 80.

[2] St John xiv 30–31 'The prince of the world cometh and he hath nothing in me,' sums up the whole impression left by the Gospels. The only passage which could be alleged to the contrary is the 'Why callest thou me good?' (St Mark x 18). But this, interpreted as a repudiation of goodness, is too utterly out of keeping with our Lord's general claims It must be regarded as a question asked of the young man to test his motives and principles, see *B L.* pp 13, 198

[3] St. Matt xxiv 35   [4] St John xvi. 30

dicted by the evangelical narrative taken as it stands. The view which is truly in accordance with the narrative must lie in between these two extremes, but even within the intermediate area we cannot, I think, be contented with a view which simply puts in juxtaposition, during our Lord's earthly life, the divine and human consciousnesses—which represents Him as acting and speaking now as God and now as man, and which attributes to Him simultaneously omniscience as God and limitation of knowledge as man. It is no doubt true that as God He possessed potentially at every moment the divine as well as the human consciousness and nature. But the self-sacrifice of the Incarnation appears to have lain in great measure, *so far as human words can express it*, in His refraining from the divine mode of consciousness within the sphere of His human life, that He might really enter into human experience. It is not enough, for example, to recognize that our Lord was ignorant of the divine secret of the day and hour of the end, in respect of His human nature, unless we recognize also that He was so truly living under human conditions as Himself to be ignorant. The Son Himself, as He reveals Himself to men in manhood, did not know.

II.

THE HISTORY OF CHRISTIAN OPINION, OUTSIDE THE CANON, ON THE SUBJECT OF OUR LORD'S HUMAN CONSCIOUSNESS.

§ 1.

Preliminary. On the permanence in the Incarnation of the Godhead of Christ.

I have mentioned above that all theologians of the Church from Irenaeus downwards affirm that Christ in becoming incarnate did not cease to be God or to exercise the cosmic functions of the Word. His human birth. it is frequently expressed, was no diminution or destruction of what He was before. 'Hoc enim quod ex carne atque in carne venit, ortus eius fuit, non imminutio; et natus tantum est non demutatus; quia licet in forma Dei manens formam servi assumpserit, infirmitas tamen habitus humani non infirmavit naturam Dei.' This passage from Cassian (*de Incarn.* vi. 19) may stand as an example of innumerable others from all periods of Christian theology The Christian consciousness has, as a fact, from its beginning down to the Reformation, and for the most part since then, found it an inconceivable supposition that the cosmic functions of the Son and His divine functions—such as His share in the eternal

The Consciousness of our Lord.

procession of the Holy Ghost—should be interrupted by the Incarnation. But it is important to notice that, granted this, there is still room for difference in statements of the truth, according as the divine and cosmic functions (and accompanying consciousness) of the Son are or are not brought into juxtaposition with the human function (and consciousness) so as practically to overwhelm them. The following quotations will illustrate the difference and also the general theological assumption.

IRENAEUS, *con. Haer* v. 18. 3 'Mundi enim factor vere Verbum Dei est : hic autem est Dominus noster qui in novissimis temporibus homo factus est, in hoc mundo exsistens et secundum invisibilitatem continet [-ens?] quae facta sunt omnia et in universa conditione infixus [1] quoniam Verbum Dei gubernans et disponens omnia ; et propter hoc in sua visibiliter [2] venit et caro factum est et pependit super lignum, uti universa in semetipsum recapituletur . . . Ipse est enim qui universorum potestatem habet a Patre quoniam Verbum Dei et homo verus, invisibilibus quidem participans rationabiliter et sensuabiliter [3] legem statuens universa quaeque in suo perseverare ordine ; super visibilia autem et humana regnans manifeste.'

Here Irenaeus certainly asserts that the Incarnation did not interrupt the cosmic activity of the Word. 'In the last times,' he informs us, 'He was made man, while all the same existing in the world and invisibly sustaining all creation. It was because of the universal cosmic

---

[1] i e implanted in the whole creation.
[2] The sense requires us to read *visibiliter*, not *invisibiliter*, here
[3] This must represent νοητῶς or νοερῶς, and means 'in a manner perceptible to the reason' (not the senses). The translator of Irenaeus translates νοῦς by *sensus*.

government entrusted to Him that He rendered Himself visible and was made flesh and hung upon the cross, in order to accomplish a work of recovery, which was necessary to recapitulate all things into Himself.' But when previously Irenaeus had spoken of the human consciousness of Christ, he markedly abstained (as will appear shortly, when the passages are quoted) from bringing this universal activity of the Word into juxtaposition with His human life and experience

ORIGEN, speaking of the Incarnation of the Son (*de Princip.* iv. 30, Rufinus' translation) writes :

'In quo non ita sentiendum est quod omnis divinitatis eius maiestas intra brevissimi corporis claustra conclusa est, ita ut omne Verbum Dei et sapientia eius ac substantialis veritas ac vita vel a Patre divulsa sit vel intra corporis eius coercita et conscripta brevitatem, nec usquam praeterea putetur operata.'

On the other hand, like Irenaeus, though perhaps with more of the hesitation begotten of his philosophy, he inclines (as will appear) to give a real meaning to the divine self-emptying in the assumption of manhood.

EUSEBIUS, *Dem Evang.* vii. 1 ἵν' οὖν καὶ διὰ σωμάτων αἰσθήσεως τῆς τῶν νοητῶν καὶ ἀσωμάτων ἐννοίας ἐπιλαβώμεθα, τὸν ἡμῖν συγγειῆ καὶ γνώριμον [λόγον] αὐτὸς ὁ θεὸς λόγος ἀνελάμβανε, καὶ πάντα γε δι' αὐτοῦ τὰ σωτήρια τοῖς αὐτηκόοις καὶ αὐτόπταις τῶν ἐνθέων αὐτοῦ λόγων τε καὶ ἔργων προεβάλλετο. καὶ ταῦτ' ἔπραττε ταῖς τοῦ σώματος ἀνάγκαις ὁμοίως ἡμῖν οὐδαμῶς καταδεσμούμενος οὐδέ τι χεῖρον ἢ μεῖζον αὐτὸς ἑαυτοῦ τῆς θεότητος ὑπομένων, οὐδ' οὕτως οἷα ἀνθρώπου ψυχὴ τῷ σώματι πεδούμενος ὡς μὴ ἐνεργεῖν δύνασθαι τὰ θεῖα, μὴ δὲ πανταχῇ παρεῖναι θεοῦ λόγον ὄντα καὶ τὰ πάντα πληροῦντα καὶ διὰ πάντων ἥκοντα· ἀλλ' οὐδὲ ῥύπον ἢ φθορὰν ἢ μίασμα

The Consciousness of our Lord.

ἐξ ἧς ἀνείληφε σαρκὸς ἐπενηνεγμένος, ὅτι δὴ ἀσώματος ὢν τὴν φύσιν καὶ ἄϋλος καὶ ἄσαρκος οἷα θεοῦ λόγος, ἐνθέῳ δυνάμει καὶ λόγοις ἡμῖν ἀρρήτοις πᾶσαν ὑπῄει τὴν οἰκονομίαν, τῶν οἰκείων μεταδιδούς, ἀλλ' οὐκ ἀντεπαγόμενος τῶν ἀλλοτρίων. οὐκοῦν τί φοβεῖσθαι χρὴ τὴν ἔνσαρκον οἰκονομίαν, ἐπεὶ μὴ ἐμολύνετο ὁ ἀμόλυντος, μὴ δὲ ἐκ τῆς σαρκὸς ὁ ἀμίαντος ἐμιαίνετο, μὴ δὲ συνεφθείρετο τῇ τοῦ σώματος οἰκείᾳ φύσει ὁ ἀπαθὴς τοῦ θεοῦ λόγος, ἐπεὶ μὴ δὲ ἡλίου πάθοιεν ἄν τι ἀκτῖνες νεκρῶν καὶ παντοίων σωμάτων ἐπαφώμεναι;

The sense of this passage may be given briefly thus:

'The Word was incarnate in order to present spiritual and rational realities to us men under forms of sense. But in doing this His own divine nature was subjected to no change He was not fettered to the necessities of the body which He assumed. He was not involved, like a man's soul, in his body, so as not to be able to operate divinely in the whole universe. He suffered no defilement in his immaterial and impassible essence, nor contracted any attributes alien to it while He was imparting His own, any more than the sun contracts the defilements of the objects which its light illuminates.'

This passage is typical of Eusebius' thought. We may compare it with another, *Dem. Evang* iv. 13 (*Patr. Graec* xxii pp. 284 ff) Here he is again emphasizing that while Christ was conversing among men He was at the same time filling all things and subsisting in the Father (p. 288 a). He describes Him as 'imparting what is His own to the manhood, but not receiving its attributes in exchange' (τὰ μὲν ἐξ αὐτοῦ μεταδιδοὺς τῷ ἀνθρώπῳ, τὰ δὲ ἐκ τοῦ θνητοῦ μὴ ἀντιλαμβάνων), He calls the manhood an 'instrument which he held out before Him' (δι' ὀργάνου οὗ προὐβέβλητο ἀνθρωπίνου), and compares His relation to it to that of a musician to his lyre (285 c) who is not himself affected by the blows which strike the strings (288 b). The metaphor of the sun again appears the nature of the Word is no more involved in the passions of the body which He assumed, than the sun's rays are defiled by the objects which they touch (288 c).

Such a line of thought is typical not of Eusebius only but of many of the more philosophical fathers. Current philosophy was, perhaps, overmuch occupied with the impassibility of God. At any rate to guard the conception of the divine impassibility, philosophical Christians —and Eusebius among them—go dangerously far in minimizing the meaning of the Incarnation. It is overmuch assimilated to the immanence of the divine reason in the universe. The above metaphor of the sun (not used by Eusebius alone [1]) is surely very inadequate to express the relation of the Word to His own manhood. In fact Eusebius is here speaking much more the language of current philosophy than of the New Testament writers. His first thought is of the impassibility of the Word and His cosmic function. In the New Testament writers, on the other hand—for St. Paul and St. John and the author of the Epistle to the Hebrews—the Son of God made man, the Word made flesh, is the primary thought. He being what He was, really did humble

---

[1] See reffs in Newman, *Tracts Theol and Eccl* p 314 Cf a fragment of a letter *ad Caesarium* attributed to St Chrysostom (*Opera*, ed Migne, tom xiii p 497) where the divine Son is said to suffer in the passion no more than the sun suffers when a tree is cut down which it is completely penetrating with its rays St John Damasc *de Fid Orth* iii 26 repeats the metaphor and argument, which is also found in Alcuin, *de Fid. s. Trin.* iii. 16

The Consciousness of our Lord.

Himself to conditions of human suffering and trial and death, for us men and for our salvation. So preoccupied are they with the thought that they do not for the time seem to ask the question—what is the relation of this humiliation to those cosmic functions of the Word, which, antecedently and subsequently to the humiliation, they have full in view? I should contend then that in this passage Eusebius is making primary metaphysical considerations which should be kept strictly secondary, and allowing a philosophical deduction to obscure the full meaning of the Gospel revelation.

ATHANASIUS, *de Incarnatione*, 17. 4, 5 οὐ δὴ τοιοῦτος ἦν ὁ τοῦ θεοῦ λόγος ἐν τῷ ἀνθρώπῳ· οὐ γὰρ συνεδέδετο τῷ σώματι, ἀλλὰ μᾶλλον αὐτὸς ἐκράτει τοῦτο, ὥστε καὶ ἐν τούτῳ ἦν καὶ ἐν τοῖς πᾶσιν ἐτύγχανε καὶ ἔξω τῶν ὄντων ἦν καὶ ἐν μόνῳ τῷ πατρὶ ἀνεπαύετο· καὶ τὸ θαυμαστὸν τοῦτο ἦν, ὅτι καὶ ὡς ἄνθρωπος ἐπολιτεύετο καὶ ὡς λόγος τὰ πάντα ἐζωογόνει καὶ ὡς υἱὸς τῷ πατρὶ συνῆν.

Here Athanasius, almost repeating the words of Eusebius in the passage just referred to, simply asserts that the Incarnation did not limit the Word in Himself. He was still in the universe and in the bosom of the Father. With this position, as a necessary philosophical conclusion, there is—it seems to me—no fault to be found so long as the Gospel revelation of the meaning of the Incarnation is kept in the foreground. But Athanasius like Eusebius goes on—

ὅθεν οὐδὲ τῆς παρθένου τικτούσης ἔπασχεν αὐτός, οὐδὲ ἐν σώματι ὢν ἐμολύνετο· ἀλλὰ μᾶλλον καὶ τὸ σῶμα ἡγίαζεν. οὐδὲ γὰρ ἐν τοῖς πᾶσιν ὢν τῶν πάντων μεταλαμβάνει, ἀλλὰ πάντα μᾶλλον ὑπ' αὐτοῦ ζωογονεῖται καὶ τρέφεται.

Then follows the metaphor of the sun, employed exactly as by Eusebius. Here again then I cannot but think that the philosophical interest overpowers the evangelical truth: as again in c. 41, where, in order to make Christian truth easy for 'the Greeks,' the Incarnation is assimilated to the ἐπίβασις of the Word upon nature. On the other hand Athanasius later in his life strongly insisted on the Word having really identified Himself with the humanity which He assumed. see *Ep. ad Epictetum*, as referred to on p. 124.

PROCLUS of Cyzicus, *Orat.* i 9 (*P. G.* lxv. p 690 c) ὁ αὐτὸς ὢν ἐν τοῖς κόλποις τοῦ πατρὸς καὶ ἐν γαστρὶ παρθένου· ὁ αὐτὸς ἐν ἀγκάλαις μητρὸς καὶ ἐπὶ πτερύγων ἀνέμων· ὁ αὐτὸς ἄνω ὑπὸ ἀγγέλων προσεκυνεῖτο καὶ κάτω τελώναις συνανεκλίνετο· τὰ σεραφὶμ οὐ προσέβλεπε καὶ Πιλάτος ἠρώτα ... ὧδε πλάνος ἐσυκοφαντεῖτο καὶ ἐκεῖ ἅγιος ἐδοξολογεῖτο.

'He, the same, was in His Father's bosom and in the womb of the Virgin, in His mother's arms and on the wings of the winds; He was being worshipped by the angels in heaven and He was supping with publicans on earth; whom the Seraphim dare not gaze at, Pilate was questioning ... *Here* He was being maligned as a cheat, while *there* He was being glorified as the Holy One.'

This is a passage from a memorable and splendid sermon[1] preached in reply to Nestorius' follower Anastasius in the Cathedral of St Sophia at Constantinople. Proclus is emphasizing that the incarnate person is no other than the eternal Son, and he puts into strong rhetorical juxtaposition the humiliating sufferings of the manhood and the glories of the Godhead, as belonging

[1] See Bright's *Early Church History*, p. 313. Cf. Hilary, *de Trin* x. 54.

The Consciousness of our Lord.

simultaneously to the same person. I would only contend that there is nothing in the New Testament to justify this sort of language, and that it gives an unnatural meaning—if meaning at all—to such a fact as our Lord's cry of desolation upon the cross, if within the sphere where that cry was uttered, He was personally living in the exercise of the beatific vision, if that vision was (so to speak) side by side with the experience upon the cross. When, as in this case, the abstract movement of human thought is necessarily baffled by the conditions of the subject, it is specially necessary to keep close to *the facts*, in this case the revealed facts, and to let the language follow closely upon them.

I would conclude then, on this preliminary matter, that it is necessary, if we would be true to the New Testament in thinking or writing of the incarnate Christ, to put into the foreground and to emphasize the human state as it is described in the Gospels. The truth of the New Testament is impaired or destroyed if the divine state is put into immediate juxtaposition with this Only as there is real reason to believe that the apostolic writers did contemplate the continuance of the cosmic functions of the Word, and as the thought of the Church has found it impossible to conceive the opposite, it is right to explain that the real κένωσις within the sphere of the Incarnation must be held compatible with the exercise of divine functions in another sphere. On the question whether this is conceivable by us, more will need to be said later on

§ 2.

Early tradition and speculation on the special subject of the human consciousness of Christ.

The 'churches' were started on their career with a 'tradition' of faith which it was their office to guard. This tradition was conceived to embody the teaching of the apostolic founders on the matters which constituted 'the faith once for all committed to the saints.' This idea of tradition, to which the New Testament bears frequent testimony, has been mentioned before [1]. All that we now have to inquire is whether in the earliest churches this tradition was conceived to contain any information on the subject of our Lord's human consciousness, or whether the subsequent development of Christian thought upon the subject was due simply to the influence of certain 'texts' in the apostolic writings and to conclusions drawn from the general idea of the Incarnation.

The divinity of Christ—that He was the Son of God made man—is assumed by the subapostolic representatives of the churches of Rome and Antioch, Clement and Ignatius [2]. It is assumed, not as matter of controversy,

[1] See above, p. 41.
[2] Clement, *ad Cor.* 2 τὰ παθήματα αὐτοῦ, 1 e τοῦ θεοῦ (= Christ); Ignatius, *Eph* 1 ἐν αἵματι θεοῦ, *Rom.* 6 τοῦ πάθους τοῦ θεοῦ See further Lightfoot's notes on Clem *ad Cor* 2. I ought to add that since Lightfoot decided for θεοῦ not Χριστοῦ as the true reading in this place, the ancient Latin version published by D Germanus Morin in *Anecdota Maredsolana* has increased the evidence on the other side. If Χριστοῦ is to be used, however, there still

The Consciousness of our Lord.

but as truth which can be alluded to, i.e as matter of traditional acceptance common to the churches of Rome and Antioch with those churches—of Greece and Asia—to which Clement and Ignatius were writing[1]. Considering what the teaching of St. Paul and St John on the subject of the Incarnation had been, this could hardly have been otherwise. When we first get formulated summaries of 'the tradition,' i e. creeds, longer or shorter, this principle is the centre of the Christian theology.

Thus the creed of Irenaeus, often repeated in substance, is 'in one God Almighty, from whom are all things; and in one Son of God, Jesus Christ, our Lord, through whom are all things, and in His dispensations, by which the Son of God became man, and in the Spirit of God[1].' And the 'rule of faith' as stated

---

remains evidence of the faith of Clement and his church (1) In the fact that he quotes and depends upon the language of the Epistle to the Hebrews (Heb 1 5) about the person of Christ, c 36 (2) In his reference to Christ as of Jacob, *according to the flesh*, τὸ κατὰ σάρκα, c. 32 (3) In doxologies addressed apparently to Christ, cc 20, 50 (4) In the Trinitarian phrase, ζῇ ὁ θεὸς καὶ ζῇ ὁ κύριος Ἰησοῦς Χριστὸς καὶ τὸ πνεῦμα τὸ ἅγιον ἥ τε πίστις καὶ ἡ ἐλπὶς τῶν ἐκλεκτῶν, c 58, cf c 46

It should be added that the *Shepherd* of Hermas contains in the clearest form the principle of the Incarnation (not so clearly the doctrine of the Trinity) as accepted Christian truth. The Son of God, begotten before all creation as the counsellor of His Father in creation, was in the last days manifested for the salvation of man (*Sim* ix 12)

It is noticeable that Ignatius is contending not for the Godhead of Christ, but for His true humanity. The note of *contention* for the divinity of Christ appears first in the so-called second Epistle of Clement, probably a homily of the Corinthian Church belonging to the first half of the second century, but later than Ignatius Here the preacher, having no doubt the Ebionites in his mind, begins 'Brethren, we must think of Jesus Christ as of God, as of the Judge of quick and dead. and we must not have mean views of our salvation, for if we think meanly of Him we expect also to receive but a mean reward'

[1] Iren *con Haer* iv 33. 7 εἰς ἕνα θεὸν παντοκράτορα, ἐξ οὗ τὰ πάντα, πίστις

by Origen is, so far as it bears on the Incarnation, as follows [1]:

'The particular points clearly delivered in the teaching of the apostles are as follows First, that there is one God ... Secondly, that Jesus Christ Himself who came [into the world] was born of the Father before all creatures; that after He had been the minister of the Father in the creation of all things—for *by Him were all things made*—in the last times, emptying Himself [of His glory] He became man and was incarnate, although God, and while made man remained the God which He was; that He assumed a body like to our own, differing in this respect only that it was born of a virgin and of the Holy Spirit ...'

But this common doctrine of the Incarnation may bring with it one of several different answers to the question of our Lord's consciousness in His mortal life On this latter subject there was no tradition, and the early Church was left, as we are, to the examination of 'texts' and the formation of opinions. This appears from the three earliest statements on the subject.

IRENAEUS, assuming the principle of the Incarnation, emphasizes the reality of our Lord's entrance into

ὁλόκληρος καὶ εἰς τὸν υἱὸν τοῦ θεοῦ Ἰησοῦν Χριστόν, τὸν κύριον ἡμῶν, δι' οὗ τὰ πάντα, καὶ τὰς οἰκονομίας αὐτοῦ, δι' ὧν ἄνθρωπος ἐγένετο ὁ υἱὸς τοῦ θεοῦ, πεισμονὴ βεβαία καὶ εἰς τὸ πνεῦμα τοῦ θεοῦ

[1] Origen, *de Princ* pref 4 'Species vero eorum quae per praedicationem apostolicam manifeste traduntur istae sunt Primo quod unus Deus est . Tum deinde quia Iesus Christus ipse qui venit, ante omnem creaturam natus ex Patre est Qui cum in omnium conditione Patri ministrasset, *per ipsum* enim *omnia facta sunt*, novissimis temporibus se ipsum exinaniens, homo factus, incarnatus est cum Deus esset et homo factus mansit quod erat Deus Corpus assumpsit nostro corpori simile, eo solo differens quod natum ex virgine et Spiritu sancto est'

The Consciousness of our Lord.

human experience. That he should have done this is no more than what we might expect from the greatest of the opponents of Gnosticism. 'Gnosticism' is a vague term, but a general characteristic of the phases of speculation and belief, which are grouped under the name, is a radical disbelief in the compatibility of the spiritual and the material, of God and nature, and, therefore, a radical antagonism to the root-principle of the Incarnation. Thus opposition to Gnosticism leads the Church teachers to a healthy emphasis, as on other things, so also on the reality of the human 'flesh' of Jesus. God really was made man. The Supreme did really enter into nature and manhood. Tertullian chiefly emphasizes this in regard to physical processes and sufferings and in regard to the actual human birth and human sufferings of the Son of God. But Irenaeus emphasizes it more broadly. He claims that God the Son of God, did truly enter into all that makes up the nature of man in body, mind and soul. Not only, then, did He reveal God to man, but He 'exhibited man to God[1]' He really went through human struggles and won a human victory. 'He struggled and overcame · He was man fighting for his fathers, and by His obedience paying the debt of their disobedience : for He *bound the strong* (adversary) and loosed the weak (captives) and gave deliverance to His creatures, destroying sin[2].' And in order to fight the human fight fully,

[1] iv 20 7 'Deo autem exhibens hominem' This activity of the Word is not, however, confined to the Incarnation by Irenaeus

[2] iii 18. 6, 7 'Luctatus est enim et vicit, erat enim homo pro patribus certans et per obedientiam inobedientiam persolvens , alligavit enim fortem et solvit infirmos et salutem donavit plasmati suo, destruens peccatum. . . .

110   *Dissertations.*

'He passed through every age, from infancy to manhood, restoring to each communion with God.' And in order that His human struggle may be believed to have been real, St. Irenaeus postulates a *quiescence* of the divine Word 'while He was tempted and dishonoured, and crucified and slain,' as on the other hand its 'co-operation with the man (or manhood) in His victory and endurance and goodness, and resurrection and ascension[1].' Irenaeus thus emphasizes the reality of

Quapropter et per omnem venit aetatem, omnibus restituens eam, quae est ad Deum communionem' Cf also ii 22 4, an interesting passage, where great stress is laid on our Lord *being truly what He seemed*, and not violating the law of human life. 'Triginta quidem annorum exsistens quum veniret ad baptismum, deinde magistri aetatem perfectam habens, venit Hierusalem, ita ut ab omnibus iuste audiret magister non enim aliud videbatur et aliud erat, sicut inquiunt qui putativum introducunt; sed quod erat hoc et videbatur Magister ergo exsistens, magistri quoque habebat aetatem, non reprobans nec supergrediens hominem, neque solvens legem in se humani generis, sed omnem aetatem sanctificans per illam, quae ad ipsum erat, similitudinem. Omnes enim venit per semetipsum salvare, omnes, inquam, qui per eum renascuntur in Deum, infantes et parvulos et pueros et iuvenes et seniores Ideo per omnem venit aetatem, et infantibus infans factus, sanctificans infantes, in parvulis parvus, sanctificans hanc ipsam habentes aetatem, simul et exemplum illis pietatis effectus et iustitiae et subiectionis, in iuvenibus iuvenis, exemplum iuvenibus fiens et sanctificans Domino Sic et senior in senioribus, ut sit perfectus magister in omnibus, non solum secundum expositionem veritatis, sed et secundum aetatem, sanctificans simul et seniores, exemplum ipsis quoque fiens; deinde et usque ad mortem pervenit, ut sit *primogenitus ex mortuis, ipse primatum tenens in omnibus,* princeps vitae, prior omnium et praecedens omnes'

[1] iii 19 3 ὥσπερ γὰρ ἦν ἄνθρωπος, ἵνα πειρασθῇ, οὕτως καὶ λόγος, ἵνα δοξασθῇ ἡσυχάζοντος μὲν τοῦ λόγου ἐν τῷ πειράζεσθαι . καὶ σταυροῦσθαι καὶ ἀποθνήσκειν συγγινομένου δὲ τῷ ἀνθρώπῳ ἐν τῷ νικᾷν καὶ ὑπομένειν καὶ χρηστεύεσθαι καὶ ἀνίστασθαι καὶ ἀναλαμβάνεσθαι Irenaeus' expression here admits of criticism. By the divine Word he must be understood to mean the *powers* of the divinity, if this passage is to be brought into agreement with his general doctrine And his ascription of the elements of weakness only to the manhood, the element of victory to the Godhead, is not, as we shall see, justifiable from Scripture But these defects of statement do not affect our present purpose. It ought of course to be remembered that

The Consciousness of our Lord.

our Lord's human experiences. And, in accordance with this, the reality of our Lord's human ignorance Then he rebukes the would-be omniscience of the Gnostics

'Unreasonably puffed up, you audaciously declare that you know the unutterable mysteries of God; unreasonably—seeing that even the Lord, the very Son of God, allowed that the Father alone knew the actual day and hour of judgement, saying plainly *of that day and hour knoweth no man, neither the Son, except the Father only.* If therefore the Son did not blush to refer to the Father the knowledge of that day, but said what is true; neither let us blush, to reserve to God those points in inquiries which are too high for us For no one is above his master. . . . For if any one ask the reason why the Father, though in all things holding communion with the Son, was declared by the Lord alone to know the day and hour; he could not at present find one more suitable, or proper, or less perilous than this (for our Lord is the only true master)—that we may learn through Him, that the Father is over all For *the Father*, He says, *is greater than I.* And that even in respect of knowledge the Father is put over [the Son] is announced to us by our Lord, in order that we too, so long as we belong to the fashion of this world, may leave

a good deal of confusion of language (and thought) is due to the use of ὁ ἄνθρωπος, and still more of *homo*, for the manhood Sometimes *homo* is used where what is clearly meant is *not* 'man' but 'manhood,' e. g. in Hilary, *de Trin* ix 7 *homo noster* = our manhood But the use of the concrete term to express the abstract coincides with a frequent confusion of thought between the ideas of 'man' and 'manhood' When opposition to Nestorianism led to clear definition the confusion of thought is over, though even then the use of *homo* for manhood does not cease Thus e g the *contra Eutychen et Nestorium*, assigned to Boetius, a treatise devoted to defining exactly the distinct meanings of 'person' and 'nature' in the Incarnation, still uses the phrase (c 7) *vestitus homine* as = 'clothed with the *manhood*.'

to God perfect knowledge and such investigations [as the Gnostics were presuming to undertake] ¹.'

It might appear as if St. Irenaeus attributed this ignorance to the Son simply as Son; but the phrase, 'so long as we belong to the fashion of this world,' and a previous expression² 'while we are still in this world,' show that he was thinking of human ignorance generally, and therefore of our Lord's ignorance as belonging simply to that mortal state which He assumed in assuming humanity To the *person* of the Son incarnate then, as He was among men, Irenaeus certainly attributes limitation of knowledge³.

¹ ii. 28 6–8 'Irrationabiliter autem inflati, audaciter inenarrabilia Dei mysteria scire vos dicitis; quandoquidem et Dominus, ipse Filius Dei, ipsum iudicii diem et horam concessit scire solum Patrem manifeste dicens: *de die autem illa et hora nemo scit, neque Filius, nisi Pater solus* Si autem scientiam diei illius Filius non erubuit referre ad Patrem, sed dixit quod verum est, neque nos erubescamus quae sunt in quaestionibus maiora secundum nos reservare Deo, *nemo* enim *super magistrum est*   . Etenim si quis exquirat causam, propter quam in omnibus Patei communicans Filio, solus scire horam et diem a Domino manifestatus est, neque aptabilem magis neque decentiorem nec sine periculo alteram quam hanc inveniat in praesenti (quoniam enim solus verax magister est Dominus), ut discamus per ipsum super omnia esse Patrem. *Etenim Pater*, ait, *maior me est* Et secundum agnitionem itaque praepositus esse Pater annuntiatus est a Domino nostio ad hoc, ut et nos, in quantum in figuia huius mundi sumus, perfectam scientiam et tales quaestiones concedamus Deo '

² See ii 28 7 'nos adhuc in terra conversantes '

³ In the same chapter in which he speaks of this ignorance of the Son, he ascribes to Him, in His eternal being, the knowledge of the meaning of the divine generation, unknown to the highest created existences (ii 28. 6), and to the Son, as exalted Christ (apparently), the knowledge of the mysteries of sin and of the fall (ii 28. 7) The context generally, and Irenaeus' theology as a whole, lead us to conclude with Bull (*Defence of the Nicene Creed*, in *Library of Anglo-Catholic Theol* 1. 176), though not exactly for his reasons, and with Dorner (*Doctrine of the Person of Christ*, Clark's Library, 1 p 309) that Irenaeus ascribes true limitations of knowledge to the incarnate Son, in His mortal life

The Consciousness of our Lord.

Meanwhile, Irenaeus' contemporary at Alexandria, CLEMENT, was apparently asserting that the incarnate Christ was omniscient because He was God.

'While the Lord was actually being baptized, a voice sounded upon Him from heaven in witness to the beloved, *Thou art my beloved Son; to-day have I begotten thee* [1]. Let us inquire of these wise men [the Gnostics]· Is Christ *begotten again to-day* [in baptism] already perfect or—what would be most strange—is He deficient? If the latter, He must acquire information. But, as He is God, it is not likely He would acquire any information whatever For no one could be greater than the Word or teacher of the only teacher. Will they, then, unwillingly confess that the Word, begotten as He was of the Father, perfect of the perfect, was *begotten again* [in baptism] according to the forecast of revelation perfectly? And if He was perfect, why was the perfect one baptized? He needed, they say, to fulfil the profession which belonged to man. Quite true. I say the same Does He then become perfect in the act of His being baptized by John? It is plain that this is so Did He then learn nothing from him? Nothing. But He is perfected by the font alone and sanctified by the descent of the Spirit. So it is [2].'

[1] St Mark 1 11, assimilated to Ps 11 7.
[2] Clem *Paedagog* 1 6 25 (Dindorf) αὐτίκα γοῦν βαπτιζομένῳ τῷ κυρίῳ ἀπ' οὐρανῶν ἐπήχησεν φωνὴ μάρτυς ἠγαπημένου υἱός μου εἶ σὺ ἀγαπητός, ἐγὼ σήμερον γεγέννηκά σε. πυθώμεθα οὖν τῶν σοφῶν σήμερον ἀναγεννηθεὶς ὁ Χριστὸς ἤδη τέλειός ἐστιν ἢ ὅπερ ἀτοπώτατον ἐλλιπής, εἰ δὲ τοῦτο, προσμαθεῖν τι αὐτῷ δεῖ. ἀλλὰ προσμαθεῖν μὲν αὐτὸν εἰκὸς οὐδὲ ἐν θεὸν ὄντα. οὐ γὰρ μείζων τις εἴη ἂν τοῦ λόγου, οὐδὲ μὴν διδάσκαλος τοῦ μόνου διδασκάλου μή τι οὖν ὁμολογήσουσιν ἄκοντες τὸν λόγον τέλειον ἐκ τελείου φύντα τοῦ πατρὸς κατὰ τὴν οἰκονομικὴν προδιατύπωσιν ἀναγεννηθῆναι τελείας, καὶ εἰ τέλειος ἦν, τί ἐβαπτίζετο ὁ τέλειος, ἔδει, φασί, πληρῶσαι τὸ ἐπάγγελμα τὸ ἀνθρώπινον. παγκάλως φημὶ γάρ· ἅμα τοίνυν τῷ βαπτίζεσθαι αὐτὸν ὑπὸ Ἰωάννου γίνεται τέλειος, δῆλον ὅτι οὐδὲν οὖν πρὸς αὐτοῦ προσέμαθεν, οὐ γὰρ τελειοῦται δὲ τῷ λουτρῷ μόνῳ καὶ τοῦ πνεύματος τῇ καθόδῳ ἁγιάζεται οὕτας ἔχει.

The passage is not, perhaps, quite clear in its meaning; but Clement appears to attribute to our Lord both divine omniscience, which cannot learn from outside, as well as a perfect (human) enlightenment acquired in His baptism, the like of which he attributes, as against the Gnostics, to all baptized Christians He appears then to think of our Lord on earth as exercising both the divine omniscience of the Godhead and the perfect enlightenment of the manhood. But we should hardly expect from Clement, who went as far on the road of Docetism as to deny the existence in our Lord of any, even the most innocent, human emotions or appetites [1], a very full realization of his real humanity.

ORIGEN, who succeeded Clement in the Catechetical School of Alexandria, gives us more to dwell upon. So far as tradition goes, what it gave to Origen was (as we have seen) the principle that the Son of God divesting Himself, but none the less remaining God, became truly and really man by a human birth. We should expect Origen to fill up this outline by scrupulous attention to the letter of Holy Scripture. It cannot be too often emphasized that Origen's errors—so far as his opinions are certainly errors—were mainly due to an over-scrupulous literalness in the interpretation of Holy Scripture, that for instance his doctrine that the Son was not the absolute Goodness, as He was the absolute Wisdom, was due to his interpretation, more literal than true, of the text 'There is none good but one, that is

---

[1] He was ἀπαξαπλῶς ἀπαθής. He neither experienced the appetite of hunger, nor the emotions of joy and grief (*Strom* vi 9 71) In *Strom* iii 7.59 Valentinus is quoted, and apparently with approval, as denying in our Lord the natural physical process of digestion.

The Consciousness of our Lord.

God.' We turn then with interest to Origen's commentary on such a critical passage as St. Matt. xxiv. 36, which unfortunately remains to us only in an old and very bad Latin version [1]: *De die autem illa et hora nemo scit, neque angeli caelorum, neque Filius, nisi Pater solus.* After noticing that this text serves to rebuke those who pretend to know too much about the last things, Origen remarks that the Saviour appears, according to this passage, to join Himself to those who do not know the day and hour. How is this consistent with His perfect knowledge of the Father (St. Matt. xi. 27)? How did it come about that the Father concealed this from Him? He proceeds to give two main interpretations, which we can more or less discern through the dimness of the bad Latin translation.

(a) Some will have the courage to attribute this to the proper human development ascribed to our Lord by St. Luke (ii. 52). According to this interpretation He too. the man Christ Jesus, must wait His time for perfect knowledge [2]. Therefore now, 'before He had fulfilled His dispensation,' it was no wonder if He was ignorant of this one point alone. After the resurrection, when God highly exalted Him and bestowed upon Him the name which is above every name, He uses different language: 'It is not *for you to know* the times and the seasons.' For by this time He knew all that the Father knew.

---

[1] Huet, *Origeniana,* lib III. cap 2. qu 3. § 12 ascribes this translation, not without reason, to a companion of Cassiodorus

[2] '*Homo qui secundum Salvatorem* intelligitur proficiens,' &c. — (I suppose) 'the man who (or the manhood which) in the case of the Saviour' Cf his 'secundum historias' (in *Tom* xv 5 of the same commentary) which = ' in the case of the O. T. stories.'

Origen however further suggests that by the words which follow—'which the Father has put in His own power'—it is implied that the Father Himself, waiting upon the outcome of human conduct, has not fixed the day of the end, but keeps it open[1].

(β) He then gives another interpretation, which he

[1] *in Matth Comment Series* 55 (Lommatzsch iv p 329) 'Et se ipsum Salvator, secundum hunc locum, coniungit ignorantibus diem illam et horam. Et rationabiliter est quaerendum quomodo qui confidit se cognoscere Patrem dicens *Nemo novit Patrem nisi Filius, et cui voluerit Filius revelare*, Patrem quidem novit, diem autem et horam consummationis non novit? et quare hoc abscondit Pater a Filio? Omnino enim ratio esse debet, quod etiam a Salvatore tempus consummationis absconditum sit, et ignoret de eo Audebit autem aliquis dicere, quoniam homo qui secundum Salvatorem intelligitur proficiens sapientia et aetate et gratia coram Deo et hominibus, qui proficiens proficiebat quidem super omnes scientia et sapientia, non tamen ut veniret iam quod erat perfectum, priusquam propriam dispensationem impleret Nihil ergo mirum est, si hoc solum nescivit ex omnibus, id est, diem consummationis et horam Forsitan autem et quod ait nescire se diem consummationis et horam, ante dispensationem suam dixit, quia nemo scit, neque angeli, neque Filius, nisi solus Pater Post dispensationem autem impletam nequaquam hoc dixit, postquam *Deus illum superexaltavit, et donavit ei nomen quod est super omne nomen* Nam postea et Filius cognovit scientiam a Patre suscipiens, etiam de die consummationis et hora, ut iam non solum Pater sciret de ea, sed etiam Filius Et in *Actibus* quidem *Apostolorum* convenientes apostoli interrogaverunt eum dicentes: *Domine, si in hoc tempore restitues regnum Israel?* Ille autem dixit ad eos *Non est vestrum nosse tempora vel momenta quae Pater posuit in sua potestate* Et quoniam in sua potestate tempora et momenta consummationis mundi et restitutionis regni Israel posuit, ideo quod nondum fuerat praedefinitum a Deo, nemo poterat scire Si autem ita est, praefinivit quidem consummationem facere mundi, non autem et tempora et momenta praefinivit quae posuit in sua potestate, ut si voluerit ea augere, sic iudicans augeat ea, si autem abbreviare, abbreviet, nemine cognoscente Et ideo de temporibus et momentis consummationis mundi in sua posuit potestate, ut consequenter humano generi in suo arbitrio constituto talia vel talia agenti definiat iudicium debitum Multa et in prophetis est invenire ad utilitatem audientium scripta, in praeceptis et denunciationibus, quasi Deo non praefiniente quicquam de iis, sed puniente quidem si peccaverint, salvante autem si praecepta servaverint Et sicut in illis non introduxit scriptura Deum praefinientem, sed secundum utilitatem audientium proloquentem, sic intelligendum est et de die consummationis et hora'

The Consciousness of our Lord. 117

describes as 'more celebrated than the above.' It is that Christ is speaking in the person of the Church. 'For while the Church, which is His body, does not know that day and hour, so long neither the Son Himself is said to know it; in order that He may then be understood to know when all His members also know.' This interpretation is paralleled by the interpretation of 1 Cor xv. 28, according to which the subjection of the Christ means the subjection of the Church in Christ[1]. The sense thus given is modified by the suggestion that to 'know' means to experience. It is the experience of the glory of the last day which lies in the mind of the Father alone, unrealized alike by the Head and the members of the Church. But Origen seems to return to the suggestion of a real ignorance or incompleteness of some sort in Christ, owing to His having put Himself in our place· 'But the consummation of each single person .. the Father alone knows ; for the Son, accompanying and preceding His followers, and willing (their salvation) is, so to speak, about to come, and delays that they who seek

---

[1] *ib* 'Alia expositio, quae famosior est iis quae iam tradita sunt, aliud dicit de eo quod scriptum est· *Neque Filius, nisi solus Pater.* Dicit, inquit, alicubi de Salvatore apostolus, et de rebus in fine saeculi ordinandis, hoc modo *Cum autem subiecta illi fuerint omnia, tunc et ipse Filius subiectus erit ei qui sibi subdidit omnia, ut sit Deus omnia in omnibus* Et videtur per haec dicere subiectionem Filii fieri subiectionem omnium qui ei erant subiiciendi, et adventum eorum per Filium ad Deum, et perfectionem Si ergo bene dicitur hoc de Filii subiectione ad Patrem futura, ut tunc hi, qui futuri sunt Christi et adhaeserunt ei, cum ipso Christo Patri subiiciantur : quare non et de die illa et hora neminem scire, neque Filium, similiter exponemus ? Donec enim ecclesia, quae est corpus Christi, nescit diem illam et horam, tam diu nec ipse Filius dicitur scire diem illam et horam, ut tunc intelligatur scire, quando scierint et omnia membra eius' Cf. *de Princip* ii 8 5.

to follow Him may be able to do so and be found with Him at that day and hour ¹.'

In another passage, where we have the original Greek to examine, Origen appears to postulate a real entrance of the Son into human ignorance. He is conceived to have really emptied Himself and descended to actual human limits. Origen is considering how the words of the prophet (Jer. i. 6), 'I am a child: I cannot speak,' can be applied to Christ. He replies by referring to the testimony of the Gospel. ' Jesus, while yet a child, before He became a man, since He had "emptied Himself," is seen to "advance." Now no one who is already perfect advances, for to advance implies the need of advance. Therefore He advanced in stature, in wisdom, in favour with God and man. For because He had emptied Himself in coming down to us, therefore, having emptied Himself, He proceeded to take again that of which He had emptied Himself, such self-emptying having been a voluntary act. What wonder then if He advanced in wisdom and stature and in favour with God and man, and that it should be truly said of Him by Isaiah [vii. 15, 16], that "He shall choose the good and refuse the evil, *before He knows evil and good*²"?'

¹ *ib* 'Et diem ergo consummationis huiusmodi et corruptionis saeculi nemo scit, neque angeli caelorum, neque Filius Dei, de sanctis Deo melius providente, ut simul fiant in beatitudine quae futura est post diem et horam consummationis illius . Et uniuscuiusque autem consummationem . solus scit Pater quoniam Filius comitans, et praecedens ante sequentes, et volens, ut ita dicam, venturus est, et tardat, ut possint eum sequi qui certant sequi eum, et sequentes eum inveniantur cum eo in die illa et hora.'

² *in Ier hom* 1. 7 εἰ δὲ καὶ ἀπὸ εὐαγγελίου δεῖ λαμβάνειν παράδειγμα, Ἰησοῦς οὐκ ἀνὴρ γενόμενος, ἀλλ' ἔτι παιδίον ὤν, ἐπεὶ ἐκένωσεν ἑαυτόν, προέκοπτεν· οὐδεὶς γὰρ προκόπτει τετελειωμένος, ἀλλὰ προκόπτει δεόμενος προκοπῆς· οὐκοῦν προέκοπτεν ἡλικίᾳ, προέκοπτε σοφίᾳ, προέκοπτε χάριτι παρὰ θεῷ καὶ

The Consciousness of our Lord.

This learning on the part of the Son is like a grown man's learning to talk like a child. Because he is full grown, he has to put violence on himself to talk with children after their manner. So the Son sets Himself to learn what lies below Him. Subsisting in the majesty of the glory of God, He does not speak human words, He does not, as it were, know how to speak to those below. Therefore it is that when He comes into the human body, He says to the Father ' I cannot speak: I know indeed things too great for human speech. But Thou wishest me to speak to men. I have not yet acquired human speech. I have Thy speech, I am Thy Word, I can speak to Thee; but I know not how to speak to men for I am a child [1].'

Further on the language of the Incarnation is described, in St. Paul's phrase, as the 'foolishness of God.' The self-emptying of the Incarnation is a coming down of the divine Word into conditions in which the divine wisdom must become what, compared to its own essential character, is foolishness, though as compared to all human wisdom it is ' wiser than men [2].'

ἀνθρώποις   εἰ γὰρ ἐκένωσεν ἑαυτὸν καταβαίνων ἐνταῦθα, καὶ κενώσας ἑαυτὸν ἐλάμβανε πάλιν ταῦτα ἀφ' ὧν ἐκένωσεν ἑαυτόν, ἑκὼν κενώσας ἑαυτόν   τί ἄτοπον αὐτὸν καὶ προκεκοφέναι σοφίᾳ καὶ ἡλικίᾳ καὶ χάριτι παρὰ θεῷ καὶ ἀνθρώποις, καὶ ἀληθεύεσθαι περὶ αὐτὸν τό· Πρὶν ἢ γνῶναι αὐτὸν καλὸν ἢ πονηρόν, ἐκλέξεται τὸ ἀγαθὸν καὶ ἀπειθεῖ πονηρίᾳ,

[1] ib 8 μανθάνει οὖν, καὶ οἱονεὶ ἀναλαμβάνει ἐπιστήμην οὐ μεγάλων, ἀλλ' ὑποδεεστέρων   καὶ ὥσπερ μανθάνω, βιαζόμενος ἐμαυτὸν ψελλίζειν, ὅτε παιδίοις διαλέγομαι   οὐ γὰρ ἐπιστάμενος παιδιστί, ἵν' οὕτως εἴπω, λαλεῖν, βιάζομαι τέλειος ὤν, οὕτως καὶ ἐν τῇ μεγαλειότητι τῆς δόξης τοῦ θεοῦ τυγχάνων, οὐ λαλεῖ ἀνθρώπινα, οὐκ οἶδε φθέγγεσθαι τοῖς κάτω   ὅτε δὲ ἔρχεται εἰς σῶμα ἀνθρώπινον, λέγει κατὰ τὰς ἀρχάς   Οὐκ ἐπίσταμαι λαλεῖν, ὅτι νεώτερός εἰμι.

[2] ib hom viii 8 μέλλει τι ἐπιτολμᾶν ὁ λόγος καὶ λέγειν   ὅτι τὸ ἐπιδημῆσαν τῷ βίῳ ἐκένασεν ἑαυτόν, ἵνα τῷ κενώματι αὐτοῦ πληρωθῇ ὁ κόσμος   εἰ δὲ ἐκένωσεν ἐκεῖνο τὸ ἐπιδημῆσαν τῷ βίῳ, αὐτὸ ἐκεῖνο τὸ κένωμα σοφία ἦν· ὅτι τὸ μωρὸν τοῦ

120   *Dissertations.*

We may notice one other passage from Origen bearing on the subject because it is highly ambiguous and, in company with other passages, illustrates the tentative uncertainty of Origen's view. In Jerome's version of the Homilies on St. Luke, the comment of Origen on the words in St. Luke ii. 40 and 52, Jesus 'waxed strong, being filled with wisdom' and 'Jesus increased in wisdom, &c.,' is twofold. On the first passage he declares that His wisdom was for a boy supernatural: '*Replebatur sapientia.* This is beyond human nature, nay, beyond the whole rational creation.' 'We doubt not that something divine appeared in the flesh of Jesus[1].' On the second he comments as follows: 'Was He not wise before, that He should increase in wisdom? or is it that, as He had emptied Himself when He took "the form of a servant," so now He was resuming that which He had lost, and was being filled with excellences which He seemed to have lost when a little before He had taken the body[2]?'

θεοῦ σοφώτερον τῶν ἀνθρώπων ἐστίν. A passage (quoted by Newman, *Tracts Theol Eccl* p 314) might, taken by itself, be interpreted to deny the reality in Christ of a truly human activity 'omne quod agit, quod sentit, quod intelligit, Deus est' (*de Princ* ii 6 6); but in its context it would appear that Origen is only vindicating such a union of Christ's human soul with God as renders possible His moral unalterableness The words which follow are. ' et ideo non convertibilis aut mutabilis dici potest quae inconvertibilitatem ex Verbi Dei unitate indesinenter ignita possedit.' In such a passage as *con. Cels* iii 41, it appears that the transformation of the humanity into an ethereal and divine quality there spoken of refers to the period after the resurrection; cf *con Cels.* ii 63–67, and Huet, *Origeniana*, l ii c 2 qu 3 17

[1] *in Luc hom* xix '*Puer* . . *replebatur sapientia* Hoc hominum natura non recipit, ut ante duodecim annos sapientia compleatur Aliud est partem habere sapientiae, aliud sapientia esse completum Non ambigimus ergo, divinum aliquid in carne Iesu apparuisse et non solum super hominem, sed super omnem quoque rationalem creaturam.'

[2] *in Luc hom.* xx 'Numquid sapiens non erat, ut sapientior fieret? An

The Consciousness of our Lord.

These passages from Irenaeus, Clement, and Origen, have been dwelt on and quoted at length because they seem to prove—

(1) That the 'apostolic tradition' as understood by these great fathers, had nothing to say in regard to the consciousness of the incarnate Son. Men were left then, as now, to the examination of our Lord's words and to conclusions from the principles involved in the Incarnation.

(2) That there were different opinions and tones of thought on this great subject in the second century. There were those who, like Irenaeus and (generally) Origen, took the language of the Gospels as strictly true, and believed in the limitation of our Lord's consciousness, whether through a 'quiescence' of the divine activity, or as a sympathetic entry on the part of the eternal Word into a consciousness lower than His own. There were those on the other hand who would argue, like Clement, that Christ, as God, could not grow in knowledge, and who, accepting the 'more celebrated' interpretation of our Lord's words, ascribed ignorance to Him, not in Himself but in His Church.

<small>quoniam evacuaverat se formam servi accipiens, id quod amiserat resumebat et replebatur virtutibus quas paullo ante, assumpto corpore, visus fuerat relinquere?' The *visus fuerat* (and *videbatur* above) indicate a hesitation in Origen's mind, which is apparent in other places, as to the nature of the κένωσις. See, for instance, *con Cels* iv 15 At the end of this passage he declares the Word unaffected in His own nature by the affections of the human flesh and mind, and indeed uses language which would make the humanity a mere transitory veil of His divine glory In other passages where the truth of the human mind is better guarded, the tone is very Nestorian, and coloured by the idea of the pre-existence of all souls, including the soul of Jesus, e g. *de Princip* iv 31.</small>

§ 3.

The anti-Arian writers who admit a human ignorance.

It has been worth while dwelling at length on these passages, not only because they indicate the absence of any original tradition on the subject we are dealing with, but also because they represent, strange as it may seem, the highest level of ecclesiastical thought on this subject for a long time to come. In the third and fourth centuries the theological attention of the Church was diverted from the Incarnation proper to the doctrine of the Trinity. The conflict was against Unitarian Sabellianism on the one hand, which would have annihilated the 'distinction of persons,' and the extreme subordinationism on the other which was countenanced by some language of Origen and Dionysius of Alexandria, and which afforded an excuse for what was none the less the essentially different Arian position according to which the Son was no more than the highest of the creatures[1]. As a consequence of this long and complicated controversy, the Trinitarian terminology was arrived at by which the Church affirmed the existence of three 'persons' (ὑποστάσεις or *personae*) coeternal, coequal and

[1] Of recent years a fresh interest has been given to the question of the origin and meaning of Arianism, by the writings of Gwatkin and Harnack The summary of Robertson in *Athanasius* (*Nicene and Post-Nicene Fathers*) pp xxi–xxx is admirable. One cannot but hope that it may exist shortly in a more accessible form.

The Consciousness of our Lord. 123

coessential in the one essence or substance of the Godhead. This controversy was carried on mainly as regards the person of the Son, and as a result no aspect of His essential relation to the Father was left untouched; but very little was contributed as regards the doctrine of His incarnation, or specially as regards His human consciousness. When the Arians however produced texts such as 'Jesus increased in wisdom,' 'of that day and hour knoweth no man, neither the Son,' as evidence of the essential inferiority of the Son, Athanasius referred them to our Lord's *humanity*, on the assumption that in respect of His humanity there was a real growth and a real limitation of knowledge. This assumption—though it may be said to have been made incidentally, by way of setting aside the proposed texts as irrelevant to the discussion of the Godhead, rather than by way of positive treatment, and though it is not made without vacillation—is still clearly made by Athanasius, and it is implied that it is a common assumption of Churchmen. A concession, similar to Athanasius' assumption of a human ignorance, is to be found in Gregory of Nazianzus, but it is not very clear. and St. Basil, while not himself assenting, allows such a concession of human ignorance. The passages referred to are as follows:

ATHANASIUS, in *Orat. adv. Arian.* iii. 51–54, comments on St Luke ii. 52 προέκοπτεν τῇ σοφίᾳ. His chief contention is that this is no advance of the Word or Wisdom as such, but only in respect of the humanity He assumed: διὰ τοῦτο, ὡς προείπομεν, οὐχ ἡ σοφία, ᾗ σοφία ἐστίν, αὐτὴ καθ' ἑαυτὴν προέκοπτεν· ἀλλὰ τὸ ἀνθρώπινον ἐν τῇ σοφία προέκοπτεν, ὑπεραναβαῖνον κατ' ὀλίγον τὴν ἀνθρωπίνην φύσιν καὶ θεοποιούμενον καὶ ὄργανον αὐτῆς πρὸς τὴν ἐνέργειαν τῆς θεότητος καὶ τὴν ἔκλαμψιν αὐτῆς γινόμενον καὶ φαινόμενον πᾶσιν. διὸ οὐδὲ εἶπεν ὁ λόγος προέκοπτεν, ἀλλὰ ὁ Ἰησοῦς, ὅπερ ὄνομα γενόμενος ἄνθρωπος ὁ κύριος ἐκλήθη, ὡς εἶναι τῆς ἀνθρωπίνης φύσεως τὴν προκοπὴν οὕτως ὡς ἐν τοῖς ἔμπροσθεν εἴπομεν. Here Athanasius does recognize a human advance: more than a mere increased manifestation of the Godhead in the human body which he had spoken of in the previous chapter (52), τοῦ σώματος ἄρα ἐστὶν ἡ προκοπή· αὐτοῦ γὰρ προκόπτοντος, προέκοπτεν ἐν αὐτῷ καὶ ἡ φανέρωσις τῆς θεότητος τοῖς ὁρῶσιν. He also recognizes that the subject of the advance is the eternal person, because He appropriated or identified with Himself the human nature which He assumed Thus speaking of the human states of trouble, fear, progress, &c., he says οὐκ ἦν ἴδια φύσει τοῦ λόγου ταῦτα, ᾗ λόγος ἦν, ἐν δὲ τῇ τοιαῦτα πασχούσῃ σαρκὶ ἦν ὁ λόγος (c. 55); οὐδὲ γὰρ οὐδὲ ἔξωθεν ὄντος τοῦ λόγου ἐγίνετο ἡ προκοπή, οἷά ἐστιν, ἣν εἰρήκαμεν· ἐν αὐτῷ γὰρ ἦν ἡ σὰρξ ἡ προκόπτουσα, καὶ αὐτοῦ λέγεται (c. 53); ἀνάγκη ἐν πάσχοντι σώματι καὶ κλαίοντι καὶ κάμνοντι γενομένου αὐτοῦ, αὐτοῦ λέγεσθαι μετὰ τοῦ σώματος καὶ ταῦτα ἅπερ ἐστὶν ἴδια τῆς σαρκός (c. 56). Compare the language of the *Epistle to Epictetus*, c. 6, as to the Word 'appropriating' (ἰδιοποιεῖσθαι) the properties of the body, as being His own body.

His language as to St Mark xiii. 32 (οὐδεὶς οἶδεν... οὐδὲ ὁ υἱός) is perhaps more explicit. First, it is not *qua* Son that Christ is ignorant. See *Orat. adv Ar.* iii. 44 διὰ τοῦτο καὶ περὶ ἀγγέλων λέγων, οὐκ εἴρηκεν ἐπαναβαίνων ὅτι οὐδὲ τὸ πνεῦμα τὸ ἅγιον· ἀλλ' ἐσιώπησε, δεικνὺς κατὰ δύο ταῦτα ὅτι, εἰ τὸ πνεῦμα οἶδεν, πολλῷ μᾶλλον ὁ λόγος, ᾗ λόγος ἐστίν, οἶδεν, παρ' οὗ καὶ τὸ πνεῦμα λαμβάνει· καὶ ὅτι, περὶ τοῦ πνεύματος σιωπήσας, φανερὸν πεποίηκεν ὅτι περὶ τῆς ἀνθρωπίνης αὐτοῦ λειτουργίας ἔλεγεν οὐδὲ ὁ υἱός.

But *the Christians recognize* that this expression 'the Son knows not' is spoken by Christ truly as man (c. 45); οἱ δὲ φιλόχριστοι καὶ χριστοφόροι γινώσκομεν ὡς οὐκ ἀγνοῶν ὁ λόγος ᾗ λόγος ἐστὶν ἔλεγεν οὐκ οἶδα, οἶδε γάρ· ἀλλὰ τὸ ἀνθρώπινον δεικνὺς ὅτι τῶν ἀνθρώπων ἴδιόν ἐστι τὸ ἀγνοεῖν καὶ ὅτι σάρκα ἀγνοοῦσαν ἐνεδύσατο, ἐν ᾗ ὢν σαρκικῶς ἔλεγεν· οὐκ οἶδα. Cf. c. 43 ὡς μὲν λόγος γινώσκει ὡς δὲ ἄνθρωπος ἀγνοεῖ ... εἰδὼς ὡς θεός, ἀγνοεῖ σαρκικῶς. οὐκ εἴρηκε γοῦν, οὐδὲ ὁ υἱὸς τοῦ θεοῦ οἶδεν, ἵνα μὴ ἡ θεότης ἀγνοοῦσα φαίνηται· ἀλλ' ἁπλῶς οὐδὲ ὁ υἱός· ἵνα τοῦ ἐξ ἀνθρώπων γενομένου υἱοῦ ἡ ἄγνοια ᾖ. C. 46 ὥσπερ γὰρ ἄνθρωπος γενόμενος μετ' ἀνθρώπων πεινᾷ καὶ διψᾷ καὶ πάσχει, οὕτως μετὰ μὲν τῶν ἀνθρώπων ὡς ἄνθρωπος οὐκ οἶδεν, θεϊκῶς δὲ ἐν τῷ πατρὶ ὢν λόγος καὶ σοφία οἶδεν.

In c. 47 however he assimilates our Lord's profession of ignorance to St. Paul's, when he says 'whether in the body or out of the body, I know not' (see 2 Cor. xii. 2), and he assumes that St. Paul really knew the conditions under which the revelation was given to him, though he concealed his knowledge. Thus in this passage he seems to make our Lord's profession of ignorance only 'economic.' On the other hand in c. 48 he reaffirms that in professing ignorance Christ did not lie, 'for He spoke humanly—as man I do not know' (καὶ οὔτε ἐψεύσατο τοῦτο εἰρηκώς· ἀνθρωπίνως γὰρ εἶπεν, ὡς ἄνθρωπος, οὐκ οἶδα).

Agreeably to the hesitation exhibited by Athanasius in these passages, when he is commenting on our Lord's questions, 'where have ye laid him?' 'how many loaves have ye[1]?' he both admits a possible ignorance as appertaining to our Lord's manhood, and at the same time explains the questions as not in fact involving ignorance. See *Orat. adv. Ar.* iii. 37 ὅταν ἐρωτᾷ ὁ κύριος οὐκ ἀγνοῶν... ἐπερωτᾷ, ἀλλὰ γινώσκων ὅπερ ἠρώτα αὐτός... ἂν δὲ φιλονεικῶσιν ἔτι διὰ τὸ ἐπερωτᾶν, ἀκουέτωσαν ὅτι ἐν μὲν τῇ θεότητι οὐκ ἔστιν ἄγνοια, τῆς δὲ σαρκὸς ἴδιόν ἐστι τὸ ἀγνοεῖν, καθάπερ εἴρηται.

ST. GREGORY NAZIANZEN, *Orat.* xxx. 15, says with reference to St. Mark xiii. 32, ᾗ πᾶσιν εὔδηλον ὅτι γινώσκει μὲν ὡς θεός, ἀγνοεῖν δέ φησιν ὡς ἄνθρωπος, ἄν τις τὸ φαινόμενον χωρίσῃ τοῦ νοουμένου[2]. He notices that ignorance is attributed not to the 'Son of God' but to 'the Son' simply; and this he says gives us opportunity— ὥστε τὴν ἄγνοιαν ὑπολαμβάνειν ἐπὶ τὸ εὐσεβέστερον, τῷ ἀνθρωπίνῳ, μὴ τῷ θείῳ, ταύτην λογιζομένους. But he goes on (c. 16) to suggest that another interpretation is tenable which makes the words mean only that *the Son does not know apart from the Father.* Indeed, taking the passage as a whole, it must be admitted that he is not disposed to think of our incarnate Lord as in any sense really ignorant.

Previously (c 5) he has interpreted the subjection of the Son (1 Cor. xv. 28) as the subjection of us in Him: He presents us to God, ἑαυτοῦ ποιούμενος τὸ ἡμέτερον.

[1] St John xi 34, St Mark vi. 38
[2] Later writers, Eulogius of Alexandria (see p 159) and John of Damascus, *de Fide Orthod* iii 21, take Gregory to mean by this phrase that Christ was only ignorant in His humanity, if you consider the humanity as an outward object in abstraction from the Godhead to which in fact you know it to have been united . and this is not an unfair interpretation of the passage

The Consciousness of our Lord.

(Cf. Gregory of Nyssa *adv. Eunom.* xi. 14, *P. G.* xlv. p. 557 ἀλλὰ καὶ πάντων τῶν ἀνθρώπων τὴν πρὸς τὸν θεὸν ὑποταγήν, ὅταν ἑνωθέντες οἱ πάντες ἀλλήλοις διὰ τῆς πίστεως ἓν σῶμα τοῦ κυρίου τοῦ ἐν πᾶσιν ὄντος γενώμεθα, τοῦ υἱοῦ πρὸς τὸν πατέρα ὑποταγὴν ὁ ἀπόστολος λέγει.) So the cry 'My God, my God, why hast thou forsaken me?' is the cry of *our sinful* human nature deserted by God, now taken upon the lips of Him who was bringing us near to God; He, the Christ, was not deserted (οὐ γὰρ αὐτὸς ἐγκαταλέλειπται, . . . ἐν ἑαυτῷ δὲ τυποῖ τὸ ἡμέτερον).

ST. BASIL considers the meaning of St. Mark xiii. 32 at length (*Ep.* 236), and while he prefers to interpret 'No man knoweth, nor do the angels, nor did the Son know *except* the Father, i. e. the cause of the Son's knowing is from the Father' (c. 2), he admits that 'one who refers the ignorance to Him who in His incarnation took everything human upon Himself, and advances in wisdom and favour with God and man, will not fall outside the orthodox apprehension of the matter' (τὸ τῆς ἀγνοίας ἐπὶ τὸν οἰκονομικῶς πάντα καταδεξάμενον καὶ προκόπτοντα παρὰ θεῷ καὶ ἀνθρώποις σοφίᾳ καὶ χάριτι λαμβάνων τις, οὐκ ἔξω τῆς εὐσεβοῦς ἐνεχθήσεται διανοίας)[1].

Among westerns ST. AMBROSE has been quoted as admitting a real increase of knowledge in Christ as man. Cf. *de Incarn.* vii. 72 '*Iesus proficiebat aetate et sapientia et gratia apud Deum et homines* Quomodo

---

[1] It should be noted that St Basil's argument in part depends on the position that St. Matthew, who says 'the Father *only* knows' (ὁ πατὴρ μόνος, xxiv 36), does not admit the words 'neither the Son', but according to the true reading St Matthew and St Mark both have these latter words.

proficiebat Sapientia Dei? Doceat te ordo verborum. Profectus est aetatis et profectus sapientiae, sed humanae est. Ideo aetatem ante praemisit ut secundum hominem crederes dictum, aetas enim non divinitatis sed corporis est. Ergo si proficiebat aetate hominis, proficiebat sapientia hominis. sapientia autem sensu proficit quia a sensu sapientia.' He protests that to recognize real human increase in Christ is not to divide the Christ but to distinguish the substance of the flesh (manhood) and of the Godhead, cf *Expos. in Luc.* ii. 63, 64[1]. On the other hand St Ambrose, when (*de Fide*, v. 16. 193) he comes to deal with the words 'of that day and hour knoweth no man ... neither the Son,' after first suggesting that the words *nec Filius, as not being represented in the old Greek codices*, are an interpolation[2], and after, secondly, suggesting that 'the Son' means 'the Son of Man' or Christ in His humanity, goes on finally to deny the ignorance of Christ altogether, like all late westerns, and to make the profession merely economic; see v. 17. 219 'Ea est in scripturis consuetudo divinis, ... ut Deus dissimulet

---

[1] The distinction of the two natures is expressed in *Expos in Luc* x 61, as if the humanity did not really belong to the person of the Son Commenting on *Tristis est anima mea,* he writes 'Tristis autem est non ipse, sed anima Non est tristis sapientia, non divina substantia, sed anima' Cf Hilary *de Trin* ix 5, where it is argued that the things said by Christ, 'secundum hominem,' are not to be taken as said 'de se ipso,' i e of the divine nature

[2] It is often assumed, as by Dr Liddon, *Divinity of our Lord* (Longmans, ed. 12) p. 467, that St Ambrose is here referring to Mark xiii 32 In this case St. Ambrose's statement would be a simple mistake But in fact, as shown by the words *nisi solus Pater,* he is referring to St Matt xxiv 36, where many—though not the best—Greek codices do omit οὐδὲ ὁ υἱός The reading is discussed by Jerome in a passage quoted p 135 This fact however does not improve Ambrose's argument, for he has simply left Mark xiii. 32, where the reading is undoubted, out of sight.

The Consciousness of our Lord.

se nescire quod novit[1]. Et in hoc ergo unitas divinitatis et unitas dispositionis in Patre probatur et Filio, si quemadmodum Deus Pater cognita dissimulat, ita Filius etiam in hoc imago Dei quae sibi sunt nota dissimulet.' Again, v. 18. 220 'Mavult Dominus nimio in discipulos amore propensus, petentibus his quae cognitu inutilia iudicaret, videri ignorare quae noverat, quam negare: plusque amat nostram utilitatem instruere quam suam potentiam demonstrare.' He goes on however to mention the interpretation of some 'less timid than himself' who, while denying that the Son of God in His divine nature could be ignorant, affirm that in respect of His assumption of humanity He could both grow in knowledge and be ignorant of the future. I may add that Ambrose appears to deny that our Lord prayed for Himself. 'non utique propter suffragium,' he says, 'sed propter exemplum' (*Expos. in Luc.* v. 10). Cf. v. 42 'orat Dominus non ut pro se obsecret sed ut pro me impetret.' The above quotations show that St. Ambrose cannot be reckoned with Athanasius as affirming the reality of a human ignorance in our Lord. But perhaps he is hardly consistent with himself.

[1] Ambrose is referring to passages such as Gen xi 5, where God is represented as *coming down to earth to see*, as if He did not know. Such expressions belong, one can hardly doubt, originally to a period when God's spiritual omnipresence was very imperfectly realized.

§ 4.

Anti-Arian writers especially of the west.

These admissions by anti-Arian writers of a real human ignorance are, though valuable, still in a measure unsatisfactory, and that for two reasons.

(1) The theologians who make these admissions do not really face the question of the relation of the divine person to the human conditions into which He entered. What is meant when it is said, '*the Son was ignorant in respect of His manhood*'? Does this mean that within the sphere of His incarnate life the Son Himself was submitting to conditions of limitation? Or does it mean that He simply annexed a human consciousness to the divine, so that always, in every act He was conscious with the divine consciousness, whatever else He may have been? This question, neither theologically nor exegetically, is met full face.

(2) Anti-Arian theology shows a rapid tendency to withdraw the admission of a human ignorance. Already, as has been said, Basil and Gregory, even in a measure Athanasius, lead the way in retiring upon a more or less forced interpretation of our Lord's words. Ephraim Syrus writes boldly—in his commentary upon Tatian's *Diatessaron*—'Christ, though He knew the moment of His advent, yet that they might not ask Him any more about it, said *I know it not*[1].' Didymus of Alexandria

---

[1] *Evang Concordant Expos* (Aucher and Moesinger, Venice, 1876) p. 16.

The Consciousness of our Lord. 131

introduces into a beautiful passage about the divine condescension the idea of the merely 'economic' ignorance [1]. St. Cyril will be found on the whole to follow him ; and St. Chrysostom, trained though he was in the literalism of Antioch, adopts the same view [2].

This withdrawal is due in part no doubt to the fatal tendency which haunts the Church to extreme reaction from perilous error ; in part also it is to be accounted for by the metaphysical tendency of the time to ascribe to God not only unchangeableness of essential being, purpose, and power, such as Scripture ascribes to Him, but also unchangeableness in such rigid 'metaphysical' sense as would exclude all idea of self-accommodation, and therefore all idea of real self-limitation, on God's part to human conditions [3]. The tendency to explain away our Lord's express words, which those theologians exhibit who are responsible for this withdrawal, meets in the East with at least one vigorous protest from Theodoret [4]

In a phrase which commends itself to modern consciences he wrote: 'If He knew the day and, wishing to

---

[1] *in Psalm* lxviii 6 (*P G* xxxix. p. 1453) καὶ γὰρ διδάσκαλος τελείαν ἔχων ἐπιστήμην διὰ συγκαταβάσεων τοῖς εἰσαγομένοις ταῦτα φαίνεται γινώσκων (i. e. appears to know those things *only*) ὧν εἰσὶν ἐκεῖνοι χωρητικοί

[2] *in Matt hom* lxxvii 1 and 2 He argues at length in the usual strain against the *real* ignorance

[3] See below, p 173

[4] *Repr. xii Capp Cyril* c 4 (*P G* lxxvi 412 a) εἰ δὲ οἶδε τὴν ἡμέραν, κρύπτειν δὲ βουλόμενος ἀγνοεῖν λέγει, ὁρᾷς εἰς ποίαν βλασφημίαν χωρεῖ τὸ συναγόμενον ἡ γὰρ ἀλήθεια ψεύδεται The passage is an argument for the distinct reality of our Lord's manhood from the phrases in the Gospels which attribute to Him prayer, ignorance, and the sense of being deserted of God. Such expressions cannot be attributed to the Word, Theodoret argues, but to the manhood which the Word assumed.

conceal it, said He was ignorant, see what blasphemy is the result of this conclusion. Truth tells a lie.'

But the protest fell flat. Neither the interest in accurate exegesis, nor the enthusiasm for truth to fact as distinct from truth which is edifying, was adequate to sustain it. It is reheard in a remarkable phrase of a writer reckoned as Leontius of Byzantium, to be mentioned later, but the 'explanation' protested against prevailed, and in the end there is no protest.

Hilary, Ambrose[1], and Jerome led the way in the west with the doctrine of our Lord's 'economic' ignorance, the doctrine, that is, that our Lord knew, but represented Himself as ignorant for purposes of edification. Augustine retains this way out of the difficulty caused by St. Mark xiii. 32, but in interpreting our Lord's growth in wisdom and His cry of desolation upon the Cross he seems to regard Christ as spoken of or speaking in the person of His Church, not for Himself, thus returning to a mode of 'explanation' with which Origen had already made us familiar. Moreover St. Augustine seems to have regarded any belief in our Lord's actual human ignorance as *heretical*. When a monk from Gaul appeared in Africa, named Leporius, accused of Pelagian and quasi-Nestorian views, Augustine induced him to abandon his error; accordingly he is made to recant among other things his previous assertion of a real ignorance in Christ as man, and made to recant it as positively heretical.

The following passages will be found to justify the assertions of the above paragraph:

[1] As explained above, § 3.

HILARY *de Trinit* ix 62 'Non patitur autem in nobis doctor gentium Paulus hanc impii erroris professionem, ut ignorasse aliquid unigenitus Deus existimetur: ait enim, *instituti in dilectione, in omnes divitias adimpletionis intellectus, in agnitionem sacramenti Dei Christi, in quo sunt omnes thesauri sapientiae et scientiae absconsi.* Deus Christus sacramentum est, et *omnes sapientiae et scientiae* in co *thesauri* latent Portioni vero et universitati non potest convenire quia neque pars omnia intelligitur, et omnia partem non patiuntur intelligi. Filius enim si diem nescit, iam non omnes in eo scientiae thesauri sunt diem non ignorat, omnes in se scientiae thesauros continens Sed meminisse nos convenit, occultos in eo istos scientiae thesauros esse, neque idcirco, quia occulti sint, non inesse cum per id quod Deus est, in eo insint, per id vero quod sacramentum est, occultentur. Non occultum autem neque ignoratum est nobis sacramentum Dei Chiisti, in quo absconsi omnes scientiae thesauri sunt. Et quia sacramentum ipse est, videamus an in his, quae nescit, ignorans sit. Si enim in ceteris professio ignorandi non habet nesciendi intelligentiam [1]: ne nunc quidem quod nescit ignorat. Nam cum ignoratio eius, secundum quod omnes thesauri in eo scientiae latent, dispensatio [2] potius quam ignoratio sit, habes causam ignorandi sine intelligentia nesciendi [3].'

---

[1] i e is not to be understood as implying absence of knowledge, e g God in the O T is often spoken of in terms suggesting partial ignorance

[2] i e an economy

[3] i e you have the reason of his (professed) ignorance, without having to explain it as equivalent to absence of knowledge Cf. ix 71 'idcirco nescire se dicat ne et alii sciant' and x 37 'non ergo sibi tristis est neque sibi orat, sed illis quos monet orare pervigiles' It must be noted that in fact St Paul's expressions in Col ii. 2, 3, and 9, 10, refer to our Lord in the state of glory—'the head of all principality and power' We cannot directly answer the question, Would St. Paul have applied these

There is, it is true, one passage [1] of doubtful genuineness in the *de Trinitate* (ix. 75) in which our Lord's nescience is assimilated to His hunger and thirst, sadness and fear, as an affection properly belonging to the manhood which He assumed. But supposing the passage to be genuine, it must be remembered that Hilary, unlike most other fathers, tends to explain away all our Lord's human affections. He emphasizes that in Him the Godhead was the centre of personality to both soul and body ('ut corporis sui sic et animae suae princeps Deus,' 'Deus Verbum consummavit hominem viventem,' x. 15); he considers that in consequence even His 'human' nature was superhuman ('natura quae supra hominem est,' x. 44); he points as evidence of this to His walking on the water, glorifying His body in the transfiguration, passing through closed doors after the resurrection (x. 23), and he draws the general conclusion that though His human body was susceptible of physical impressions of all sorts from without, yet He did not, in and for Himself, feel physical pain or mental grief or anxiety. He received the 'impetus passionis,' but did not experience the 'dolor passionis' 'Habens ad patiendum quidem corpus et passus est, sed naturam non habens ad dolendum' (x. 23). 'Non est itaque in ea natura quae supra hominem est humanae trepidationis anxietas' (x. 44). 'Habens quidem in se sui corporis

expressions to our Lord in the state of His humiliation? Hilary draws no distinction between the state of Christ's body or soul before and after the resurrection

[1] Another passage of similar import in x 8 (Erasmus' text) is interesting, but certainly not genuine. Hilary is again quoted on his general idea of the Incarnation on p. 147.

The Consciousness of our Lord.

veritatem, sed non habens naturae infirmitatem' (x. 35). In dying His manhood was not overcome by death, but He, the Lord of life, who lifted the human body which He had assumed out of the power of death, Himself 'gave up' His human spirit and soul by His own act into the Father's hands (x. 11).

JEROME writes thus *in Matt.* xxiv. 36 (ed. Vallarsi, vii. p. 199):

'*De die autem illa et hora nemo scit, neque angeli caelorum, nisi solus Pater.* In quibusdam latinis codicibus additum est, *neque Filius*. cum in graecis, et maxime Adamantii et Pierii exemplaribus, hoc non habeatur adscriptum : sed quia in nonnullis legitur, disserendum videtur. Gaudet Arius et Eunomius, quasi ignorantia magistri gloria discipulorum sit, et dicunt: non potest aequalis esse qui novit et qui ignorat. Contra quos breviter ista dicenda sunt: cum omnia tempora fecerit Iesus, hoc est, Verbum Dei (*omnia* enim *per ipsum facta sunt et sine ipso factum est nihil*) in omnibus autem temporibus etiam dies iudicii sit · qua consequentia potest eius ignorare partem cuius totum noverit? Hoc quoque dicendum est: quid est maius, notitia Patris an iudicii? si maius novit, quomodo ignorat quod minus est? Scriptum legimus *omnia quae Patris sunt mihi tradita sunt*; si omnia Patris Filii sunt, qua ratione unius sibi diei notitiam reservavit, et noluit eam communicare cum Filio? Sed et hoc inferendum : si novissimum diem temporum ignorat, ignorat et pene ultimum[1] et retrorsum omnes. Non enim potest fieri ut qui primum ignorat sciat quid secundum sit. Igitur quia putavimus non ignorare Filium consummationis diem, causa reddenda est cur ignorare dicatur. Apostolus super Salvatore scribit: *in quo sunt*

[1] i.e the last day but one

omnes thesauri sapientiae et scientiae absconditi. Sunt ergo omnes thesauri in Christo sapientiae et scientiae, sed absconditi sunt. Quare absconditi sunt? Post resurrectionem interrogatus ab apostolis de die manifestius respondit · *non est vestrum scire tempora vel momenta quae Pater posuit in sua potestate.* Quando dicit *non est vestrum scire* ostendit quod ipse sciat, sed non expediat nosse apostolis, ut semper incerti de adventu iudicis sic quotidie vivant quasi die alia iudicandi sunt Denique et consequens evangelii sermo idipsum cogit intelligi, dicens quoque Patrem solum nosse, in Patre comprehendit et Filium, omnis enim pater filii nomen est.'

This passage is an excellent instance of the way in which *a priori* reasoning was allowed to override real exegesis.

ST. AUGUSTINE'S line may be illustrated by *de Trin* i 12 23, on St. Mark xiii. 32 ' hoc enim nescit quod nescientes facit [1], id est, quod non ita sciebat ut tunc discipulis indicaret , sicut dictum est ad Abraham, *nunc cognovi quod times Deum,* id est, nunc feci ut cognosceres' Cf *Enarr. in Ps.* vi 1 'ita dicatur nescire Filius hunc diem, non quod nesciat, sed quod nescire faciat eos, quibus hoc non expedit scire, id est, non eis hoc ostendat'

In regard to St Luke ii. 52 St. Augustine seems to hesitate (*de div. quaest. lxxxiii,* qu. 75. 2°), but to incline to the position that 'pietas' would not admit of a real increase of knowledge in the 'homo dominicus,' and so to ascribe it to His body the Church [2]. This, however,

---

[1] i e 'that He does not know which He makes others not to know'
[2] An interpretation also to be found in Pseudo-Hieronymus, *Breviarium*

The Consciousness of our Lord. 137

is only touched upon allusively. In *de pecc. merit. et remiss.* ii. 48 he speaks quite clearly against the attribution to the infant Christ of an infant's ignorance.

'Quam plane ignorantiam nullo modo crediderim fuisse in infante illo, in quo Verbum caro factum est ut habitaret in nobis; nec illam ipsius animi infirmitatem in Christo parvulo fuerim suspicatus quam videmus in parvulis. Per hanc enim etiam cum motibus irrationabilibus perturbantur nulla ratione, nullo imperio; sed dolore aliquando vel doloris terrore cohibentur; ut omnino videas illius inobedientiae filios'

Here however St Augustine plainly passes from mere ignorance to what is in the germ a sinful impatience. In *de Trin.* iv. 3 6, like Gregory Nazianzen, Hilary, and others, he interprets the cry 'My God, My God, why hast thou forsaken me?' as the cry of the 'old Adam' in the redeemed, expressed by Christ as Head of the body 'interioris enim hominis nostri sacramento data est illa vox pertinens ad mortem animae nostrae significandam.'

An account of Leporius will be found in the *Dict of Christian Biography*. His retractation, or *Libellus Emendationis*, is, so far as touches our present question, as follows (*Bibl Max. Vett. Patr.* vii p. 3)

'Ut autem et hinc nihil cuiquam in suspicione derelinquam, tunc dixi, immo ad obiecta respondi, Dominum nostrum Iesum Christum secundum hominem ignorare

---

in Psalm xv 7 (Vallars vii app p 34) *Benedicam dominum qui tribuit mihi intellectum*—'vox capitis cum membris,' i e the expressions attributing human conditions of knowledge to our Lord are true of Him, taken as including His mystical body.

Sed nunc non solum dicere non praesumo, verum etiam priorem anathematizo prolatam in hac parte sententiam; quia dici non licet etiam secundum hominem ignorasse Dominum prophetarum.'

St. Augustine, with other African bishops, signed this retractation as an evidence of its genuineness, and sent Leporius back to Gaul with a warm letter of recommendation. See Aug. *Ep.* 219.

§ 5.

The Apollinarian controversy.

It might have been supposed that the controversy on the question raised by Apollinarius of Laodicea would have counteracted the tendency just described, by emphasizing the complete rational and spiritual humanity of Christ. In fact, however, its effect in this way was not as great as might have been anticipated.

There is indeed no evidence of a divine providence watching over the fortunes of the Church more marked than that which is to be found in the decisive and reiterated refusals of the Church to admit any opinion to be Christian which explained away the reality, or the natural and spiritual completeness, of our Lord's manhood. The divine providence is in this especially manifest because current theological opinion in its zeal against anything which seemed to imperil our Lord's Godhead was continually running the risk of onesidedness[1]. There was no equally strong zeal in regard to the manhood or the verity of the human picture in the Gospels. This is made evident by the meagreness of the Catholic literature directed against Apollinarius as compared to that directed against Arius. For in the nature of the case there is no justification for this. Men were quite as liable to be misled in one direction as in the other. Apollinarius' doctrine was markedly interesting and developed with the highest ability. And if Churchmen had been at all deeply occupied in the picture of Christ presented in the Gospels, they would have found there a wealth of argument with which to confront the new teaching. The meagreness of the literature against Apollinarius is due, then, at least in some measure, to lack of strong interest in the subject. Athanasius indeed never loses his theological balance and impartiality. The small part of his writings which is directed against Apollinarian views shows him presenting as firm a front on this side as on the other[2]. But besides Athanasius the chief opponent of Apollinarius is Gregory of Nyssa. And we feel how small a part of his interest and intellectual power was really given to the task of vindicating the

---

[1] Thus Apollinarius himself and Marcellus of Ancyra were 'extreme Athanasians', see also just below as to Gregory of Nyssa. On Hilary of Poitiers see above, § 4.

[2] See Athan. *con Apoll.* 1. 16–18, on the verity of our Lord's human soul. The strongest passage is one in which he maintains the voluntary but real and natural 'trouble' in our Lord's mind (c. 16) διὰ τοῦτο γὰρ καὶ ὁ κύριος ἔλεγεν νῦν ἡ ψυχή μου τετάρακται καὶ κατώδυνός ἐστιν. τὸ δὲ νῦν, τοῦτ' ἔστιν, ὅτε ἠθέλησεν ὅμως μέντοι τὸ ὂν ἐπεδείκνυτο· οὐ γὰρ τὸ μὴ ὂν ὡς παρὸν ὠνόμαζεν, ὡς δοκήσει λεγομένων τῶν γινομένων· φύσει γὰρ καὶ ἀληθείᾳ τὰ πάντα ἐγένετο.

completeness of our Lord's manhood in spirit as well as body, and the real existence and action in Him, the Word made flesh, of the human mind and spirit.

Some passages indeed from Gregory's writings are valuable in this sense. For example he does contend that the reality of our Lord's assumption of manhood involves His real assumption of the human mind and spirit. He recognizes among the signs of His true spiritual humanity the reality of His temptation, of His growth in knowledge, and of His human ignorance. Here he is a worthy and even more decisive successor of Athanasius. He also points out (what is very rarely noticed) that the miracles of our Lord are not purely divine acts, but acts which at least might have been wrought by a humanity empowered by God. Finally, he recognizes at times that the Incarnation involves on God's side a self-accommodation to alien conditions; and he finds in this divine self-humiliation the special evidence of the highest sort of power in that God can accommodate Himself to conditions such as do not belong to His own nature. We can only lament that these great thoughts were so little developed and emphasized. The fact is that Gregory's chief interest was in the other aspect of the Incarnation—that in which it is an exaltation of the manhood in virtue of its union with the divine nature. In this direction he constantly runs to excess, speaking of the manhood, at least after the resurrection, as transubstantiated into the Godhead and lost in it. And on the other hand, with reference to the period of our Lord's humiliation, in his zeal to maintain the impassibility of the Godhead, his language has frequently a Nestorian sound, as if the passible man were a different person from the impassible God.

The following passages from GREGORY OF NYSSA will prove the above statements.

That a real temptation argues a real human spirit— a complete human nature—is asserted in *adv Apoll.* 11 ἐπάναγκες κατὰ τὴν τοῦ ἀποστόλου ἀπόφασιν[1], τὸν κατὰ πάντα πεπειρασμένον τοῦ ἡμετέρου βίου καθ' ὁμοιότητα χωρὶς ἁμαρτίας (ὁ δὲ νοῦς ἁμαρτία οὐκ ἔστι) πρὸς πᾶσαν ἡμῶν οἰκείως ἔχειν τὴν φύσιν. Cf. *adv. Eunom.* iii. 4, vi. 3 (*P. G.* xlv. pp 597, 721).

The reality in our Lord of natural, including mental, growth asserted—*adv. Apoll.* 14 φησὶν ὁ Λουκᾶς ὅτι προέκοπτεν Ἰησοῦς ἡλικίᾳ καὶ σοφίᾳ καὶ χάριτι, τελειούμενος ὡς ἐπὶ τὸ μέτρον προῆλθε τῆς ἀνθρωπότητος, ὁδῷ βαδίζων διὰ τῆς φύσεως. And 28 τὴν δὲ ἑνωθεῖσαν τῇ θείᾳ σοφίᾳ τῆς σαρκὸς ἡμῶν μοῖραν ἐκ μετοχῆς δέξασθαι τὸ ἀγαθὸν τῆς σοφίας οὐκ ἀμφιβάλλομεν, πειθόμενοι τῷ εὐαγγελίῳ οὑτωσὶ διεξιόντι ὅτι Ἰησοῦς δὲ προέκοπτεν ἡλικίᾳ καὶ σοφίᾳ καὶ χάριτι. ὥσπερ ἐν τῷ σώματι ἡ κατ' ὀλίγον προσθήκη τροφῆς συνεργίᾳ πρὸς τὸ τέλειον τῆς φύσεως πρόεισιν, οὕτως καὶ ἐν τῇ ψυχῇ ἡ ἐπὶ τὸ τέλειον τῆς σοφίας πρόοδος δι' ἀσκήσεως τοῖς μετιοῦσι προστίθεται

The reality of human ignorance in our Lord—*adv. Apoll* 24 πῶς δὲ καὶ ἀγνοεῖ ὁ ἔνσαρκος αὐτοῦ θεὸς[2] τὴν ἡμέραν καὶ τὴν ὥραν ἐκείνην; πῶς δὲ οὐκ ἐπίσταται τὸν τῶν σύκων καιρόν; ... τίς ὁ ἀγνοῶν, εἰπάτω; τίς ὁ λυπούμενος; τίς ὁ ἐν ἀμηχανίᾳ στενοχωρούμενος; τίς ὁ ἐγκαταλελεῖφθαι παρὰ τοῦ

---

[1] Heb iv 15.
[2] i e the God who, according to an opinion ascribed to Apollinarius, was eternally 'in the flesh,' and never assumed a true *human* nature.

θεοῦ βοήσας [1]; these things cannot belong to the eternal Godhead: ἀλλὰ κατ' ἀνάγκην τὰς ἐμπαθεῖς ταύτας καὶ ταπεινοτέρας φωνάς τε καὶ διαθέσεις τῷ ἀνθρωπίνῳ προσμαρτυρήσει [2], ἄτρεπτόν τε καὶ ἀπαθῆ τοῦ θεοῦ τὴν φύσιν, καὶ ἐν τῇ κοινωνίᾳ τῶν ἀνθρωπίνων παθημάτων διαμεμενηκέναι συνθήσεται (i.e. these utterances of humiliation are the real expression of properly human experiences undergone by the eternal Word, who yet remained unchanged in His own essence).

That our Lord's miracles might have been done in the power of a God-inspired humanity—*adv. Apoll.* 28, Apollinarius had asked, 'Who but God is it who works with power the things of God?' To this Gregory replies that such a question derogates from the power of God and is childish. τὸ γὰρ ἐν ἐξουσίᾳ τὰ τοῦ θεοῦ ποιεῖν καὶ ἀνθρώπων ἐστὶν ἠξιωμένων θείας δυνάμεως οἷος ἦν ὁ Ἠλείας ... ὥστε οὐδὲν ὑπὲρ ἄνθρωπον τὸ ἐν ἐξουσίᾳ τοῦ θεοῦ ποιεῖν τι τῶν θαυμάτων ἐκ θείας δυνάμεως· ἀλλὰ τὸ αὐτὸν εἶναι τὴν ὑπερέχουσαν δύναμιν [3]. But cf. *adv. Eunom.* v. 5 (p. 705), where the miracles of our Lord are ascribed to His Godhead in the more usual way.

That the special marvel of divine power lies in the self-accommodation of the Son of God to the conditions alien to His own nature—*adv. Eunom.* v. 3 (p. 693) οὐδὲν κατὰ τὴν ἑαυτοῦ φύσιν κινούμενον ὡς ἐπὶ παραδόξῳ θαυμάζεται· ἀλλὰ ὅσα τοὺς ὅρους ἐκβαίνει τῆς φύσεως, ταῦτα μάλιστα πάντων ἐν θαύματι γίνεται, ... διὸ καὶ πάντες οἱ τὸν λόγον κηρύσσοντες, ἐν τούτῳ τὸ θαῦμα τοῦ μυστηρίου

---

[1] St Mark xiii 32, xi 13, xv. 13
[2] i e 'he must ascribe'
[3] i e what is superhuman is not the working of the miracles, but the being Himself the supreme power.

καταμηνύουσιν ὅτι θεὸς ἐφανερώθη ἐν σαρκί . . . ὅτι ἡ ζωὴ θανάτου ἐγεύσατο· καὶ πάντα τὰ τοιαῦτα βοῶσιν οἱ κήρυκες, δι' ὧν πλεονάζεται τὸ θαῦμα τοῦ διὰ τῶν ἔξω τῆς φύσεως τὸ περιὸν τῆς δυνάμεως ἑαυτοῦ φανερώσαντος. And v. 5 (p. 705) κενοῦται γὰρ ἡ θεότης ἵνα χωρητὴ τῇ ἀνθρωπίνῃ φύσει γένηται. Cf. *Orat. Cat Mag.* 24 πρῶτον μὲν οὖν τὸ τὴν παντοδύναμον φύσιν πρὸς τὸ ταπεινὸν τῆς ἀνθρωπότητος καταβῆναι ἰσχῦσαι πλείονα τὴν ἀπόδειξιν τῆς δυνάμεως ἔχει ἢ τὰ μεγάλα τε καὶ ὑπερφυῆ τῶν θαυμάτων. τὸ μὲν γὰρ μέγα τι καὶ ὑψηλὸν ἐξεργασθῆναι παρὰ τῆς θείας δυνάμεως κατὰ φύσιν πώς ἐστι καὶ ἀκόλουθον . . . ἡ δὲ πρὸς ταπεινὸν κάθοδος περιουσία τίς ἐστι τῆς δυνάμεως, οὐδὲν ἐν τοῖς παρὰ φύσιν κωλυομένης.

Cf. *adv. Apoll.* 20: In His divine nature Christ was inaccessible to weak humanity and incomprehensible by it, but He became such that our perishable humanity could possess and endure Him then, ὅτε ἐκένωσε, καθώς φησιν ὁ ἀπόστολος, τὴν ἄφραστον αὐτοῦ τῆς θεότητος δόξαν καὶ τῇ βραχύτητι ἡμῶν συγκατεσμίκρυνεν (i e. He narrowed His Godhead by accepting human limitation).

On the other hand, for the transubstantiation of the manhood into God, see *adv. Apoll.* 25, and 42 ad finem. The human is swallowed up in the divine as a drop of vinegar in the ocean and changed into the divine substance; there remains no physical property of body. It is to this latter passage that Hooker refers (*E. P.* v. 53. 2) as consisting of 'words so plain and direct for Eutyches that I stand in doubt they are not his whose name they carry.' So in *adv. Eunom.* v. 4, 5 (pp. 697, 705–6) it is affirmed that Christ was always God, but was not man either before His virgin birth or after His ascension.

For quasi-Nestorian language see especially *adv. Eunom* v. 5 (p. 700 d, 705—commenting on Acts ii. 36), *adv. Apoll.* 54 ad fin, and *Orat. Cat Mag.* He continually uses the word συνάφεια, which subsequently became typical of Nestorianism to express the relation of the humanity to the divinity in Christ. But this quasi-Nestorian language does not express the main tendency of Gregory's thought.

§ 6.

The Nestorian controversy.

There was indeed one school of theology in which opposition to Apollinarianism was hearty enough, and associated with a literal interpretation of the New Testament—the school of Antioch, of which the most prominent representative is Theodore of Mopsuestia. He himself had nothing more at heart than the assertion of the real moral freedom and spiritual humanity of Christ—His real temptation, His real struggles. Naturally therefore he was also ready to recognize the reality of His limited knowledge as man. He seems, if we may believe Leontius of Byzantium, to have gone to a length which there is nothing in the Gospels to justify, and to have asserted that our Lord in His temptation did not know who was tempting Him[1]. But unhappily, in

[1] Leont Byz *adv Incorrupticolas et Nestor* III 32 (*P. G.* lxxxvi p 1373) καὶ πειραζόμενος οὐκ ἐγίνωσκεν ὅστις εἴη ὁ πειράζων αὐτόν

The Consciousness of our Lord. 145

spite of the great theological reputation in the enjoyment of which he lived and died, he was working, as afterwards appeared more plainly, on a false line. He was—not by a mere careless use of language but deliberately—placing a centre of independent personality in the humanity of Jesus and distinguishing the man Jesus from the eternal Word who in a unique manner indwelt him. Nestorius was only following out this line of thought when he openly declared that the infant born of Mary was not, personally, the Son of God.[1]

The Church repudiated, with all haste and emphasis, this disastrous, and also intensely unpopular, heresy. Christ was personally God. In Him very God, remaining very God, had taken a human nature in its completeness; and He operated in the human nature, appropriating and making His own the acts and sufferings of the manhood from birth to death and through death to glory. So had rung out the theology of Athanasius, especially in his later period as represented by his letter to Epictetus of Corinth; the note had been sounded simultaneously by Hilary in the west and was taken up as by others so with pre-eminent power by Cyril of Alexandria, the great opponent of Nestorianism. Here is the verity of the Incarnation at its very heart. God, the very God, condescends to take a human nature to live and to suffer in it. In Christ

---

[1] The real Nestorianism of Theodore appears nowhere more clearly than in the extracts given by Justinian from his work against Apollinarius. He there distinctly denies that the Word was made man and affirms that He assumed the man Jesus. He describes the man Jesus as declaring that the Word, as well as the Father, indwells him—$\theta\epsilon\grave{o}s$ $\delta\grave{\epsilon}$ $\lambda\acute{o}\gamma os$ $\grave{\epsilon}\nu$ $\grave{\epsilon}\mu o\grave{\iota}$ $\acute{o}$ $\tau o\hat{v}$ $\theta\epsilon o\hat{v}$ $\mu o\nu o\gamma\epsilon\nu\acute{\eta}s$. See Justin. *Epist. adv. Theod.* in *P. G.* lxxxvi pp. 1050-1.

Jesus then God is manifesting Himself under human conditions. Does this involve a real self-limitation on God's part? Yes, is in some sense the repeated answer of both Hilary and Cyril[1]. Hilary has striking passages about the divine 'self-emptying' involved in the Incarnation; and Cyril also has strong statements as that the very God, in being made man, 'let Himself down to the limit of the self-emptying' and 'suffered the measures of the humanity to prevail in His own case[2].'

But both Hilary and Cyril refuse to apply the idea of the self-emptying so as to admit the reality of intellectual growth or limitation of knowledge in the incarnate Lord. This is certainly the case with Hilary, as has already appeared, and on the whole must be allowed in regard to Cyril. He too falls back upon a merely 'economic' ignorance. This particular tendency was facilitated by a general tendency, which must be admitted to exist in much of Cyril's writing, to allow the apprehension of the real manhood of our Lord to be weakened by the emphasis on His Godhead. 'Under his treatment [of St. John's Gospel],' says Dr. Westcott[3], 'the divine history seems to be dissolved into a docetic drama.' This is a somewhat startling expression of opinion from one who is apt to measure his words. But it can hardly be said to exceed the truth.

The following citations will be found to justify the remarks just made.

---

[1] So also of Gregory of Nyssa, see above, § 5

[2] See passages quoted below. One may notice also how Cyril, like most fathers, habitually recognizes that ignorance, as much as hunger and thirst, *belongs to* human nature. cf *Thesaur* 22 (*P. G* lxxv p 373).

[3] *Speaker's Comm.* St. John, p xcv.

The Consciousness of our Lord.

HILARY'S doctrine of the self-emptying of the Incarnation is striking, but not easy to grasp.

(a) He maintains constantly that in becoming incarnate the eternal Son remains what He was before.

iii. 16 'Non amiserat quod erat sed coeperat esse quod non erat non de suo destiterat sed quod nostrum est acceperat. profectum ei [i. e. naturae humanae] quod accepit eius claritatis expostulat unde non destitit' (of that glory whence He did not withdraw He asks advance for that nature which He received, St John xvii. 5).

ix 66 'Nec Deus destitit manere qui homo est.'

xii. 6 'Neque enim defecit ex sese qui se evacuavit in sese'. cf. v. 18, x 66.

(β) Nevertheless he postulates, though with some inconsistency of language, a real self-emptying. Thus at one time he declares the Son to have abandoned the form of God, meaning by that equality with God. at another he denies that He abandoned the form of God (in the same sense): at another he affirms the abandonment of the divine form, but identifies this with the 'glory' or divine mode of existence (*habitus*) Generally he may be said to affirm an abandonment of the divine glory and a retention of the divine nature and power.

viii 45 'Ad susceptionem se formae servilis per obedientiam exinanivit, exinanivit autem se ex forma Dei, id est ex eo quod aequalis Deo erat.'

xi. 48 'In forma enim Dei manens formam servi assumpsit'. cf. xii. 7.

ix. 14 'Evacuatio formae non est abolitio naturae: quia qui se evacuat non caret sese.'

ix. 51 'Erat [in Christ incarnate] naturae proprietas,

sed Dei forma iam non erat quia per eius exinanitionem servi erat forma suscepta'

ix 4 'Deo itaque proprium fuit contrahere se usque ad conceptum et cunas et infantiam nec tamen Dei potestate decedere'

Cf ix. 38 'habitus demutatione': 39 'se exinanierat de forma gloriae'

(γ) He goes so far as to suggest a real *offensio* of the divine unity between the Father and the Son

ix 38 'Novitas temporalis, licet maneret in virtute naturae, amiserat tamen cum forma Dei naturae Dei secundum assumptum hominem unitatem. . . . Reddenda apud se ipsum Patri erat unitas sua, ut naturae suae nativitas in se rursum glorificanda resideret, quia dispensationis novitas offensionem unitatis intulerat, et unitas ut perfecta antea fuerat, nulla esse nunc poterat, nisi glorificata apud se fuisset carnis assumptio'

ix 39 'Ut in unitate sua maneret ut manserat, glorificaturus eum apud se Pater erat; quia gloriae suae unitas [*v l* unitatem] per obedientiam dispensationis excesserat'

(δ) He conceives this self-emptying as an act of supreme self-restraint, and therefore as the fulness of power.

xi. 48 'In forma enim Dei manens formam servi assumpsit, non demutatus sed se ipsum exinaniens et intra se latens et intra suam ipse vacuefactus potestatem dum se usque ad formam temperat habitus humani, ne potentem immensamque naturam assumptae humilitatis non ferret infirmitas, sed in tantum se virtus incircumscripta moderaretur, in quantum oporteret eam usque ad patientiam connexi sibi corporis obedire Quod autem se ipsum intra se vacuefaciens continuit.

detrimentum non attulit potestati, cum intra hanc exinanientis se humilitatem virtute tamen omnis exinanitae intra se usus sit potestatis' Cf xii 6

CYRIL'S doctrine of the κένωσις and the limits he assigns to it will appear in the following citations

(a) As to St Mark xiii. 32, adv. Anthropomorph 14 (P. G. lxxvi pp 1101, 1104).

'The only-begotten Word of God bore with the manhood all that appertains to it, except sin only But ignorance of the future properly suits the limits of humanity. So then, so far as He is thought of as God, He knows all that the Father knows; but so far as He is also man, He does not cast off even the appearance of ignorance because it is suitable to humanity (οὐκ ἀποσείεται τὸ καὶ ἀγνοῆσαι δοκεῖν διὰ τὸ πρέπειν τῇ ἀνθρωπότητι). Just as He received bodily sustenance, though He was the life and power of all, not despising the limit of His self-emptying, and has been recorded to have slept and been weary, so also, though He knew all things, He does not blush to attribute to Himself the ignorance which is suitable to humanity. For everything that belongs to humanity became His, except sin only. Thus when His disciples would have learnt what was above them, He pretends for their profit not to know, inasmuch as He is man (σκήπτεται χρησίμως τὸ μὴ εἰδέναι καθ' ὃ ἄνθρωπος), and He says that not the very angels knew, that they may not be grieved at not being entrusted with the mystery.'

Cf. *Thesaurus*, assert. 22 (P G lxxv p. 376) ὥσπερ οὖν οἰκονομίας τινὸς ἕνεκεν τὸ μὴ εἰδέναι ποῦ κεῖται Λάζαρος ἔφασκεν, οὕτω καὶ περὶ τῆς ἡμέρας καὶ τῆς ὥρας, κἂν λέγῃ μὴ εἰδέναι, χρήσιμόν τι καὶ ἀγαθὸν οἰκονομῶν τοῦτο ποιεῖ οἶδε γὰρ ὡς θεός. Again, p. 377, οἰκονομεῖ γάρ τοι Χριστὸς μὴ εἰδέναι λέγων τὴν ὥραν ἐκείνην καὶ οὐκ ἀληθῶς ἀγνοεῖ and cf. his reply to Theodoret's 'reprehension' mentioned above, p. 131 (*P. G.* lxxvi p. 416), where he starts with the fundamental proposition that as God He knows all, but in His manhood only what the indwelling Godhead revealed and the conclusion is that He personally knew the day of the end, because He was God, but assumes the ignorance of manhood 'economically.' Other passages are collected by Dr A. B Bruce, *Humiliation of Christ*, pp 366–372. Their drift is unmistakeable.

(β) As to St. Luke ii. 52, Cyril appears at times to recognize in our Lord a reality of human growth in knowledge; but when speaking exactly, tends to make it only an increased manifestation of an already existing knowledge Cf *Quod unus sit Christus* (*P. G.* lxxv. p 1332):

'For the wise evangelist, when introducing the Word made flesh, exhibits Him as economically letting His own flesh have its way, so as to go through the laws of its own nature (δείκνυσιν αὐτὸν οἰκονομικῶς ἐφέντα τῇ ἰδίᾳ σαρκὶ διὰ τῶν τῆς ἰδίας φύσεως ἰέναι νόμων) It belongs to humanity to advance in stature and wisdom, and, I may add, in grace, the understanding in each case keeping pace in a way with the measures of the body. The understanding of those who are already grown children differing from that of infants, and so on. It was not impossible or unattainable for Him who was God, the Word begotten of the Father, to raise the body united to Him to its full height even from its very swaddling-clothes and to bring it to full development And in the same way it would have been easy and practicable for Him to exhibit a marvellous wisdom even in the infant But this would have been akin to mere wonder-working, and unsuitable to the conditions of the economy For the mystery was accomplished noiselessly. Therefore economically He suffered the measures of the humanity to prevail in His own case (ἀλλ' ἦν τὸ χρῆμα τερατοποιίας οὐ μακράν, καὶ τοῖς τῆς οἰκονομίας λόγοις ἀνάρμοστον· ἐτελεῖτο γὰρ ἀψοφητὶ τὸ μυστήριον. ἠφίει δὴ οὖν οἰκονομικῶς τοῖς τῆς ἀνθρωπότητος μέτροις ἐφ' ἑαυτῷ τὸ κρατεῖν).'

I have left 'economy' and 'economically' untranslated, because οἰκονομία, starting from meaning the process by which God communicates and reveals Himself in such a way as to be intelligible to man, passes imperceptibly into meaning a process of divine reserve which is in fact deception. It does not necessarily carry with it any sense of unreality, for Cyril says that the suffering of Christ 'belongs to the economy' (τὸ μὲν πάθος ἔσται τῆς οἰκονομίας, *schol de Incarn* 13, t lxxv. p. 1388). And in the above paragraph it might seem to have the nobler meaning. But the following passage is more explicit

Thesaurus, assert. 28 (t lxxvi p. 428) 'A certain law of nature does not allow a man to have wisdom to a degree which would be out of correspondence with his bodily stature, but our understanding keeps pace and advances in a way with our bodily growth. Now the Word made flesh was man as has been written; and He was perfect, being the Wisdom and Power of God. And since it was necessary in a way that He should accommodate Himself to the custom of our nature (τῷ τῆς φύσεως ἡμῶν ἔθει παραχωρεῖν πως ἐχρῆν), to avoid being thought a portent by those who saw Him as man, while His body was gradually growing therefore He concealed Himself and kept daily appearing wiser to those who saw and heard Him . . . But because He was ever wiser and more gracious to those who saw Him, therefore He was said to advance, the advance being in fact relative to those who admired, rather than to Himself (ὡς ἐντεῦθεν ἤδη τὴν τῶν θαυμαζόντων προκόπτειν ἕξιν ἢ τὴν αὐτοῦ).' Cf p. 429 ὅτιπερ καὶ ὄργανον εἴη [τὸ ἀνθρώπινον] τῆς ἐν αὐτῇ θεότητος, κατὰ βραχὺ πρὸς τὴν ἔκφασιν αὐτῆς διὰ τῶν ἔργων ὑπηρετοῦν, and *scholia* 13, t lxxv. p 1388.

In another passage, *adv. Nestor*. t. lxxvi. p 154, he definitely distinguishes this view from that of a *real* advance postulated by Nestorius. The above quotations are mostly to be found in Bruce (*l. c*), whose discussion of the matter is I think, exhaustive He also (p 425) points out how Cyril had in view and repudiated (1) an idea of the 'depotentiation' of God incarnate, such as some extreme Lutherans have held, and (2) the attempt to distinguish the nature from the personality of the Word, and to assert that in the Incarnation the nature remained in the glory of God, but not the personality, see *adv. Nest.* 1. 1, *adv. Anthropomorph* 18, t. lxxvi pp. 1108 ff.

In general one must allow, I think, that there is in St Cyril, side by side with a real apprehension of our Lord's manhood especially in its physical aspects—of hunger, thirst, pain, &c —a tendency to allow its spiritual and intellectual reality to be merged in his emphasis on the Godhead He had no sympathy with Apollinarius' formal denial of the human spirit in Jesus, but his language is sometimes markedly akin to Apollinarius' language when he speaks of the manhood as simply the

The Consciousness of our Lord. 153

instrument or veil, through which the Godhead communicates or discloses itself, and it is remarkable that the phrase adopted by Cyril, which afterwards afforded an excuse for Monophysitism—the μία φύσις τοῦ θεοῦ λόγου σεσαρκωμένη—is derived from a treatise *de Incarn. Verbi Dei*, ascribed by Cyril to Athanasius [1], but which appears in fact to have been written by Apollinarius; see Robertson, *Athanasius (Nicene and Post-Nicene Fathers)*, p lxv. There is no doubt that in the early part of the fifth century the more moderate disciples of Apollinarius succeeded in disseminating writings of their master under the famous names of Athanasius, Julius, and Gregory Thaumaturgus This was disclosed first at the Council of Chalcedon, and later, in the early part of the sixth century, by Leontius of Byzantium if indeed he is the writer of the *adversus Fraudes Apollinistarum* [2] The tract from which Cyril derived his famous phrase was one of these Apollinarian treatises ascribed to Athanasius. The whole matter of Apollinarian propaganda under assumed names has been the subject of recent investigation by C. P. Caspari, *Alte und neue Quellen zur Geschichte des Taufsymbols* (Christiania, 1879); and by Draseke, *Apollinarios von Laodicea (Texte und Untersuch.* vii. 3, 4) The whole discussion is reviewed in the *Ch Quart. Review* (Oct. 1893, *Apollinarius of*

---

[1] See *Dict of Chr Biography*, 1 p 770

[2] Loofs (*Text u Unt* III 1, 2), who has recently investigated Leontius of Byzantium and his works, thinks that its author was an older contemporary of Leontius, 1 e that it was written c A D 512 But the grounds assigned for this date are not over-convincing It may well have been by Leontius and written about 531 See the last investigator of the subject, P W Rugamer (a Roman Catholic), *Leontius von Byzanz* (Wurzburg, 1894), pp 14 ff

Laodicea). I must add that Cardinal Newman's Tract (*Tracts Theol and Eccl.*) on St. Cyril's formula, in spite of its interest and learning, is really in great part an apology for minimizing the meaning of our Lord's manhood.

§ 7.

The Monophysite controversy.

The heresy of Eutyches was in part due to a misunderstanding of Cyril's teaching, in part it was a revival of a certain still current aspect of Apollinarianism to which some of Cyril's language had been too closely akin. Speaking generally, Eutychianism, and the 'Monophysite' doctrine which was a modification of it, postulated, in varying degrees[1], a transubstantiation in the person of Christ of the manhood into God. As against such teaching, the definition of Chalcedon secured dogmatically the distinct and permanent reality of our Lord's manhood, and the later decision of the third council of Constantinople dogmatically secured the presence in Him of a distinct human will and energy, linked hypostatically to the divine will and energy, but not swallowed up in it. But from the point of view of our present inquiry it must be noticed

(1) that these definitions did not lead to any perma-

[1] In varying degrees because some Monophysites, like the Agnoetae or even the Severians, generally recognized the reality of the manhood in the 'composite nature' of Christ to a very great extent See the excellent account of the Severians in Dorner's *Person of Christ*, iv ii vol 1 pp 133-143.

The Consciousness of our Lord.

nent reaction among catholic theologians in favour of recognizing the reality of our Lord's mental growth or limitation in knowledge as man.

(2) that there was no real help given by the orthodox thought of the time towards solving the question of the relation of the divine and human natures, which the dogma of Chalcedon left simply juxtaposited in the unity of Christ's person [1].

(1) This is best shown by the attitude of the Church towards the Agnoetae. This sect—which is also known as the 'Themistians' from its chief representative Themistius—arose among the Monophysites on the moderate or Severian wing, i.e. among those who maintained the naturally corruptible nature of our Lord's body, about A D 540 or somewhat later [2]. Its characteristic tenet was the limitation of our Lord's human knowledge, and its adherence to this was based upon the natural interpretation of the often-discussed passages of the Gospels, such as St. Mark xiii. 32, St John xi 34. The Monophysite origin of the sect would countenance the hypothesis (to which Dr. Liddon adheres [3]) that they affirmed ignorance of our Lord in the only nature which Monophysites could consistently recognize in Christ, viz. the divine. But men are not always consistent, and

---

[1] So far, I think, Dorner is right But not in his criticisms on the Chalcedonian formula considered *per se*, *l. c* pp 113-119 That was in no contradiction to Ephesus and was a most necessary supplement to it Further the function of a dogmatic decision is not to supply the philosophy of the subject see *Bampton Lectures*, 1891, p 110

[2] Leontius Byz *de Sectis*, v 6 'while Theodosius (the Monophysite patriarch of Alexandria) was living at Byzantium as a private person,' i e after his banishment from Alexandria, c 537.

[3] *Divinity of our Lord*, p 468, quoting Suicer.

moreover the Severian Monophysites in their view of the 'composite nature' of Christ allowed a great deal of reality to the humanity. At any rate the evidence does not seem to warrant this hypothesis. If the language of Eulogius, the patriarch of Alexandria, who wrote against the Agnoetae about A. D. 590, is ambiguous[1], that of the treatise *de Sectis*, ascribed to Leontius of Byzantium, is quite distinct—λέγουσιν ἀγνοεῖν τὸ ἀνθρώπινον τοῦ Χριστοῦ, ἠγνόει ὁ Χριστὸς ὡς ἄνθρωπός που[2] : and

---

[1] See just below, p 158. John of Damascus is also ambiguous in his account of Themistius, see *de Haer* 85

[2] *de Sectis*, x 3 (cited below) The Greek title of the work is Λεοντίου σχολαστικοῦ Βυζαντίου σχόλια ἀπὸ φωνῆς Θεοδώρου, τοῦ θεοφιλεστάτου ἀββᾶ καὶ σοφωτάτου φιλοσόφου, κ τ λ That is to say it is a work compiled by the Abbot Theodore from the *scholia* of Leontius Theodore must have written after the accession of Eulogius of Alexandria, which he mentions, in 579, and the scholia were probably compiled about the middle of the century See Loofs, *l c* and Rugamer, *l c* pp 25 and 30

The passage in question is probably due to Leontius (so Rugamer as against Loofs), at least the passage in what is apparently Leontius' earliest work (c 531)—*adv Nestorianos et Eutychianistes*, iii 32—directed against a Nestorian view of Christ's ignorance, is no argument against it For the latter passage is directed against an extreme view of Christ's 'ignorance' and one in which ignorance is identified with sin; and is also separated by perhaps nearly twenty years from the passage in the *de Sectis* Even in the earlier work Leontius is jealous for the verity of our Lord's manhood, especially on its physical side—contending for instance that κατὰ βραχὺ ἐν τῇ παρθενικῇ μήτρᾳ προέκοπτε νόμῳ κυήσεως, ὡς πρὸς τὴν ἀπηρτισμένην τοῦ βρέφους τελείωσιν *con Nest et Eut* ii p 1328 c). But on this subject he seems to have changed his mind, *adv Nestorian* iv p 1669 and his later view was followed by orthodox divines, who postulated an instantaneous formation of the embryo, e g John Damasc οὐ ταῖς κατὰ μικρὸν προσθήκαις ἀπαρτιζομένου τοῦ σχήματος ἀλλ' ὑφ' ἓν τελειωθέντος (*de Fid Orthod* iii 2) So St Thomas Aquinas, *Summa,* p iii qu 33 art 1

It is remarkable that a writer such as Leontius, of whom so much remains of great interest, whom Cardinal Mai describes as 'in theologica scientia aevi sui facile princeps,' and who has been the subject of so much recent discussion in Germany, should be all but passed over in silence in the *Dict of Chr Biography.*

The Consciousness of our Lord.

the words of Sophronius of Jerusalem are equally distinct[1]. And like these easterns, so the western, Pope Gregory, in his correspondence with Eulogius regards the question at issue to be our Lord's ignorance as man. This he, with Eulogius, is emphatic in denying They both admit that humanity as such, and therefore Christ's humanity by itself, would be ignorant. But they say that in fact, as united to the Godhead in one person its ignorance was removed If He was ignorant 'ex humanitate,' He was not so 'in humanitate' If He professes ignorance as man He is speaking as Head for the members and economically.

It would appear that this particular matter was never specifically considered by any oriental council But the Agnoetae certainly formed a sect of their own and were reckoned as heretics, with the special characteristic of affirming the limitation of knowledge in Christ We notice however that the orthodox Leontius emphatically takes the side of the Agnoetae. and declares, with an exaggeration which is no doubt somewhat strange, that almost all the fathers held to our Lord's human ignorance

The following passages should be examined in this connexion

LEONTIUS OF BYZANTIUM, *de Sectis*, act x 3 (*P G* lxxxvi p. 1261) 'Now the Agnoetae believe just as the Theodosians with this difference, that the Theodosians deny that the humanity of Christ was ignorant and the Agnoetae affirm it For they say, ' He was in

---

[1] *Epist Syn ad Sergium* (*P G* lxxxvii 3, p. 3192 d) ἀγνοεῖν τὸν Χριστὸν οὐ καθὸ θεὸς ὑπῆρχεν ἀΐδιος, ἀλλὰ καθὸ γέγονεν κατὰ ἀλήθειαν ἄνθρωπος

all points like us. And if we are ignorant, it is plain that He too was ignorant. And He Himself in the Gospels says, *no man knoweth the day nor the hour, neither the Son, but the Father only* And again, *where have ye laid Lazarus?*" All these utterances, they say, are signs of ignorance. It is said in reply that Christ spoke these things "economically," to divert the disciples from learning from Him the hour of the end. Observe, they say, after the resurrection, when He is again asked by them, He no longer says *neither the Son*, but *none of you* [1]. But we [2] say that we must not be too exact on these matters (οὐ δεῖ πάνυ ἀκριβολογεῖν περὶ τούτων). On this principle neither did the Synod [3] busy itself with this sort of opinion (οὐδὲ ἡ σύνοδος τοιοῦτο ἐπολυπραγμόνησε δόγμα), but it must be known that most of the Fathers, yes almost all, appear to say that He was ignorant For if He is said to have been of one substance with us in all respects, and we are ignorant, it is plain that He too was ignorant. And the Scripture says about Him, *He advanced in stature and wisdom*; that is plainly, learning what He was ignorant of' Cf. Act. v. 6.

EULOGIUS, the patriarch of Alexandria, is quoted by Photius. *Bibliotheca,* cod. 230 (*P. G.* ciii pp. 1080 ff), as writing against the Agnoetae to the following effect. He denies that Christ was ignorant either in His manhood or (still more) in His Godhead. He gives 'explanations' of the texts cited for the opposite view. Christ may have been speaking economically; or, again, nothing hinders us from interpreting His words κατ' ἀναφοράν, i. e. in such a way as to refer them back from the Head who spoke them to the members of the body

---

[1] Acts 1 7 'it is not for you, &c' [2] i. e. Leontius.
[3] The reference appears to be to Chalcedon.

The Consciousness of our Lord. 159

for whom He spoke. He cried out as deserted in our name So He may have professed ignorance in our name. 'No man can, without recklessness, ascribe real ignorance to Him either in His Godhead or in His manhood (οὔτε γὰρ κατὰ τὴν θεότητα οὔτε κατὰ τὴν ἀνθρωπότητα τὴν ἄγνοιαν λέγειν ἐπ' αὐτοῦ θράσους ἐπισφαλοῦς ἠλευθέρωται)' We may indeed ascribe ignorance ideally to Christ's humanity, *qua* humanity considered by itself (which it was not), like Gregory the theologian[1]. He adds,

'If some of the fathers admitted the asserted ignorance in the manhood of our Saviour, they did not advance this as a positive opinion, but with a view to warding off the madness of the Arians, for as the Arians ascribed the human affections to the Godhead, they thought it a better expedient to refer them to the manhood than to allow them to divert them to the Godhead. Not but what if any one were to say that they too spoke anaphorically [i. e of Christ *for us*], he will be accepting the safer explanation (εἰ καί τινες τῶν πατέρων τὴν ἄγνοιαν ἐπὶ τῆς κατὰ τὸν σωτῆρα παρεδέξαντο ἀνθρωπότητος, οὐχ ὡς δόγμα τοῦτο προήνεγκαν, ἀλλὰ τὴν τῶν Ἀρειανῶν μανίαν ἀντιφερόμενοι, οἳ καὶ τὰ ἀνθρώπινα πάντα ἐπὶ τὴν θεότητα τοῦ μονογενοῦς μετέφερον, ὡς ἂν κτίσμα τὸν ἄκτιστον λόγον τοῦ θεοῦ παραστήσωσιν, οἰκονομικώτερον ἐδοκίμασαν ἐπὶ τῆς ἀνθρωπότητος ταῦτα φέρειν ἢ παραχωρεῖν ἐκείνους μεθέλκειν ταῦτα κατὰ τῆς θεότητος. εἰ δὲ κατὰ ἀναφορὰν κἀκείνους δοίη ταῦτά τις εἴπειν, τὸν εὐσεβέστερον λόγον ἀποδέξεται).'

GREGORY THE GREAT, *Epist.* x. 39 (*ad Eulogium, Patr. Lat.* lxxvii. p. 1097), says that the text St. Mark xiii. 32

'Is most certainly to be referred to the Son, not as

[1] See passage quoted, p 126

He is Head, but as to His body which we are (non ad eundem Filium iuxta hoc quod caput est, sed iuxta corpus eius quod sumus nos, est certissime referendum).' He adds that Christ 'in natura quidem humanitatis novit diem et horam iudicii, sed tamen hunc non ex natura humanitatis novit: quod ergo in ipsa novit, non ex ipsa novit, quia Deus homo factus diem et horam iudicii per deitatis suae potentiam novit'

Like Theodoret's in earlier days, the protest of Leontius against explaining away our Lord's words is isolated Thus, the great Greek schoolman, John of Damascus, who in the eighth century formulated the theology of the Greeks, repudiates as Nestorian any assertion of real increase in our Lord's knowledge as man, or real limitation in His knowledge of the future

JOHN DAMASCENE, *de Fide Orthod* iii 12–23 His human nature by its own essence does not possess the knowledge of the future, 'but the soul of the Lord, because of its unity with the person of God the Word and its hypostatic identity, was enriched, as I said, as with the other divine miracles, so with the knowledge of the future (διὰ τὴν πρὸς αὐτὸν τὸν θεὸν λόγον ἕνωσιν καὶ τὴν ὑποστατικὴν ταυτότητα κατεπλούτησεν, ὡς ἔφην, μετὰ τῶν λοιπῶν θεοσημειῶν καὶ τὴν τῶν μελλόντων γνῶσιν).'

He goes on to determine that it is Nestorian to call Chr st by the name 'servant (δοῦλος) of the Lord[1],' and

---

[1] St Thomas (*Summa*, p iii qu 20 art 1) allows the expression So Petavius (*de Incarn* vii 7–9) and others Other western theologians have agreed more or less decisively with John of Damascus that our Lord, as man, is not to be called *servus*, chiefly because the expression was insisted upon by the Adoptionists and repudiated by Pope Hadrian I and other opponents of this heresy see de Lugo, *de Myst Incarn* xxviii 2

The Consciousness of our Lord. 161

that in spite of the frequent use of the similar phrase παῖς κυρίου in the Acts of the Apostles, of which he takes no notice; and Nestorian, again, to attribute real intellectual growth to our Lord in His manhood

'He is said to advance in wisdom and stature and grace, because He grows in fact in stature, and through His growth in stature, brings out into exhibition the wisdom which already existed in Him . . But those who say that He grew in wisdom and grace, as (really) receiving increase in these, deny (in fact) that the flesh was united to the Word from the first moment of its existence, nor do they allow the union to be hypostatic, but assent to Nestorius, . . . For if the flesh from the first moment of its existence was united to the Word of God, or rather subsisted in Him, and possessed hypostatic identity with Him, how could it have been otherwise than perfectly enriched with all wisdom and grace? (προκόπτειν δὲ λέγεται σοφίᾳ καὶ ἡλικίᾳ καὶ χάριτι, τῇ μὲν ἡλικίᾳ αὔξων, διὰ δὲ τῆς αὐξήσεως τῆς ἡλικίας τὴν ἐνυπάρχουσαν αὐτῷ σοφίαν εἰς φανέρωσιν ἄγων . . . οἱ δὲ προκόπτειν αὐτὸν λέγοντες σοφίᾳ καὶ χάριτι ὡς προσθήκην τούτων δεχόμενον οὐκ ἐξ ἄκρας ὑπάρξεως τῆς σαρκὸς γεγενῆσθαι τὴν ἕνωσιν λέγουσιν, οὐδὲ τὴν καθ' ὑπόστασιν ἕνωσιν πρεσβεύουσι, Νεστορίῳ δὲ τῷ ματαιόφρονι πειθόμενοι, σχετικὴν ἕνωσιν καὶ ψιλὴν ἕνωσιν τερατεύονται· εἰ γὰρ ἀληθῶς ἡνώθη τῷ θεοῦ λόγῳ ἡ σὰρξ ἐξ ἄκρας ὑπάρξεως μᾶλλον δὲ ἐν αὐτῷ ὑπῆρξε καὶ τὴν ὑποστατικὴν ἔσχε ταυτότητα, πῶς οὐ τελείως κατεπλούτησε πᾶσαν σοφίαν καὶ χάριν ;)'

Here is abstract reasoning, as so often in theology and philosophy, winning its triumph over facts. In the west the Agnoetic view was revived by the Nestorianizing Adoptionists, and treated therefore, in the west as in the east, as simply a fragment of Nestorianism.

AGOBARD, bishop of Lyons, records[1] how Felix of Urgel, the Adoptionist leader, 'began to teach certain people to believe that our Lord Jesus Christ was, according to the flesh, truly ignorant of where Lazarus lay and of the day of judgement and of the subject of the conversation of the two disciples (on the road to Emmaus), &c When I heard this,' he adds,

'I approached him in the presence of those whom he was seeking to convince and asked him whether this was really his opinion. And when he sought to establish his view I denounced him and expressed abhorrence of his corrupt teaching and I showed the others, as best I could, how anxiously they should repudiate such ideas, and in what sense those passages of Scripture ought to be understood : and I caused passages chosen from the holy fathers to be read to Felix himself which contradicted his blasphemies. And when they had been read, he promised to apply himself with all diligence to his own correction.'

(2) The definition of Chalcedon affirmed the juxtaposition of the divine and human natures in Christ each with its separate and distinct operation, but contributed nothing positive towards the solution of the question : how is this duality of natures and operations related to the unity of the person ? How, for example, did the one person Christ, being God, exercise a human consciousness, involving as it does human limitations ? The tendency was to regard the divine and human natures simply as placed side by side ; to speak of Christ

---

[1] See Agobard *adv Felicem Urgel.* c. 5, and the note in *Patr. Lat* civ p 37.

as acting now in the one and now in the other—or, more specifically, to attribute the powerful works and words of the incarnate person to His Godhead and His sufferings and 'humble' sayings to His manhood. The following is a typical passage from the great Tome of Leo[1]:

'The nativity of the flesh is a manifestation of human nature the birth from a virgin is an indication of divine power[2]. The infancy of the babe is exhibited by the lowliness of the cradle the greatness of the Highest is declared by the voices of angels. He whom Herod impiously designs to slay is like humanity in its beginnings; but He whom the Magi rejoice to adore upon their knees is Lord of all. . . . To hunger, to thirst, to be weary, and to sleep is evidently human But to satisfy five thousand men with five loaves, and to give to the Samaritan woman living water, of which whoso drinketh is secure from further thirst, to walk on the surface of the sea with feet not sinking, and to allay the swelling waves by rebuking the tempest—this without doubt is divine. As then (to omit not a little), it belongs not to the same nature to weep for a dead friend with the sensation of compassion, and

---

[1] It should be noted that the dogmatic authority of a letter approved by a Council as a whole is not identical with the dogmatic authority of the actual formula decreed by the Council; e g the letters of St. Cyril are not dogmas in the sense in which it is a dogma that the term *theotocus* is rightly applied to the Blessed Virgin The letters were approved as embodying the truth which the Council affirmed. Thus again St Leo's tome was accepted at Chalcedon as embodying the truth of the permanence and distinct reality of Christ's human nature in the Godhead which assumed it But all the phrases and passages in it are no more of dogmatic authority than the reading of 1 John iv. 3 *qui solvit Iesum* (ὁ λύει τὸν Ἰησοῦν) adopted in the tome (c 5)

[2] i e an indication that Christ, the child, was God.

to raise the same friend to life again at the authority of a word ; ... or to hang upon the cross and to make all the elements tremble, turning daylight into night ; or to be pierced with nails, and to open the gates of paradise to the faith of the thief; so it belongs not to the same nature to say *I and the Father are one*, and to say *the Father is greater than I*[1].'

In his notes on this passage Dr. Bright[2] quotes some parallels (which, in fact, abound), e g. St Athanasius, *adv. Arian*. iii 32 ' In the case of Lazarus He uttered a human voice, as man ; but divinely, as God, did He raise Lazarus from the dead.' And St. Gregory Nazianzen, ' Orthodox writers clearly make a distinction between the things which belong to Christ—they assign to what is human the facts that He was born, was tempted, hungered, thirsted, was weary, and slept ; and they set down to the Godhead the facts that He was glorified by angels, that He overcame the tempter and fed the people in the wilderness and walked on the surface of the sea.' He quotes further the formula of reunion between St. Cyril and the Easterns, ending with the words ' We know that theologians have treated some of the expressions concerning our Lord as common, as referring to one person, and have distinguished others as referring to two natures, and have taught us to refer to Christ's Godhead those which are appropriate to deity (θεοπρεπεῖς) and to the manhood those which imply

---

[1] *Ep ad Flav.* c 4 This is a working out in example of the general principle 'Agit utraque forma cum alterius communione quod proprium est , verbo scilicet operante quod verbi est et carne exsequente quod carnis est Unum horum coruscat miraculis, aliud succumbit iniuriis'

[2] *St Leo on the Incarnation* (Masters, 1886) pp. 230 ff.

humiliation,' and he proves that this practice was endorsed by St. Cyril.

Now in regard to this tendency, to distribute to the two natures the words and acts of Christ, we may remark that up to a certain point it must be accepted by all who believe in Christ's Godhead. Thus 'I and my Father are one thing' (St. John x. 30) is ῥῆμα θεοπρεπές. It could only be spoken by one who, however truly incarnate, was Himself God St. John viii. 40 'Me, a man who hath told you the truth which I have heard from God,' is ἀνθρωποπρεπές. It could only be spoken by one who, whatever else he was, was really man. But beyond the rare words of our Lord about His own essential being, such as the one just cited or St. Matthew xi. 27 'No one knoweth the Father save the Son'—beyond such words and the accompanying divine claim on men which such words are necessary to interpret and justify, there is very little recorded in our Lord's life—may I say nothing?—which belongs to the divine nature *per se* and not rather to the divine nature acting under conditions of manhood. He had come to reveal God and to make His claim felt not as a messenger but as the Son. For this purpose He spoke as what He was, the Son. But He came to reveal God and make His claim felt, under conditions and limitations of manhood, and His powerful works, no less than His humiliations, are in the Gospels attributed to His manhood. Thus His miracles in general, and in particular the raising of Lazarus, are attributed by our Lord to the Father, as answering His own prayer, and to the Holy Spirit as 'the finger of God,' and St. Luke describes His miracles generally as the result of 'the power of the Lord' present with Him[1]. *This is a point on which—it must be emphatically said—accurate exegesis renders impossible to us the phraseology of the Fathers exactly as it stands.* So Dr. Westcott remarks 'It is unscriptural, though the practice is supported by strong patristic authority, to regard the Lord during His historic life, as acting now by His human and now by His divine nature only. The two natures were inseparably combined in the unity of His person. In all things He acts personally; and, as far as it is revealed to us, His greatest works during His earthly life are wrought by the help of the Father through the energy of a humanity enabled to do all things in fellowship with God (comp. John xi. 41 f.)[2].'

§ 8.

Mediaeval and scholastic theology.

By the time of Augustine in the west, and by the time of John of Damascus at least in the east, the theological determination against the admission of a real growth in our Lord's human knowledge or a real ignorance in His human condition, such as the Gospel documents describe, must be regarded as fixed[3]. I must however indicate

---

[1] St. John xi. 41, St. Matt. xii. 28, St Luke v 17, and see above, p 80.
[2] *Ep. to the Hebrews*, p 66.
[3] Apparent exceptions do not on examination seem to hold, e g St Bernard, commenting on Mark xiii 32 (*de Grad Hum* cc 3, 10), seeks to

The Consciousness of our Lord 167

a certain greater definiteness which was given to the denial. In the earlier mediaeval period writers speak of Christ in general terms as possessing even in His human soul the divine omniscience. Thus Fulgentius in the sixth century asserts that Christ, in virtue of the hypostatic union, certainly had in His human soul the full knowledge of the Godhead: He knows as man all that He knows as God, though not in the same manner; for as God He knows naturally, as man He knows in such a way as still to remain human[1]. And Alcuin (c. 790) asserts that 'the soul of Christ may not be held to have lacked in any respect the full knowledge of the Godhead, inasmuch as it formed one person with the Word[2].' This however, as Cassiodorus pointed out[3], was clearly

avoid imputing mendacity to Christ by admitting a real ignorance of the day and hour in respect of *His human experience* 'etsi suae divinitatis intuitu, aeque omnia praeterita scilicet praesentia atque futura perlustrando, diem quoque illum palam habebat, non tamen ullis carnis suae sensibus experiendo agnoverat.' But when commenting on Luke ii 52 (*hom super Missus est* ii. 10), he denies to our Lord, because He was God, all real growth as in human knowledge · 'non secundum quod erat, sed secundum quod appareret intelligendum est .. constat ergo quia semper Iesus virilem animum habuit, etsi semper in corpore vir non apparuit' Ch 9 'vir [i e a grown man] igitur erat Iesus necdum etiam natus, sed sapientia non aetate, animi vigore non viribus corporis, maturitate sensuum non corpulentia membrorum, neque enim minus fuit sapientia Iesus conceptus quam natus, parvus quam magnus.' All that he would admit then of ignorance of the day and hour is that He had not realized it in terms of human sensibility, or (like Gregory) that ignorant *ex humanitate*, He knew *in humanitate*

[1] Fulg *ad Ferrand Ep* xiv 26-32 (*P L* lxv p 420) 'novit anima Christi quantum illa [deitas] sed non sicut illa.' On the other hand, in the *ad Trasimund.* i 8 (p 231) he seems to admit a real *growth* in the knowledge of our Lord's human soul, according to Luke ii. 52

[2] *de Fide S Trin* ii 11, 12 (*P L.* ci p 31) 'non aestimandum est animae Christi in aliquo plenam divinitatis deesse notitiam, cuius una est persona cum Verbo' He goes on to explain that Christ said that He did not know what He causes others not to know (as Augustine).

[3] Cassiod. *in Psalm.* cxxxviii 5 (*P L* lxx p. 985, quoted by Peter

to ignore the truth that the human faculty essentially falls short of the divine. Thus Peter Lombard decides[1] that while Christ's human soul 'knew all things that God knows,' it did not apprehend them so clearly and perspicuously as God.

Later, again, St. Thomas Aquinas is found carrying definition further, and laying it down that Christ possessed both divine and human knowledge; and further, the human soul of Christ possessed knowledge of three kinds:

(i) *scientia beata*, i.e. the perfect human participation in the beatific vision, or the divine light by which Christ as man knew things as they exist in the eternal Word;

(ii) *scientia indita vel infusa*, by which Christ possessed the perfect knowledge of things as they are relatively to mankind;

(iii) *scientia acquisita*, the knowledge of things derived from experience. On this subject Aquinas professes that he has changed his opinion, and decides that Christ, though he already *ab initio* possessed perfect knowledge in His human soul by *scientia infusa* without reference to experience, also acquired that very same knowledge by sensitive experience[2]. This latter point remained in controversy between Thomists and Scotists, but it is purely

Lombard) 'Veritas humanae conditionis ostenditur, quia assumptus homo divinae substantiae non potest adaequari vel in scientia vel in alio.' Therefore Christ in the person of the Psalmist cries ' *Mirabilis facta est scientia tua ex me et non potero ad eam.*'

[1] Petr Lomb. *Sentent* III. dist. 14 The opposite of Peter Lombard's proposition was condemned at Basle *Sess* xxii 'anima Christi videt Deum tam clare et intense quantum clare et intense Deus videt se ipsum.'

[2] See *Summa*, p. III qu ix ff We are inclined to ask with an objector mentioned by de Lugo 'quid ergo multiplicandae sunt tot scientiae in Christo circa eadem obiecta?'

academic. The subject is pursued with an infinite intricacy in later scholastics such as Suarez or de Lugo But in the result it is affirmed in the strongest way and with complete unanimity that Christ's human soul was from the first moment of its creation what is commonly meant by omniscient, so that no place is left in it for faith or hope [1], and the distinction of the divine and human consciousnesses is safeguarded only by metaphysical refinements. as by the affirmation that Christ knew in His human soul at the first instant of its creation and at every moment all reality or existence of every kind, past, present and future, with all its latent possibilities, but not the abstract possibilities of existence which He knew only as God [2].

It must however be noticed (1) that there is a general sense of doubt in all the scholastic literature as to how much of all this ratiocination is *de fide*; though Petavius decides that the opinion of those who recognize actual limitation of knowledge in the human soul of Christ, 'though formerly it received the countenance of some men of highest eminence, was afterwards marked as a heresy [3].'

(2) that many of the scholastic writers, such as de Lugo,

[1] *Summa*, p III. qu VII art 3, 4
[2] St Thomas, *l c* qu x art. 2 de Lugo, *de Myst Incarn* disp XIX 1. Cf. Petavius, *de Incarn* XI 3 § 6 'The soul of Christ knew all things that are, or ever will be, or ever have been, but not what are only in *posse* not in fact'
[3] *de Incarn* XI 1 § 15 Among recent Roman Catholic writers, Dr. Hermann Schell, *Katholisch Dogmatik* (Paderborn, 1892), shows a disposition to criticize the scholastic determinations, and to assert the reality of the growth and limitations of our Lord's consciousness as man But he is, apparently, so hampered by decisions believed to be authoritative that in the result his position is hardly intelligible

profess to be deciding only what was true *as a matter of fact* about our Lord : it being admitted for instance that in abstract possibility the human mind of Christ might even have contracted actual error. This admission of the scholastics is valuable for us who feel that what we have gained from the more exact study of the Gospels is a conviction different from theirs of what was true in fact, so far as concerns the limitation of our Lord's human knowledge. This changed conviction of what was true in fact leads us to welcome their abstract admissions as to what might have been true without overthrowing the principle of the Incarnation [1].

By way of comment on these scholastic conclusions, there are two points to which it is worth while calling attention

1. The earlier mediaeval and scholastic method appears to put the dogmas of the Church in a wrong place [2]. The dogmas are primarily intended as limits of ecclesiastical thought rather than as its premises. they are the hedge rather than the pasture-ground : they block us off from lines of error rather than edify us in the truth. By them we are warned that Christ is no inferior being but very God ; and that He became at His Incarnation completely man, not in body only but in mind and spirit; and that remaining the same one and divine person He yet subsists henceforth in two distinct

---

[1] de Lugo, *de Myst Incarn.* disp. xxi 3 The inquiry is *An* [*Christi*] *cognitio fuerit vel potuerit esse falsa ?* The answer is to *fuerit*, no , to *potuerit esse*, yes; according to the *communis* and *verior* opinion. Such fallibility, it is argued, need not have interfered with His teaching office , might have been allowed by the divine nature, &c

[2] I have tried to express the point also at somewhat greater length, in *B. L.* pp 106, 108.

The Consciousness of our Lord.

natures. But thus warned off from cardinal errors, we are sent back to the New Testament, especially to the Gospels, to edify ourselves in the positive conception of what the Incarnation really meant. To Irenaeus, to Origen, to Athanasius, the New Testament is the real pasture-ground of the soul, and the function of the Church is conceived to be to keep men to it. But after a time there comes a change. The dogmas are used as the positive premises of thought. The truth about Christ's person is formed deductively and logically from the dogmas —whether decrees of councils or popes, or sayings of great fathers which are ranked as authoritative—and the figure in the Gospels grows dim in the background. Particular texts from the Gospels which seem contrary to current ecclesiastical teaching are quoted and re-quoted, but though, taken together, they might have availed to restore a more historical image of the divine person incarnate, in fact they are taken one by one and explained away with an ingenuity which excites in equal degrees our admiration of the logical skill of the disputant and our sense of the lamentably low ebb at which the true and continuous interpretation of the Gospel documents obviously lies

2. The view of the Incarnation current in the Middle Ages, which, as has been said, tended to minimize the real apprehension of our Lord's manhood, had its roots not only in a one-sided zeal for the Godhead of Jesus, but also in a certain metaphysical conception of God.

What I must call the biblical idea of the Incarnation seems to postulate that we should conceive of God as accommodating Himself to the conditions of human life in order to its development and recovery. God, the Son of God, must be conceived to exist not only according to His own natural mode of being, but also really and personally under the limitations of manhood. From this point of view the Incarnation might seem to be the supreme and intensified example of that general divine sympathy, by which God lives not only in His own life but also in the life of His creatures, and (in a sense) might fall in with a general doctrine of the divine immanence. Such an idea of divine sympathy and love is to be found in Christian theology even where we should least expect it, as in the Pseudo-Dionysius[1] where he describes God as carried out of Himself by His love for His creatures, and it is akin to Old Testament language about God. For in the Old Testament, if God is represented as wholly and personally distinct from His creatures, yet He is constantly represented also as following along with the fortunes of His people, collectively and individually, with an active and vigorous sympathy; or in other words He is conceived of morally rather than metaphysically.

---

[1] *de Div Nom* iv. 13 (*P G* iii. p 712) ἔστιν καὶ ἐκστατικὸς ὁ θεῖος ἔρως, οὐκ ἐῶν ἑαυτῶν εἶναι τοὺς ἐραστάς, ἀλλὰ τῶν ἐρωμένων ... τολμητέον δὲ καὶ τοῦτο ὑπὲρ ἀληθείας εἰπεῖν ὅτι καὶ αὐτὸς ὁ πάντων αἴτιος τῷ καλῷ καὶ ἀγαθῷ τῶν πάντων ἔρωτι δι' ὑπερβολὴν τῆς ἐρωτικῆς ἀγαθότητος ἔξω ἑαυτοῦ γίνεται, ταῖς εἰς τὰ ὄντα πάντα προνοίαις καὶ οἷον ἀγαθότητι καὶ ἀγαπήσει καὶ ἔρωτι θέλγεται.

Cf the later (fourteenth century) mystic Nicolas Cabasilas *de Vita in Christo* 6 (*P G*. cl. p 644) καθάπερ γὰρ τῶν ἀνθρώπων τοὺς ἐρῶντας ἐξίστησι τὸ φίλτρον, ὅταν ὑπερβάλλῃ καὶ κρεῖσσον γένηται τῶν δεξαμένων, τὸν ἴσον τρόπον ὁ περὶ τοὺς ἀνθρώπους ἔρως τὸν θεὸν ἐκένωσεν. I feel gratitude to Dorner (*Person of Christ*, div ii vol i pp 240 ff), for calling attention to this interesting author. But I cannot but think he overstates his doctrine in this respect

The Consciousness of our Lord.

On the other hand Greek philosophy was primarily concerned to conceive of God metaphysically. He was the One in opposition to the many objects of sense, and the Absolute and Unchangeable in opposition to the relative and mutable. In particular the divine immutability had a meaning assigned to it very different from that which belongs to it in the Bible, a meaning determined by contrast, not to the changeableness of human purpose, but to the very idea of 'motion' which, as belonging to the material, was also supposed to be of the nature of the evil. There is no doubt that this Greek metaphysical conception of God influenced Christian theology largely and not only for good [1]. In particular, through the medium of Neo-Platonism, it deeply coloured the thought of that remarkable and anonymous author who, writing about A.D. 500, passed himself off, probably without any intention to deceive, as Dionysius the Areopagite, the convert of St. Paul. With him the metaphysical conceptions of the transcendence, incomprehensibility, absolute unity and immutability of God are a master passion [2]. In his general philosophy the result of his zeal for the One is to lead him to ascribe to the manifold life of the universe only a precarious reality. In his view of the Incarnation it produces at least a monophysite tendency.

Jesus, even by His human name, is regarded as imparting illumination according to His super-essential Godhead [3], or He is spoken of as by His Incarnation

---

[1] See Hatch's *Hibbert Lectures* 1888 (Williams & Norgate) pp 239 ff
[2] See esp *de Div Nom* c xiii, and cf Dr. Westcott's *Religious Thought in the West* (Macmillan, 1891) pp 182-5
[3] *de Cael. Hier.* 1 2.

bringing us back into the unity of the divine life[1]. But Dionysius markedly shrinks from asserting a really human activity of the Incarnate; and, while accepting the real Incarnation as delivered in tradition, he is at pains to assert that not only did the Godhead suffer no alteration and confusion in this unutterable self-humiliation, but also that in respect of His humanity Jesus was still supernatural and supersubstantial[2], He performed human acts in a superhuman manner; it is hardly safe to say that he existed or acted as man, but He must be described as exhibiting in our manhood a new mode of 'theandric' activity[3]. On the whole we feel that the humanity of Jesus is, in the Areopagite, little but the veil for that divine self-disclosure which is at the same time a self-concealment[4]. The Incarnation becomes a partial theophany.

Now the influence of this writer—presumed to be of almost apostolic authority—became exceedingly great in the west when he first appeared in the translation by Scotus Erigena[5]. Erigena himself was profoundly

---

[1] *de Eccl Hier* III 13, IV 10.

[2] *de Div Nom* II 10. Here however he is quoting Hierotheus

[3] *Ep ad Caium Monach* 4 This word θεανδρικὴ ἐνέργεια became the motto of the Monothelites Cf *de Div. Nom* II. 9, where Christ's human acts are said to belong to a 'supernatural physiology.'

[4] *Ep ad Caium*, 3.

[5] For his influence on Thomas Aquinas see the remark of his editor, Corderius, *Obs.* XII (*P. G* III pp 90 ff), 'Facile patet,' he concludes, 'angelicum doctorem totam fere doctrinam theologicam ex purissimis Dionysii fontibus hausisse, cum vix ulla sit periodus e qua non ipse tanquam apis argumentosa theologicum succum extraxerit et in Summam, veluti quoddam alveare, pluribus quaestionibus articulisque, ceu cellulis, theologico melle [? melli] servando distinctum, redegerit'

The Consciousness of our Lord. 175

affected by him [1], and he in turn diffused in a later age the influence he had received [2] Thus early scholastic philosophy is largely dominated by a neo-platonic rather than Christian idea of the Incarnation,—that the incomprehensible God partially manifests Himself under a human veil. the manhood is but the temporary or permanent robe [3] of Godhead. In an extreme form this idea came to be known as Nihilianism.

The eternal Son, it was said, became, in becoming incarnate, nothing He was not before The humanity is no addition to His person it is but the robe of Godhead, and the robe is no addition to the wearer's person, but simply gives appropriateness to His appearance. This view is stated, among others, by Peter Lombard [4].

'Sunt etiam alii qui in incarnatione Verbi non solum personam ex naturis compositam negant, verum etiam hominem aliquem sive etiam aliquam substantiam ibi ex anima et carne compositam vel factam diffitentur. Sed sic illa duo, scilicet animam et carnem, Verbi personae vel naturae unita esse aiunt, ut non ex illis duobus vel ex his tribus aliqua natura vel persona fieret sive componeretur, sed illis duobus velut indumento Verbum Dei vestiretur ut mortalium oculis congruenter

---

[1] His view of the Incarnation is best seen in *de Div Nat* v 25 27. and see further, pp. 240 n 2, 281.

[2] Not to any great extent at once or in his own lifetime The influence of Scotus and Dionysius becomes more apparent in the twelfth century.

[3] Apparently the phraseology of the 'robe' was first brought into prominence in the school of Apollinarius of Laodicea. His moderate disciple Jovius spoke of the flesh of Christ as the στολὴ καὶ περιβόλαιον καὶ προκάλυμμα μυστηρίου κρυπτομένου (in Leontius Byz *P G* lxxxvi pp 1956 b, 1960 a).

[4] *Sentt*. lib. iii dist. 6 f. Cf. dist. 10.

appareret. . . . Ipsa persona Verbi quae prius erat sine indumento, assumptione indumenti non est divisa vel mutata sed una eademque immutata permansit.' Among the authorities for this position St. Augustine is quoted, commenting on the Latin version of Philippians ii. 7 *habitu inventus est ut homo* [1]. *Habitus*, Augustine says, always means something which is an unessential accident or appendage of something else : ' manifestum est in ea re dici habitum quae accidit vel accedit alicui, ita ut eam possit etiam non habere.' But different sorts of *habitus* may be distinguished according as the accession of the *habitus* produces or does not produce a change in the possessor of it, or in the *habitus* itself. The humanity of Christ, he decides, belongs to the class of *habitus* which do not change their possessors but are themselves changed, as for example is the case with a robe And he continues, ' *Deus* enim *filius semetipsum exinanivit*, non formam suam mutans, sed *formam servi accipiens* . . . verum hominem suscipiendo *habitu inventus est ut homo*, id est habendo hominem inventus est ut homo, non sibi, sed eis quibus in homine apparuit '

Peter Lombard does not in this passage decide in favour of this view, but in fact he appears to have held it as his opinion, without positively asserting it [2]. This

---

[1] *de div quaest lxxxiii.* qu 73

[2] John of Cornwall (c 1170), Peter Lombard's pupil and in this respect opponent, is explicit on this point See *Eulogium ad Alex. iii* in *P L.* cxcix pp 1052-3 ' Quod vero a magistro Petro Abaelardo hanc opinionem suam magister Petrus Lombardus accepit, eo magis suspicatus sum, quia librum illum frequenter prae manibus habebat . . . Opinionem suam dixi Quod enim fuerit haec eius opinio certum est. Quod vero non fuerit eius assertio haec, ipse testatur in capitulo suo . . Praeterea, paulo antequam electus esset in episcopum parisiensem, mihi et omnibus auditoribus eius qui tunc aderant protestatus est, quod haec non esset assertio sua, sed opinio sola quam a magistro acceperat. Haec enim verba subiecit .

The Consciousness of our Lord.

theory that God in becoming incarnate did not become *aliquid* or *nihil factus est quod non fuerit ante* is what is called Nihilianism, and becoming widely diffused created such scandal that it was condemned by Alexander III in 1177[1]. In fact, such a plainly monophysite position could not but be condemned, but the ideas which prompted it were neither condemned nor discarded. In spite of the fact that a suspicion of heresy attached itself to the phraseology of the *vestis* or *habitus*, as applied to the humanity of our Lord, it was still employed[2]; and the metaphysical conception of the immutability of God, in a sense different to the scriptural, still held ground. The fact was not really faced that God in becoming man really submitted Himself to the conditions of human life. Just as in the theology of nature all the emphasis was (if I may so express it) on the fact that nature is in God and little on the fact that God is in nature, so in regard to the

nec unquam Deo volente erit assertio mea, nisi quae fuerit fides catholica Postea vero per quosdam homines loquaces magis quam perspicaces quae nec in cubilibus essent audienda usque hodie praedicantur super tecta'

[1] The chief theologian of the controversy was John of Cornwall His conclusion (in the *Eulogium*, c 20) is that 'Christus est aliquis homo et utique sanctissimus et beatissimus hominum, et quod Christus secundum humanitatem est aliquid, et utique verus homo animalis, verum corpus, natura, substantia, unum totum' The Pope (see Mansi, *Concil* xxi p. 1081) bids the archbishop of Rheims to summon the *magistri* of Paris and Rheims and neighbouring towns to condemn the proposition 'quod Christus non sit aliquid secundum quod est homo' I do not think it has been noticed that there is an apparent connexion between the doctrine of nihilianism in reference to Christ and that of transubstantiation in regard to the eucharist This is pointed out in the next dissertation

[2] See quotations in Landriot, *Le Christ de la Tradition* (Paris, 1888) 1 p 84 and note 1, esp. St Thom Aquinas 'sicut vestis formatur secundum formam vestientis et non mutat vestientem, inde antiqui dixerunt quod vergit in accidens.'

Incarnation all the emphasis is on the fact that behind the veil of the humanity is God, not on the fact that God was really made man

It is significant of the same tendency of thought that the theological speculation of the time tended more and more to deprive of relationship, of movement and life, the conception of the divine nature in itself. So immutably one was it necessary to conceive the Godhead to be, that Peter Lombard denied that the divine nature, as distinguished from the divine persons, can be described as either 'generating' or 'generated' or 'proceeding' Such a doctrine, which repudiates a mode of expression familiar in the fathers, produced a strenuous protest from Richard of St Victor[1] with others He defied its maintainers to produce even a single father as authorizing such a denial. The challenge was perhaps impossible to meet, but, none the less, the fourth Lateran Council in 1215—the same which affirmed transubstantiation—defended the Master of the Sentences and gave his opinion dogmatic authority[2]. Anglican writers—such as Bull and Bingham[3]—have

---

[1] *de Trin* vi 22 (*P L* cxcvi p 986) 'Procul dubio nihil aliud est Patris persona quam substantia ingenita, nihil aliud Filii persona quam substantia genita Sed multi temporibus nostris suriexere qui non audent hoc dicere, quin potius, quod multo periculosius est, contra sanctorum patrum auctoritatem . audent negare et omnibus modis conantur refellere, nullo modo concedunt quod substantia gignat substantiam . Afferant, si possunt, auctoritatem, non dicam plures sed saltem unam, quae neget substantiam gignere substantiam'

[2] Mansi, *Concil* xxii p 983 ' Illa res [divina natura] non est generans neque genita nec procedens . sed est Pater qui generat, Filius qui gignitur, et Spiritus sanctus qui procedit ut distinctiones sint in personis et unitas in natura'

[3] See Bull, *Def Fid Nic* iv 1. 9 (*Library of Anglo-Cath Theol* ii p 568):

treated the decision with little respect, and indeed it appears not only highly precarious in itself but also to have its origin in a false metaphysical conception of unity and immutability.

§ 9.

The theology of the Reformation[1].

How the scholastic theology was presenting itself to thoughtful minds at the beginning of the sixteenth century, we may judge from the attitude towards it of Erasmus[2] and Colet. Erasmus is, of course, violent in the expression of his antipathy. But that antipathy itself he had in part imbibed from Colet, or at the least Colet had confirmed it. He tells us how in the course of conversation he had at last extracted from

---

he describes Petavius as unable to 'whitewash' this view, which is a piece of 'scholastic trifling' And Bingham's *Sermon on the Trinity* (*Works*, x 377, Oxford, 1855), who quotes the fathers more or less at length

[1] In this section I have depended much upon Dorner (*Doctrine of the Person of Christ*) and Bruce (*The Humiliation of Christ*) for the history of opinion

[2] Nowhere does Erasmus' attitude towards current theology appear more strikingly than in the *Annotations* appended to his edition of the New Testament in Greek (1516), e g on 1 Tim 1 4 'ἀπεράντοις, cuiusmodi fere nunc sunt vulgarium theologorum quodlibeta Nam quo plus est eiusmodi quaestiuncularum hoc plus etiam subsidet' Again on 1 Tim 1 6 'ματαιολογία Quantum ad pronunciationem attinet mataeologia non multum abest a theologia, cum res inter se plurimum discrepent Proinde nobis quoque cavendum est ne sic sectemur theologiam ut in mataeologiam incidamus, de frivolis nugis sine fine digladiantes, ea potius tractemus quae nos transforment in Christum et caelo dignos reddant'

Colet, who showed great unwillingness to speak on the subject, a condemnation even of Aquinas[1] Erasmus had been excepting Aquinas from a general condemnation of scholastics 'Colet turned his full eye upon him in order to learn whether he really was speaking in earnest; and concluding that it was so, ' What," he said, with a sort of inspired force (*tanquam afflatus spiritu quodam*), " do you extol to me such a man as Aquinas? If he had not been possessed with arrogance, he would not have defined everything with so much temerity and pride; and if he had not had something of the worldly spirit he would not have corrupted the whole doctrine of Christ with his profane philosophy."'

This is no doubt a hard unsympathetic judgement on Aquinas personally, but coming from a man like Colet it is an important judgement on the method which he represents The experience of the scholastic system inspired in Colet's mind a passionate desire to return to simplicity—to the Bible and the Apostles' Creed[2]. And no one can interpret the Reformation rightly, on its

[1] Erasmus, *Ep* 435, *Opera* (Lyons, 1703) iii p 458 and cf Seebohm, *Oxford Reformers* (Longmans, 1869) pp 102 ff Froude, *Life and Letters of Erasmus* (Longmans, 1894) pp 106, &c

[2] Seebohm, *l c* p 106 See Erasmus, *Ep* 207 'Optarim frigidas istas argutias aut amputari prorsus aut certe solas non esse theologis, et Christum illum simplicem ac purum penitus inseri mentibus hominum id quod hac potissimum via fieri posse existimo si linguarum adminiculis adiuti in ipsis fontibus philosophemur' *Ep* 329 ' Quae pertinent ad fidem quam paucissimis articulis absolvantur' *Ep* 613 (to Archbp of Palermo) ' Ea [pax] vix constare poterit, nisi de quam potest paucissimis definiamus et in multis liberum relinquamus suum cuique iudicium, propterea quod ingens sit rerum plurimarum obscuritas, et hoc morbi fere innatum sit hominum ingeniis ut cedere nesciant simul atque res in contentionem vocata est, quae postquam incaluit, hoc cuique videtur verissimum quod temere tuendum susceperit.' The whole of this letter is of the greatest interest

religious side, who does not bear in mind the existence of a wide-spread and passionate desire to get back to the Christ of the Gospels and the primitive Church.

In the case of Luther, this return to the Christ of the Gospels at once produced a belief in properly human limitations of knowledge in our Lord's manhood. 'According to the plain sense of Luke's words (ii 52), in the simplest manner possible, it really took place that the older Christ grew, the greater He grew · the greater, the more rational, the more rational, the stronger in spirit and the fuller of wisdom before God, in Himself and before the people. These words need no gloss. Such a view too is attended with no danger and is Christian, whether it contradicts the articles of faith imagined by scholastics or not is of no consequence[1].' So he emphasizes the human reality of our Lord's temptation and desolation This ethical reality of our Lord's manhood he interpreted, not by any theory of the divine self-emptying—for he made the *already human Christ* the nominative to ἐκένωσεν in Phil ii 6— but by a view which tends in the Nestorian direction. His language seems to postulate a separate personality for the human nature of Christ, and though he believes the man Jesus to have been indissolubly united to the Godhead from the first, yet he conceives the effects of the union to have been only gradually imparted to him[2]. This quasi-Nestorian tendency, however, was checked in

---

[1] Luther's *Opera*, '*Kirchenpostille*' (Walch, xi pp 389-90) See Dorner, *l c* div ii vol ii pp 91 ff

[2] See Dorner, *l c* pp 95-100, and note 8, p 391 In the above passage I have adopted Dorner's view of Luther's early theory, which his references seem to me to justify But see Bruce, *l c* lect. iii. note A, p 373.

Dissertations.

Luther by the sacramental controversy Driven to defend the doctrine of the real presence of our Lord's body and blood in the sacrament of the eucharist by a theory of the ubiquity of our Lord even in His humanity, he was led to speak of this ubiquity as resulting from the union of the divine and human natures, and of the *communicatio idiomatum* from one to the other as existing from the beginning of the Incarnation[1]. This led to a development of thought in a Monophysite rather than a Nestorian direction and this rival tendency, which renders Luther's Christology very difficult to understand as a whole, became dominant in the Lutheran schools It resulted in the formation of a Christology based on ubiquitarianism, which Dr A B Bruce, without undue severity, pronounces to be, to an amazing extent, 'artificial, unnatural, and incredible[2].'

Meanwhile the Reformed (Zwinglian) theologians, in strong opposition to the Lutheran interpretation of the *communicatio idiomatum*[3], were emphasizing the distinct

---

[1] Dorner, *l c* pp 127, 132-4, 138-9
[2] Bruce, *l c* p 83
[3] To the doctrine they held, see Niemeyer, *Collectio Confessionum* (Leipzig, 1840), pp 485 (*Confessio Helvetica posterior*), 632 (*Repetitio Anhaltina*), but in its original sense The phrase ἀντίδοσις ἰδιωμάτων was originally used —first apparently by Leontius of Byzantium—to express the transference, not so much of qualities, as of names appropriate to one of our Lord's natures to the other in virtue of the unity of His person See Leont Byz *con Nestor et Eutych* 1 (*P G* lxxxvi p 1289 c) ὅθεν ἡμεῖς κατὰ τὰς θείας γραφὰς καὶ τὰς πατροπαραδότους θεωρίας πολλάκις τὸ ὅλον ἐκ μέρους καὶ τὰ μέρη τῇ τοῦ ὅλου κλήσει προσαγορεύομεν, υἱὸν ἀνθρώπου τὸν λόγον ὀνομάζοντες καὶ κύριον τῆς δόξης ἐσταυρῶσθαι ὁμολογοῦντες, ἀλλ' οὐ παρὰ τοῦτο τῇ ἀντιδόσει τῶν ἰδιωμάτων ἀναιροῦμεν τὸν ἴδιον λόγον τῆς θατέρου ἐν ταὐτῷ ἰδιότητος πρὸς δὲ καὶ διὰ κυρίων ἡμῖν ταῦτα τῶν ὀνομάτων γνωρίζεται, τὴν μὲν ἀντίδοσιν τῶν ἰδιωμάτων ἐν τῇ μιᾷ ὑποστάσει θεωροῦσι, τὴν δὲ ἰδιότητα τὴν ἐν τῇ κοινότητι ἐν τῇ διαφορᾷ τῶν φύσεων ἐπιγινώσκουσιν Cf *adv Arg Sever* p 1941 a οὐ γὰρ ἀντίδοσις ἂν τῶν ἰδιωμάτων ἐγίνετο εἰ μὴ ἐν ἑκατέρῳ

The Consciousness of our Lord. 183

existence in Christ incarnate both of the human nature and of its properly human attributes, including the limitation of knowledge This limitation of knowledge was believed to have been made possible by a 'self-emptying' on the part of the eternal Word, by which the divines of this school appear to have meant a hiding or withholding of the divine attributes (omniscience, &c) from the human mind. But not much was done to elucidate the conception or to reconcile the dual consciousness of Christ—the *gemina mens*—with the unity of His person. Later writers have indeed suggested that the doctrine of a 'double life' of the Word was in the minds of some of these teachers—a distinction between the *Logos totus extra Jesum*, living His own proper life in the Godhead, and the *Logos totus in Jesu*, that is the same divine Word living another self-limited life as the incarnate Christ. This suggestion, however, is not based on very clear evidence. Of the idea itself we shall hear again in connexion with Martensen

Subsequently to the reunion of German Lutherans and Reformed in the Evangelical Church (1817), 'kenotic' views, extreme and moderate, have prevailed among

---

ἔμεινε καὶ ἐν τῇ ἑνώσει ἡ ἰδιότης ἀκίνητος Cf John Damasc *de Fid Orthodox* iii c 4, and note of P M Lequien The same idea was expressed by Gregory Naz as ἡ τῶν ὀνομάτων ἐπίζευξις, ἐπαλλαττομένων τῶν ὀνομάτων διὰ τὴν σύγκρασιν, by Gregory Nyss in the phrase ἀντιμεθίστανται τὰ ὀνόματα, and it became the commonplace of Chalcedonian theology. St Thomas Aquinas also in later days expresses the same idea, but does not use the phrase (see *Summa*, p iii qu xvi art 4 and 5) In this sense then—of names, not of qualities—the phrase was used by the Reformed , see *Repetit Anhalt* (as above) 'est enim communicatio idiomatum *praedicatio* seu *forma loquendi* qua . *tribuitur*, etc ' But, as would be supposed, theologians of all schools continually tend to pass, like Luther, from names to qualities

Protestant theologians in Germany and in Switzerland and there has been also a recurrence (on Dorner's part) to Luther's earlier view. Of these various doctrines I will describe in outline four typical specimens[1].

1. The *absolute kenotic view*, advocated in Germany by Gess[2], shall be represented by the great Neuchatel theologian, M. GODET. Commenting on St. John 1 14[3], he says,

'The proposition, "The Word became flesh," can only, as it seems to me, signify one thing, viz that the divine subject entered into the human mode of being at the cost of renouncing His divine mode of being . . . —incarnation by deprivation ($\kappa \acute{\epsilon} \nu \omega \sigma \iota \varsigma$).' The idea is further elaborated later on[4].

'Does Scripture, while clearly teaching the eternal existence of the Word, teach at the same time the presence of the divine state and attributes in Jesus during the course of His life on earth? We have seen that the formula of John 1. 14 is incompatible with such an idea. The expression, "*The Word was made flesh*," speaks certainly of a divine subject, but as reduced to the state of man, which, as we have seen, does not at all suppose the two states, the divine and the human, as co-existing in it. Such a notion is set aside by exegesis as well as by logic. The *impoverishment* of Christ, of which Paul speaks 2 Cor. viii. 9, His voluntary *self-abasement*, described Phil ii. 6, 7, equally imply His renunciation of the divine state at the moment when He entered upon human existence. The facts of the Gospel

---

[1] For fuller information see Bruce, *l c* lect iv
[2] Bruce, *l c* pp 144 ff
[3] *Gospel of St John* (Engl trans Clark) 1 p. 362. Godet intimates (p 401) that he is in substantial, but not complete, agreement with Gess
[4] pp 396 ff.

history are at one with those apostolic declarations, ... Jesus no longer possesses on earth the attributes which constitute the divine state. Omniscience He has not, for He asks questions, and Himself declares His ignorance on one point (Mark xiii 32). He possesses a pre-eminent prophetic vision (John iv. 17, 18), but this vision is not omniscience. No more does He possess omnipotence, for He prays and is heard; as to His miracles, it is the Father who works them in His favour (xi. 42, v. 36) He is equally destitute of omnipresence. His love even, perfect as it is, is not divine love. This is immutable. But who will assert that Jesus in His cradle loved as He did at the age of twelve, or at the age of twelve as He did on the cross? Perfect relatively, at every given moment, His love grew from day to day, both in regard to the intensity of His voluntary self-sacrifice, and as to the extent of the circle which it embraced. It was thus a truly human love. " The grace which is by one *man*, Jesus Christ," says St. Paul for this reason (Rom v. 15). His holiness is also a human holiness, for it is realized every moment only at the cost of struggle, through the renunciation of legitimate enjoyment and victory over the natural fear of pain (xii. 25, 27, xvii 19 a). It is so human that it is to pass over into us and become ours (xvii 19 b) All those texts clearly prove that Jesus while on the earth, did not possess the attributes which constitute the divine state, and hence He can terminate His earthly career by claiming back again the glory which He had before His incarnation (xvii. 5).

How is such a self-deprivation on the part of a divine being conceivable? It was necessary, first of all, that He should consent to lose for a time His self-consciousness *as a divine subject*. The memory of a divine life anterior to His earthly existence would

have been incompatible with the state of a true child
and a really human development. And in fact the
Gospel texts nowhere ascribe to Jesus a self-consciousness *as Logos* before the time of His baptism. The
word which He uttered at the age of twelve (Luke ii 49)
simply expresses the feeling of an intimate relation to
God and of a filial consecration to His service. With
a moral fidelity like His, and in the permanent enjoyment of a communion with God which sin did not alter,
the child could call God His Father in a purely religious
sense, and apart from any consciousness of a divine pre-
existence. The feeling of His redemptive mission must
have been developed in His earliest years, especially
through His experience of the continual contrast between
His moral purity and the sin which He saw staining all
those who surrounded Him. . . . According to the
biblical account, the Logos, in becoming incarnate, did
therefore really put off His consciousness of His divine
being, and of the state corresponding to it. This self-
deprivation was the negative condition of the Incarnation. . . .

Up to the age of thirty Jesus fulfils this task [of redemp-
tion]. By His perfect obedience and constant sacrifice of
self He raises humanity in His person from innocence to
holiness He does not yet know Himself; perhaps in
the light of Scripture He begins dimly to forecast what
He is in relation to God. But the distinct consciousness
of His dignity as Logos would not be compatible with
the reality of His human development and the accom-
plishment of the task assigned to this first period of His
life. This task once fulfilled, the conditions of His
existence change. A new work opens up to Him, and
the consciousness of His dignity as the well-beloved
Son, far from being incompatible with the work which
He has still to carry out, becomes its indispensable basis.

The Consciousness of our Lord.

To testify of God *as the Father*, He must necessarily know Himself *as the Son*. The baptism is the decisive event which begins this new phase ... Henceforward He will be able to say what He could not say before "*Before Abraham was I am*" ... Yet His baptism, while restoring to Jesus His consciousness of sonship, did not restore Him to His filial *state*, the divine *form of God* belonging to Him There is an immense disproportion between what He *knows* Himself to be and what He *is* really. Therein there will be for Him the possibility of temptation[1], therein the work of patience. Master of all, He possesses nothing. No doubt He lays out on His work treasures of wisdom and power which are in God, but solely because His believing and filial heart is constantly appealing to the fatherly heart of God

It was by His ascension that His return to the divine *state* was accomplished, and that His position was at last raised to the level of the self-*consciousness* which He had from His baptism. From that time He was clothed with all the attributes of the divine state which He possessed before His incarnation; but He was clothed with them *as the Son of Man*. *All the fulness of the Godhead* henceforth dwells in Him, but humanly, and even as Paul says, BODILY (Col ii. 9).'

'We do not think it necessary to treat here the questions which are raised as to the internal relations of the Divine Persons, by the view which we have been explaining regarding the dogma of the Incarnation. For the very reason that we hold the divine existence of the Son to be a matter of love (*the bosom of the Father*) and not of necessity as with Philo, we think that, when the Word descends into the world there to become Himself

---

[1] In his note on the temptation (St Luke iv) M Godet says, 'The Son was capable of sin, because He had renounced the divine mode of existence'

one of the beings of the universe, the Father can enter into direct relation to the world, and Himself exercise the functions of Creator and Preserver which He commonly exercises through the mediation of the Word[1].'

According to this view the Son in becoming incarnate ceases to live the life of Godhead altogether or to exercise His cosmic functions. Gess specifies further that the eternal generation of the Son and the procession of the Holy Spirit through the Son, were suspended from the time of the incarnation to that of the glorification of Christ: and further maintains that the Word, thus depotentiated, took the place of the human soul in Jesus, as actually having become a human soul[2].

I hope in what was said in the first part of this essay I have saved myself from the imputation of underrating the large element of truth there is in such views as these. But they are open to two main objections. First, they are based on an exaggerated and one-sided view of the phenomena of the Gospel. There are no facts justifying any theory at all as to the loss by our Lord during the period of childhood and growth of the consciousness of His eternal sonship and its gradual recovery. One may speculate, but there are no facts. Again, our Lord's attitude towards sin never exhibits any trace of peccability. Nor can the doctrine that the love of Jesus Christ was not strictly divine love be fairly reconciled with such language as 'He that hath seen me hath seen the Father[3].' Secondly, so far as this view postulates an

---

[1] p. 403 note cf also the statement of M Godet's view in *Defence of the Christian Faith* (Clark, Edinburgh) pp. 300-1

[2] Bruce, *l.c* pp. 148-50.   [3] St John xiv 9

The Consciousness of our Lord. 189

absolute abandonment by the Son during the period of His humiliation of His position and function in the Blessed Trinity and in the universe, it has against it the strongest considerations. To begin with, it must reckon with a weight of Church judgement such as no thoughtful Christian, Catholic or Protestant, can underrate But more than this: it is opposed to the fairly plain implications of the very apostolic writers who impress upon us the reality of the *kenosis*, St. Paul and the author of the Epistle to the Hebrews[1], while, on the ground of reason, the assumption of the surrender on the part of the Son of such a divine function as that of mediating the procession of the Holy Ghost, or such a cosmic function as maintaining the universe in being and unity, is in itself so tremendous that nothing short of a positive apostolic statement could drive one to contemplate it.

2 The *partial kenotic view*, maintained first in Germany by Thomasius[2] and later, though with great obscurity and ambiguity, by Prof Franz Delitzsch[3], shall be represented here by its recent representative in England, Dr. FAIRBAIRN[4].

'But what to the Evangelists did incarnation mean? It meant the coming to be, not of a Godhead, but of a manhood Its specific result was a human, not a divine, person, whose humanity was all the more real that it was voluntary or spontaneous, all the more natural that God, rather than man, had to do with its making To the Evangelists the most miraculous thing

---

[1] See above, pp 91–3   [2] Bruce, *l c* pp 138 ff.
[3] *Biblical Psychology* (Eng trans Clark) pp 382 ff
[4] *Christ in Modern Theology* (Hodder & Stoughton, 1893) pp. 354, 476

in Christ was His determination not to be miraculous, but to live our ordinary life amidst struggles and in the face of temptations that never ceased One principle ruled throughout the motives that governed the divine conduct governed also the human. This principle and these motives may be desciibed as the law of sacrifice. The Father denied Himself in giving the Son ; the Son denied Himself in becoming man and in living as the man He had become Looking up from below, it was all one infinite *kenosis*; looking down from above, it was all one infinite sacrifice But kenosis and sacrifice alike meant that, while He assumed the fashion of the man and the form of the servant, both the manhood and the servitude, in order to either having any significance, had to be as real as the Godhead and the sovereignty .

This act is described as a *kenosis*, an emptying of Himself. Now, this is precisely the kind of term we should expect to be used if the Incarnation was a reality. It must have involved surrender, humiliation ; there could be no real assumption of the nature, the form, and the status of the created Son, if those of the uncreated were in all their integrity retained. These two things, the surrender and the assumption, are equal and coincident ; but it is through the former that the latter must be understood We may express what it means by saying that the Incarnation, while it was not of the whole Godhead, only of the Son, yet concerned the Godhead as a whole. And this carries with it an important consequence. Physical attributes are essential to God, but ethical terms and relations to the Godhead. In other words, the external attributes of God are omnipotence, omniscience, omnipresence ; but the internal are truth and love. But the external are under the command of the internal; God acts as the Godhead is. The external alone might constitute a creator, but not a deity; the internal would make out of a deity the creator. Whatever then could be surrendered, the ethical attributes and qualities could not, but God may only seem the more Godlike if, in obedience to the ethical, He limit or restrain or veil the physical We reverence Him the more that we think the annihilation so easy to His omnipotence is made impossible by His love. No such impossibilities would be known to an almighty devil, he would glory in destruction as much as God glories in salvation. We may say then that what marks the whole life of Deity is the regulation of His physical by His ethical attributes, or the limitation of God by the Godhead. But this same principle supplies us with a factor for the solution of our problem. The salvation of the sinner was a moral necessity to the Godhead; but no such necessity demanded that each of the Divine Persons should every moment exercise all the physical attributes of God. And this surrender the Son made when He emptied Himself and assumed the form of a servant, and was made in the likeness of man. The determinative divine qualities were obeyed, and the determined limited; yet it was, as it were, the renunciation of the less in order to the realization of the more Godlike qualities "The Word became flesh, and dwelt among us," but we only the more "beheld his glory, glory as of the only begotten from the Father, full of grace and truth"' (John 1. 14).

Now this view differs from the view of M Godet, as making plainer the real continuity of divine life in the Incarnation. It maintains a real continuity of conscious life so far as the ethical qualities of the Son of God are concerned But it distinguishes His ethical from His physical attributes, and conceives Him as abandoning the latter absolutely in becoming incarnate. Thus, as much as M. Godet, Dr. Fairbairn postulates that Christ did absolutely abandon His relation of equality with God and His functions in the universe. But it is chiefly from this point of view that the view of M. Godet was criticized, and the same considerations apply to this more moderate but hardly, I think, more tenable view.

3. The theory of *the double life of the Word* This view, which has found incidental expression by Mr R. H. Hutton in England[1], is expressed most formally by the Danish Bishop MARTENSEN [2]

'In that He thus lived as a man, and as ' the Son of Man" possessed His Deity solely under the conditions imposed by a human individuality in the limited forms of a human consciousness, we may undoubtedly say of Him that He lived in humiliation and poverty, because He had renounced that majestic glory by which, as the omnipresent Logos, He irradiates the entire creation ...

We are to see in Christ, not the naked God, but *the fulness of Deity framed in the ring of humanity*; not the attributes of the divine nature in their unbounded infinitude, but the divine attributes embodied in the attributes of human nature (*communicatio idiomatum*) Instead of the omnipresence we have that blessed presence, concerning which the God-man testifies, "He that seeth me seeth the Father" (John xiv 9)[3]. in the place of omniscience comes the divinely human wisdom which reveals to babes the mysteries of the kingdom of heaven; in the place of the world-creating omnipotence enters the world-vanquishing and world-completing power, the infinite power and fulness of love and holiness in virtue

---

[1] *Theol. Essays* (Macmillan, 1888) p 269
[2] *Christian Dogmatics* (Clark's *Foreign Theol Libr.*) pp 266-7.
[3] See also Matt xxviii 20.

The Consciousness of our Lord.

of which the God-man was able to testify "All power is given to me in heaven and on earth" (Matt. xxviii. 18).

Still, there are not two Sons of God, but one Son; Christ did not add a new second Son to the Trinity; the entire movement takes place within the circle of the Trinity itself. At the same time, it must be allowed that the Son of God leads in the economy of the Father a twofold existence; that He lives a double life in His world-creating and in His world-completing activity. As the pure *Logos of Deity*, He works through the kingdom of nature by His all-pervading presence, creates the pre-suppositions and conditions of the revelation of His all-completing love. As the *Christ*, He works through the kingdom of grace, of redemption, and perfection, and points back to His pre-existence (John viii 58, xvii. 5)'

To this view—perhaps I should rather say to this attempt to adumbrate a line of thought—there is, I think, no objection except the difficulty of conceiving it. It accounts for all the scriptural language on both sides, and it is reconcilable with the authoritative decisions of the Church. As to its being rationally conceivable or suggestive something will be said later on [1].

4. In opposition to kenotic theories DORNER'S view [2] may be described as that of a gradual incarnation. He repudiates the idea of 'a lessening or reduction of the Logos Himself': he prefers to speak of 'a limitation of the self-communication of the Logos to humanity.' But how does this help us then to understand the

---

[1] See § 3, p 215 f.
[2] See *System of Christian Doctrine* (Clark's *Foreign Theol Libr*) iii pp. 308 ff , *Doctr. of the Person of Christ*, div. ii vol iii p 250

limitation of our Lord's consciousness in the flesh, if He personally is the omniscient Logos? Dorner would meet this difficulty by repudiating the doctrine of the impersonal manhood and postulating, within the life of the divine personality of the Word, a complete and therefore personal humanity as assumed by Him. Jesus was a human person—' this man '—whom the Word had from the first personally assumed into Himself and with whom He was inseparably united, but who none the less retained the personal independence of his manhood sufficiently to make possible the development of a properly human consciousness and the gradual communication to him of the divine consciousness, till at last there resulted the development of one perfect divine-human person and the Incarnation was complete and absolute. ' This incarnation,' he says, 'may be termed an increasing one in so far as through it, on the one hand, an ever higher and richer fulness becomes actually the property of the man Jesus, and he, on the other hand, becomes ever more completely the mundane expression of the eternal Son the Image of God.'

Dorner's exposition of his idea is diffuse and difficult to state, nor is it easy to make quotations that are intelligible and of reasonable length. In the above explanation of his view it has become, I fear, a little too pronounced—too Nestorian in sound. Dorner emphasizes that the Man is really, personally and inseparably united to the Word from the first: that the humanity is not more separately personal than is involved in being (according to Boetius' definition of personality) *animae rationalis individua substantia*: he regards the real personality of the Christ as a divine-human personality gradually perfected through the unity of the natures.

But however much modified—however much it has its sharp edges taken off—this view appears to me to be still at the bottom Nestorian and unscriptural. The person Jesus Christ when He was on earth remembered His eternal past. 'Before Abraham was,' He says, 'I am'. He recalls the glory which He had with the Father before the world was. His 'ego,' therefore, is the eternal Ego. Or again, 'No one knoweth the day and hour. not the angels, neither the Son' Here the speaker is the super-angelic, supra-mundane Son. He, that person, had come down from heaven and went back to heaven. There is (as far as human thought or language can take us) only one person, one ego, and that ego the eternal Son, who for us men and our salvation assumed a human nature in its completeness, and willed to live and think and pray and work and speak under its limitations. In a word we do not think Dorner's view is reconcilable fundamentally either with the dogma of Ephesus (or indeed the Nicene Creed) or with the theology of the New Testament. It has also the defect that it does not interpret but confuses the theological language to which it yet professes to hold fast Any Catholic profession of faith is, we feel sure, bound to generate in the minds of thoughtful persons reading Scripture in its light a conception of Christ's person which Dorner's view will not illuminate or tend to make rationally consistent. but will only throw into confusion.

With the more markedly and confessedly unorthodox German views we are not here concerned.

§ 10.

The Anglican theology.

The characteristic of the Anglican Church has been from the first that of combining steadfast adherence to the structure and chief formulas of the Church Catholic with the 'return to Scripture' which was the central religious motive of the Reformation. This has resulted in a theology of the Incarnation from Hooker downwards, which has been catholic, scriptural, rich in expression and application, but reserved and unscholastic in character. On the subject of our Lord's human consciousness there has been a marked unwillingness to theorize or even to speak[1]. Perhaps among the classical Anglican divines HOOKER, as he is little occupied with Scripture in detail but more with the fathers, comes nearest to the later patristic and mediaeval view.

Thus[2], speaking of the *unction* of our Lord's manhood by His Godhead, he says:

'For as the parts, degrees, and offices of that mystical administration did require which He voluntarily undertook, the beams of Deity did in operation always accordingly either restrain or enlarge themselves. From hence we may somewhat conjecture how the powers of that soul are illuminated, which being so inward unto God

---

[1] Pearson, for example, says nothing (as far as I can discover) on the subject [2] *Eccl. Pol.* v 54 6, 7

cannot choose but be privy unto all things which God worketh, and must therefore of necessity be endued with knowledge so far forth universal, though not with infinite knowledge peculiar to Deity itself[1] The soul of Christ that saw in this life the face of God was here through so visible presence of Deity filled with all manner graces and virtues in that unmatchable degree of perfection, for which of Him we read it written that " God with the oil of gladness anointed Him above His fellows "'

Bp. ANDREWES expresses not much more than an unwillingness to speculate on the subject [2]

'For *derelinqui a Deo*—the body cannot feel it, or tell what it meaneth. It is the soul's complaint, and therefore without all doubt His soul within Him was pierced and suffered, though not that which—except charity be allowed to expound it—cannot be spoken without blasphemy. Not so much, God forbid! yet much, and very much, and much more than others seem to allow, or how much, it is dangerous to define.'

Again, after quoting and dwelling upon the words of St. Leo, *non solvit unionem sed subtraxit visionem,* he continues 'And though to draw it so far as some do is little better than blasphemy, yet on the other side to shrink it so short as other some do, cannot be but with derogation to His love'

JEREMY TAYLOR[3] puts aside the question whether Christ did in reality or only in appearance increase in knowledge as one of those disputes which belong to men who 'love to serve God in hard questions.'

---

[1] It is not plain whether these words are meant to apply to our Lord's human intellect only in its glorified state

[2] *Sermons (Library of Anglo-Cath Theol)* ii 124, 147

[3] *Life of Christ,* pt 1 § 7 5 (Heber and Eden's ed. 1850, ii. p 158).

But mostly Anglican divines have assumed as a matter indubitable that there was in our Lord's humanity a real growth and limitation of knowledge, according to the plain sense of Scripture. So

BULL, in his *Defence of the Nicene Creed* [1], when he is vindicating the language of Irenaeus to this effect, remarks that 'the reformed are strangely attacked by the Papists for this opinion'

BEVERIDGE [2]. 'Our Saviour having taken our nature into His person, with all its frailties and infirmities, as it is a created being, He did not in that nature presently know all things which were to be known. It is true as God He then knew all things, as well as He had from all eternity: but we are now speaking of Him as a man, like one of us in all things, except sin.' And 'The Son Himself as man knew not' the day and hour of the end.

WATERLAND against the Arians [3]. 'There was no equivocation in [Christ] saying what was literally true that the Son, as *Son of man*, did not know the *day and hour* of the last judgment. The context itself sufficiently limits His denial to His human nature'

But I do not think these divines give us any help in relating this ignorance of Christ in His humanity to Himself, the one divine person. *The person* in Holy Scripture is said to have grown in knowledge, and declared *Himself the Son* to be ignorant of the day and hour.

Of recent years in the English Church there have been

---

[1] (*Libr of Anglo-Cath. Theol*) 1 p 176.
[2] *Works* (Parker, Oxford, 1846) viii. p 423.
[3] *Works* (ed Van Mildert, Oxford Univ. Press, 1843) ii pp. 162 f, iii. 281 f.

The Consciousness of our Lord.

representatives of almost all schools of thought on this subject—of the scholastic theology, of the kenotic views, as well as of the more usual reserved Anglican line. But it is worth while calling special attention to the language of three men whose authority carries special weight—the late Dean Church, Dr. Westcott, and Dr. Bright.

The late Dean CHURCH writes in one sermon [1]:

'Think of Him drawing human breath, fed by human food, speaking human words like yourself, being Him who at the very same moment keeps all these worlds in being.'

In another sermon thus [2]: 'When we think of His humility, we think at once of His coming among us at all. He the everlasting God coming from heaven to narrow Himself to the conditions of a creature, to give up what He was with the Father, that He might live with men.'

This writer measured his words even, we may be sure, in 'village sermons.' These passages are not a mere contradiction. But they are the words of a man who was more careful to be true to all the facts than to present a perfectly harmonized theory.

'I shrink much,' he writes elsewhere [3], 'from speculating on the human knowledge of our blessed Lord, or the limitations—and they may have been great—which He was pleased to impose on Himself, when He "emptied Himself" and became as one of us. I have never been satisfied with the ordinary explanations of the text you quote, St. Matt xxiv. 36. They seem

---

[1] *Village Sermons* (Macmillan, 1892) p 20.   [2] p 79.
[3] *Life and Letters of Dean Church* (Macmillan, 1894) p 267, cf. p. 274 f

simply to explain it away as much as any Unitarian gloss on St John i 1. To me it means that He who was to judge the world, who knew what was in man, and more, who alone knew the Father, was at that time content to have that hour hidden from Him—did not choose to be above the angels in knowing it—as He was afterwards content to be forsaken of the Father. But the whole is perfectly inconceivable to my mind, and I could not base any general theory of His knowledge on it. I think it is very likely that we do not understand the meaning of much that is said in Scripture—its sense, and the end and purport for which *at the time* it was said. But it would perplex me much to think that He was imperfect or ignorant in what He *did* say, whether we understood Him or not.'

Dr. WESTCOTT is emphatic that 'this [creative and sustaining] work [of Christ] was in no way interrupted by the Incarnation[1]'; but in dealing with the Incarnation he affirms[2]:

'The mode of our Lord's existence on earth was truly human, and subject to all the conditions of human existence ... How this "becoming [flesh]" was accomplished we cannot clearly grasp St Paul describes it as an "emptying of Himself" by the Son of God (Phil. ii. 6 f.), a laying aside of the mode of divine existence (τὸ εἶναι ἴσα θεῷ); and this declaration carries us as far as we can go in defining the mystery.'

Dr. BRIGHT writes thus [3]

'In regard to the *kenosis*, if it is once granted that during Christ's ministry among men, even at the "lowest points of self-abasement, He was still, as God, upholding

---

[1] *Ep to the Hebrews*, p 426   [2] *Gospel of St John,* pp 10-11
[3] *Waymarks in Ch. Hist.* (Longmans, 1894) appendix G, pp 392-3

all things by the word of His power," this is enough to carry the principle of the interpretation of Phil ii 6, which confines the *kenosis* to the sphere of His humanity. For, outside those limits, if He acted as God at all, He must act so altogether. Within those limits, He dispensed with manifestations of His divine majesty, except on occasions and for special ends. As a rule, He held in reserve, by a continuous self-restraint, the exercise of divine powers, and accepted the conditions of human life with all its sinless infirmities. He willed to think and feel humanly through organs of thought and feeling which, being human, were limited, and on which He did not ordinarily shed the transfiguring power of what Cyril called His " proper " or original φύσις, although whenever he taught, He spoke as the absolute " Light of men " '

In this passage Dr. Bright seems to me to go beyond the language of mere juxtaposition of the human and divine consciousnesses. 'He was truly limited in knowledge *within the sphere of His humanity*' is, it seems to me, a more valuable and suggestive phrase, more true to the New Testament picture, than 'He was truly limited *in respect of His human nature*' and ' He knew as God, He did not know as man.'

Here then we conclude our review of theological opinions on the subject of our Lord's human consciousness.

III

THE CONCLUSION OF THIS INQUIRY: THE RELATION OF THIS CONCLUSION TO CHURCH AUTHORITY: ITS RATIONALITY.

§ 1.

Conclusion from our inquiry.

The conclusions arrived at as the result of our whole inquiry can consist in nothing else than a reaffirmation of the provisional conclusions to which we were led by our examination of the language of the New Testament[1]. The great bulk of the language of ecclesiastical writers is, it is true, against us. As a matter of authority this will come up for consideration in the next section. But as a matter of argument, the theologians who refuse to recognize the real human limitations in the consciousness of the incarnate Son, from Clement of Alexandria down to our own day, have said nothing which can alter our judgement. They have hardly attempted to examine continuously the intellectual phenomena of our Lord's human life during the period of His humiliation · they have at best but taken particular texts and explained them away in the light of an *a priori* assumption as to the effect of the Godhead on the manhood, and they have unwarrantably applied expressions written of our Lord in glory to our Lord in

---

[1] See above, pp 94 ff

His mortal state. In our own day it is still far too much the habit to treat the inquiry as a matter of one or two texts. It cannot be too much emphasized that it is very far from being this What is told us of our Lord's intellectual growth in childhood, of His relation to the Holy Spirit as man both in teaching and working miracles, of His progressive 'learning' from the Father, of His asking questions and expressing surprise, of His ignorance of the day and hour of the end, of His prayers, of His dismay and agony, of His feeling Himself 'forsaken' by the Father: all that St. Paul and St. John tell us, to account for these facts, about His having 'come down' from heaven and left 'the glory,' and after His resurrection returning whence He had come—of His 'emptying Himself,' 'beggaring Himself' to take the real characteristics of humanity, and of His being, in that humanity, subsequently exalted: all this (and there is nothing which disagrees with it) forces upon us, with a consistent pressure of evidence, the conclusion that a real self-emptying was involved in the Incarnation. Nor will it suffice to say that the Son was limited in knowledge, etc, *in respect of His manhood*, so long as we so juxta-posit the omniscient Godhead with the limited manhood as to destroy the impression that He, the Christ, the Son of God, was *personally* living, praying, thinking, speaking, and acting —even working miracles—under the limitations of manhood. It may well be that the absolute truth is incomprehensible by us and does not admit of being fully interpreted by human words: but the words in which we express the mystery—from speaking about which we cannot in any case refrain—must be words which are really faithful to the revealed facts and the language of the inspired interpreters of the facts · that is to say, they must be words which express a real abandonment, on the part of the eternal Son in becoming incarnate, of divine prerogatives inconsistent with a proper human experience they must be words which express the fact that, within the period and sphere of His incarnate and mortal life, He the eternal Son was, doubtless by His own act and will, submitting Himself to the limitations proper to manhood. The real Incarnation involves a real self-impoverishment, a real self-emptying, a real self-limitation on the part of the eternal Word of God

It is useless to put in the plea of reverence to bar inquiry or exact statement on this subject. The facts of the Gospel narrative and the apostolic interpretations bearing on this point are too many and have been too much neglected to enable one to shrink back from examining them. Nor is such candid examination of what is revealed at all incompatible with an adoring reverence towards the Divine Person who is revealing Himself, or towards that tremendous mystery which accompanies and half shrouds His redemptive action

The conclusion then originally stated I do emphatically reassert with the profoundest conviction that it is not indeed the whole truth—the whole truth about God or the acts of God we cannot know—but the truth as far as human mind can receive it and human words express it: and I venture to make a fourfold appeal to the opponents of this position ·

1 That they will seriously attempt to grapple with the positive evidence for it as a whole and in its continuity. This, as far as I can ascertain, they have hitherto left undone, and have contented themselves with dealing with this or that disconnected 'text,' or with abstract argument and appeals to consequences.

2. That they will (so far as they are Anglicans) bear in mind that the whole historical position and justification of that specific form of Christianity called Anglicanism is bound up with its strenuous appeal to Scripture In that appeal we must be sincere and thorough.

3. That they will not forget that, so far as scientific theology has in and for this age a special intellectual responsibility, it is to be true to facts. Theology—Christian theology—may be said to be as really inductive as physical science that is to say it draws conclusions from facts of revelation. These facts are utterances of prophets and inspired men, but most of all the deeds and words of the incarnate Son. As truly as the facts of physical nature both justify and limit the conclusions of physical science, do these facts of revelation justify and limit the conclusions of theology; and where the facts cease to support theory, theory is, in theology as elsewhere, groundless and misleading

4. The real recognition of the suggestions of Scripture about our Lord's human state will give to the Church's teaching a great enrichment. There is no doubt, I think, that the general teaching of the Catholic Church for many centuries about our Lord has removed Him very far from human sympathies, very much

further than the Christ of the New Testament The minimizing of the meaning of His manhood is (among other things) largely accountable for the development of an exaggerated devotion to His Mother and the Saints. In proportion as the real human experiences, sufferings, and limitations of Christ during the period of His humiliation are forgotten and ignored, in that proportion men will go to seek human sympathy from on high in some other quasi-deified being. We must recover the strength which the Christian creed is meant to derive from a Christ made in all points like unto His brethren, apart from sin.

The reality of the Incarnation and of its accompanying self-limitation must be put in the forefront of Catholic theology, popular and scientific. It means—so far as human thought can grasp or words express it—a real abandonment of divine prerogative and attributes by the eternal Son within a certain sphere.

But are we to posit this abandonment as absolute? Did the Son actually cease to mediate the procession of the Holy Ghost in the divine being and to uphold the worlds in being? Such a position, I repeat, could not be maintained unless the divine revelation positively and expressly forced it upon us. But it does not; on the contrary there is reason to believe that the apostolic writers contemplated the continuance of the divine and cosmic functions through the Incarnation. We must not then disturb or destroy the picture of the incarnate state which they give us in Gospels and Epistles by bringing the absolute divine state of the Son side by side with the picture of His humiliation:

for this is exactly what the apostolic writers do not do. We must hold to the reality of the humiliation, and, if we can see no further, we must be content to hold that, even in a way we cannot conceive, this state of limitation within the sphere of the humanity must have been compatible with the exercise in another sphere, by the same divine person, of the fulness of divine power. But the rationality of such a combination is a question which must be reserved till we have dealt with the standing in regard to ecclesiastical authority of our present conclusion.

§ 2.

The relation of our conclusion to ecclesiastical authority.

We need have no hesitation in claiming that the theological conclusion we have arrived at is wholly consistent with the actual dogmatic decisions of ecumenical councils, which are the only ecclesiastical decisions bearing on the present subject, the acceptance of which can fairly be said to be required for the ministry in the Anglican Church.

That Christ is God, consubstantial with the Father in His divine nature: that He is completely man, in mind and spirit as well as body, in His human nature: that He is one only person, and that person divine, who for us men and for our salvation assumed our manhood: that the manhood as assumed remains proper manhood and retains its proper energy and attributes unabsorbed into the Godhead—these[1] are the central Church dogmas in regard to the person of Christ, and it will not take long to show that nothing said above is in any conflict with any of them. In fact it could not be suggested that any heretical tendency has been exhibited except in regard to the first and last of the above-mentioned decisions.

The first—the decree of Nicaea—asserts the Son consubstantial and coequal with the Father: it goes on by way of appendix to deny Him to be changeable or alterable[2]. Can it be said that this decree condemns any view which speaks of the Son as becoming subject to limitation, or that postulates in the Incarnation any change in the mode of being of the eternal Son?

To this question we answer, first, that the fathers of the Council had only *moral* alterability in view in their ecclesiastical decision. as it was only moral alterability which the Arians asserted of Christ[3], and any idea of moral alterability has in this discussion been expressly repudiated[4]. But further, even in regard to metaphysical alteration, it must be remembered that in the view here presented the limitation of which the incarnate Son is the subject is regarded (1) as not affecting His

---

[1] See further, for an explanation of them, *B L.* lect iv.
[2] See Heurtley s *de Fide et Symbolo*, p 6 τοὺς δὲ λέγοντας . ἢ τρεπτὸν ἢ ἀλλοιωτὸν τὸν υἱὸν τοῦ θεοῦ τούτους ἀναθεματίζει ἡ καθολικὴ καὶ ἀποστολικὴ ἐκκλησία.
[3] See Gwatkin, *Studies of Arianism* (Cambridge, 1882) p 25 'He [the Son according to the Arians] must have free will like us and a nature capable like ours of moral change, whether for evil or for good ' Cf. Bright, *Waymarks*, p 387.
[4] See above, p 96

essential being or operation in the universe, (2) as not imposed from without but an act of His own power—that divine power which declares itself 'most chiefly' in such self-renouncing 'pity' and love[1] All that is asked then is that the Son should be regarded as exhibiting a divine capacity for self-accommodation within a certain sphere in carrying out His unchanging redemptive purpose. With such a view the fathers of Nicaea were not in any way concerned. Such self-accommodation is not 'mutability,' but the self-adaptiveness, the movement, of real spiritual life As far as any charge of attributing 'mutability' to the Son in this metaphysical sense was made in the Arian controversy it was made mostly on the Arian side against the orthodox 'All generation,' the Arians said, 'is a sort of change; but God is immutable therefore God cannot be either generating or generated.' To which there is no better expressed reply than that of Victorinus Afer[2], where he refuses to identify the movement of divine life with change. Eternal life in God means eternal movement. It is only such eternal movement of life as makes intelligible such subsequent temporal 'changes' as are involved in the divine acts of creation or redemption

Nor should it be left out of sight that, so far as the self-limitation of the Son even within a certain sphere of operation may be supposed to affect His essential

---

[1] See above, pp 142, 148, for phrases quoted from Gregory of Nyssa and Hilary

[2] The argument here is quoted from Candidus the Arian to whom Victorinus Afer replied. But the argument was a commonplace of discussion see Gwatkin, *l c* p 24³; and on Candidus and Victorinus see s v VICTORINUS in *Dict. of Chr Biog.* iv. pp 1130 ff. with reff

consubstantiality with the Father, it is relative to that no less mysterious but also no less real act of self-denial on the part of the Father which the New Testament describes as His 'giving up' or 'giving' the Son. There is reciprocal self-sacrifice postulated alike in the Father and the Son [1].

As regards the last of the decisions summarized above, which is contained in the decrees of the fourth and sixth Councils, it may be said that as they assert the completeness in our Lord of both the divine and human natures and activities—the fulness of both natures being inseparably but unconfusedly united in the one person—so any position which involves incompleteness of *divine* activity or knowledge in the Incarnation is as much opposed to these decisions as one which involves a similar human incompleteness.

To this I should reply, primarily and to secure my ground, that the view expressed above involves no limitation of the divine activity of the Word absolutely in Himself or in the world, but only within a certain area. I can, therefore, affirm without any hesitation with the fourth Council that the 'one and the same Son, our Lord Jesus Christ, is both perfect in Godhead and perfect in manhood, truly God and truly man,... consubstantial with the Father according to His Godhead, and with us according to His manhood "in all points like us, apart from sin," begotten of the Father before all ages, according to His Godhead, and in these last days, the same person, for us and for our salvation, born of Mary the Virgin, the Theotokos, according to His manhood, one

---

[1] St John iii 16; 1 St John iv. 9, Rom. viii 32.

and the same person made known as Christ, Son, Lord, Only-Begotten, in two natures, unconfusedly, unchangeably, indissolubly, inseparably; the distinction of the natures being in no wise destroyed on account of the union, but each nature rather preserving its own special characteristic, and combining to form one person[1].' Or with the sixth Council, that 'We glorify in our Lord Jesus Christ, our true God, two natural energies indissolubly, unalterably, indivisibly, unconfusedly, that is the divine energy and the human energy; as Leo the theologian most clearly says, " Either form energizes in fellowship with the other as is proper to itself, the Word working what belongs to the Word, and the body accomplishing what belongs to the body [2]."'

Such decisions are in no way dissonant with a view which, maintaining the integrity and distinctness of the Godhead and of the manhood in the one person of the Son of God, maintains also, as the language of the New Testament demands, that the activity (and consciousness) of the Godhead was, by His own will, restrained and limited *within the sphere of the Incarnation*, to allow the real action of the manhood and its own proper 'energy'; and it needs to be pointed out that the special view here maintained was not at all before the mind of these councils—which were intent upon a quite different task, with which the present writer cannot be accused of lack of sympathy, that of securing against monophysite tendencies the permanence and real action of the manhood and of its faculties in our Lord's person.

---

[1] The Definition of Chalcedon (*de Fide et Symb* p 27)
[2] The decision of Constantinople III (Gieseler, *Eccl Hist.* ii. p. 176).

Indeed, it seems to me that a candid review of the theological tendencies of the fourth and fifth centuries leads a student even to an increased respect for the ecumenical councils, and an increased belief in the divine providence which superintended their decisions. For, while the theological tendencies of the time were seriously one-sided and set to emphasize the divine at the expense of the human, the conciliar decisions are deliberately and perfectly balanced. They can only become a source of peril if their true nature, as primarily negative and wholly relative to Scripture, is forgotten—if they are used, in place of the historical figure of Christ, as positive data or materials from which to obtain by abstract deduction a conception of what the Christ ought to have been. The churchman who makes a right use of the Church's decisions—who, that is, accepting the Church's creed in Christ as Son of God made man, perfect God and perfect man, goes back to the reverent but also candid study of the figure in the Gospels, will not be in any peril of finding this his central faith contradicted in the New Testament; he will but find it enriched and deepened. If he pursues his theological studies he will, I believe, find that a great deal of the 'theological comment' upon the creed, a great deal of the theology of approved Catholic writers, needs revising or moderating. But as far as the tradition expressed in the creeds is concerned—that he will find to need no revision, that, with the sacramental system and the structure of the visible Church, he will with continually increasing clearness perceive to belong to that essential permanent Christianity which is truly catholic, apostolic and scriptural.

With such a result the present writer has already elsewhere expressed himself more than satisfied[1]: and he must claim that he has with him in this satisfaction the tradition of Anglicanism. It is a note of Anglicanism to be satisfied with a very moderate amount of dogmatic requirement. A thoroughly faithful Anglican may believe that, as in civil government a certain amount of legislation is essential, but over-legislation, the over-regulation of life, is practically an evil, so in ecclesiastical government a certain amount of doctrinal requirement is necessary to protect the essence of the Church as a society based on a revelation, but that dogmatic requirement may easily outrun what the New Testament justifies and what is healthy for ecclesiastical development. The Church in each age should be free to return upon its central creed, structure, and worship, and without loss of continuity re-express its theological mind, as it has so often already done, in view of the fresh developments of the intellectual, moral, and social life of man.

The defectiveness of the theology of fathers and schoolmen on the subject which we have had under review was due to causes which belonged to their periods

1. Accurate interpretation of the text, whether of New Testament authors or of others, is in the main a growth of modern times. The fathers and schoolmen were often in advance of us in theological branches of speculation, but generally behind us in 'exegesis.'

2. Again, their philosophical categories as applied to God were abstract and *a priori*. They did not recognize

[1] See *B. L* pp 108-9.

as much as we have been taught to do that if the action of reason is implied in the very beginnings of observation and is thus logically 'prior' to experience, yet human reason has no actual contents, it contains no 'synthetic propositions,' except such as are gained through experience. that is to say as the reason is gradually awakened by experience to the perception of what is implied in the world and in itself. An *a priori* philosophy of nature or of history is sure to be at fault, and still more surely an *a priori* philosophy of God. Most certainly our human knowledge of what God is, what His omnipotence, immutability, omniscience mean, is limited strictly by what God is found to have disclosed of Himself in nature and humanity, by experience, through inspired prophets and Jesus Christ His Son.

3 No heresies excited so much antagonism as those which impugned our Lord's Godhead. By none, then, did the Church run so much risk of being driven into opposite extremes. Into such extremes she was not driven so far as her dogmatic decisions were concerned, but the effect of undue reaction is traceable in many even of her greatest schools of theology.

I should be utterly misrepresenting my own feeling if I allowed myself to be understood as disparaging in any way the fathers as theologians. In the special subject of this inquiry we do not, for the reasons just explained, see them at their best. But I do not believe that, taken on the whole, so much whether of theological or moral illumination is to be gained from any study, outside Holy Scripture, as is to be gained from the great theologians who are called, and legitimately called, 'the fathers.'

§ 3.

The rationality of our conclusion.

The conception at which we have arrived from the examination of the New Testament, and which we have found to be at least in no opposition to the authoritative dogmas of the Church Catholic, seems to involve us in thinking of the Incarnation somewhat after the manner of Bishop Martensen[1]. An old writer said of our Lord that within His humanity He 'withdrew from operation both His power and His majesty[2].' To this, as we have seen, we must add—His omniscience. But withdrawing these from operation within the sphere of the humanity He yet *Himself lived under human conditions*. And this seems to postulate that the personal life of the Word should have been lived as it were from more than one centre—that He who knows and does all things in the Father and in the universe should (reverently be it said) have begun to live from a new centre when He assumed manhood, and under new and restricted conditions of power and knowledge. Is this conceivable, or is there even any line of thought which tends in the direction of making it conceivable? Especially in regard to knowledge, does it mean anything to suggest that

---

[1] See above, pp 192-3
[2] *Potentiam suam et maiestatem ab opere retraxit*. the words are ascribed to Ambrose, but I cannot find them in his works.

He, the same eternal Son, should in one sphere not know what in another, and that His own proper sphere, He essentially knows?

There are some considerations which may assist us in this difficulty.

1. First, let us remember that supposing we can get no help towards the conceiving (or imagining) of this situation, the case is not by any means either desperate or unique. Nothing that is a fact can be irrational, but many things that are facts are beyond the power of *human* conception Certainly in the region of science what is strictly inconceivable by human reason is taken for fact. Nothing, to take a now familiar example, can be more inconceivable than the properties of the ether which physicists find themselves obliged to postulate to explain the phenomena of light. On this subject, however, let me quote the words of an acknowledged authority.

'The assumption,' says Prof. Sir George Stokes[1], 'that all space, or all at least of which we have any cognizance, must be imagined to be completely filled with a supposed medium of which our senses give us no information, already makes, we might reasonably say, a severe demand upon our credulity; and indeed there are, or at least have been, minds to which the demand appeared to be so great as to cause the rejection of that theory of light. And when we provisionally assume the existence of an ether, and use it as a working hypothesis in our further investigations, we find ourselves obliged to admit properties of this supposed ether so utterly different from

---

[1] *Natural Theology* (Gifford Lectures, 1893) pp 21 and 19. Cf. Wright's *Light* (Macmillan, 1892) pp. 380-1, and *Encycl Britann*. art ETHER.

what we should have imagined beforehand, through our previous experience, that we are half staggered.' ' How the ether can at the same time behave like an elastic solid in resisting the gliding of one portion over another, and yet like a fluid in letting bodies freely pass through it, is a mystery which we do not understand. Nevertheless, we are obliged to suppose that so it is.' The Professor goes on to point out that the properties of the supposed ether appeared both so inconceivable and so incompatible with British common sense that our countrymen were deterred from pursuing their investigations into what is now acknowledged to be one of the most important factors of the universe: ' A slashing article in an old number of the *Edinburgh Review*, ridiculing the supposed vagaries of an undulationist, had probably the effect of diminishing the share which our own country took in the great revival of physical optics in the present century.'

No wonder Professor Huxley can allow himself an inexact expression and say that 'the mysteries of the Church are child's play compared with the mysteries of nature[1].' It is an inexact expression, because in fact the life that is above us is, as we should anticipate, more mysterious than the life that is below us. Even less in what is above than in what is below us can we identify the rational with what we can imagine. And thus, in fact, the last thing which we could hope to imagine or, in this sense, to conceive would be the absolute and eternal consciousness of God, either in itself or in relation to the succession of moments in time or in relation to the lower

[1] Quoted by permission from a private letter in *B. L* p. 247

human consciousness which He vouchsafed to assume. We shall then be in no irrational position if we are obliged to confess that our imagination is absolutely baffled by the condition of things which the facts of the Incarnation seem to postulate At least we shall not, in the interest of an easier conception, abandon the facts. The facts as we can no longer doubt—the same facts which force upon us the conclusion that our Lord was the incarnate Son of God—force us to conclude that the incarnate Son was leading for the sake of real sympathy with men a life of limitation in knowledge as well as power. But here perhaps we have mentioned a word which offers us at least some *help towards* a rational conception of this mystery.

2. Sympathy, love — this is the keynote of the Incarnation. It is along this line that we can best hope to understand it And surely here—in the region of love and sympathy—we have something analogous to a double life, and a double life which affects the intellect as much as any of our powers To sympathize is to put oneself in another's place. Redemptive sympathy is the act of the greater and better putting himself at the point of view of the lower and the worse He must not abandon his own higher standing-ground if he is to benefit the object of his compassion; but remaining essentially what he was he must also find himself in the place of the lower; he must come to look at things as he looks at them; he must learn things over again from his point of view. This is, as we saw before, how Origen would have us understand the mystery of the divine condescension. It is the grown one learning to speak as

The Consciousness of our Lord.

a child : it is the Divine putting Himself at the point of view of the human.

Now no one who has had the privileges of education can attempt to be sympathetic (in a sense worthy of the name) with those who have not without finding that his superior culture is, if in one way an advantage, in another way a marked hindrance. He would give anything to be able for the time to forget · to retain indeed his ideal of knowing, but to get outside all that he actually knows; to leave it behind in order that he may really and not in mere effort of imagination look at things from the uninstructed point of view. The natures most gifted with sympathy seem actually for the moment to accomplish this. They do seem to abandon their own normal platform of knowledge and to translate themselves into alien conditions. Now we have no better guide to the methods of God than the best human sympathy and love. Only the acts of God are infinitely more perfect than our best acts, more continuous and more thorough. May not then the sympathetic entrance of God into human life have carried with it— not because it was weak but because it was powerful— something which can only be imagined or expressed by us as a real 'forgetting' or abandoning within the human sphere of His own divine point of view and mode of consciousness? And are we not helped towards some such supposition by reflecting that the attributes of God, on account of the perfection of His personal unity, are not (so to speak) separable from one another or from His personality but are identically one? May it not be that our knowledge can be at times a hindrance to us, a hindrance that we would gladly *for the time* fling away and be by far more powerful for having lost, because it is imperfectly assimilated into our personality —because it is an attribute which has not wholly become our self? May it not be that because God is perfect and His attributes inseparable from His person, therefore His knowledge is, far more than can be the case with us, under the control of His personal, essential will of love? And is not this a line of thought along which we gain real help in conceiving how the Son of God can have so loved mankind as by an act of power to enter into humanity and, remaining Himself, to live a human life from a human point of view, unembarrassed in His act of love by any impotence to control His own knowledge?

Nor, when we are discussing the conceivableness of such an act of divine sympathy, can we omit to notice that (apart from recognition of the Incarnation) it is very difficult to us to give reality to all that body of scriptural language which attributes to the absolute, omniscient God sympathy with men, sympathy of an anthropomorphic kind. It is fair to say that, if the self-limitation of the Incarnation is in itself difficult to conceive, on the other hand it reflects light upon the whole body of language which inspired men, *almost in proportion to their inspiration*, have found it necessary to use about God All real sympathy of the unconditioned for the conditioned demands, as far as we can see, real self-limitation.

3. Again, may we not advance one step more in the direction of conceiving the mystery when we set

The Consciousness of our Lord.

ourselves to think how utterly different from the divine consciousness must be the human. A thoughtful writer has recently bidden us reflect how all human knowledge (1) is at least conditioned by the senses through which alone the suggestions are presented which make thought possible, (2) is discursive, gathered laboriously piece by piece and with difficulty attaining to any comprehensive grasp which is at the same time accurate and real, (3) can never really arrive at apprehending the innermost essence of things. But the knowledge of God, though it is the ground and source of human knowledge, is as distinct in kind from it as is the divine personality distinct from the human which yet is based upon it So far as we can conceive, the divine knowledge must be (1) an absolute intuition, and therefore (2) infinitely comprehensive, and (3) infallibly penetrative of the innermost essence of things Let us but ponder for a little while on the infinite gulf which lies, in these ways, between the knowledge of God and that of man, and we shall feel how almost mutually exclusive the divine and human modes of knowing must be. We shall understand why St Paul represents to us that there is a break between the 'knowledge' we now have and the diviner knowledge we shall have beyond the veil—a break which there is not between the love, or even the faith and hope, of now and hereafter[1]. The more we ponder on this the more it seems to me we can realize how that 'birth' by which God became man, to enter into man's experience, for the sake of man's redemption, must have involved within the sphere of the humanity something which in

[1] 1 Cor xiii 8-13

human language can only be expressed as 'a sleep and a forgetting,' so strangely exclusive (as it would seem) is the human mode of consciousness of the divine [1].

4. Lastly, we are beyond question helped in the consideration of this mystery by the tendency of the deepest modern thought in regard to God's relation to nature and man as a whole. The older and more pantheistic way of regarding the immanence of God in nature ran the risk of losing the distinctive being of the creatures in the abyss of the being of God. But more exact knowledge forces us to realize more thoroughly the distinctive existence and quality of natural objects. Nature is for us infinitely more complex, more full, more real than for the ancients: so that in our age it has been easy for some even to forget God in nature. It is right neither to forget nature in God nor God in nature, but to learn from nature right notions about the method of God. God realizes His will in nature by an infinite variety of distinctive forms of life. And He loves to see each form of life realize itself in its own way. He respects the nature of each thing. 'He tastes an infinite joy in infinite ways,' by, as it were, living not only in Himself but in the separate life of each of the creatures. Nor do we realize this less if we look away from nature as it is at any moment in its infinite complexity of

[1] The thoughtful writer to whom I allude is the author of an article in the *Church Quarterly* (Oct. 1891), on 'Our Lord's knowledge as man.' I cannot however exactly accept his conclusions. He seems to me to fall back too much upon considerations of logic as opposed to considerations of sympathy. Thus he acquiesces in the mere juxtaposition of the two consciousnesses in our Lord; supposing e g that when He said He did not know, what is meant is only that the knowledge which He had as God, He had not 'translated' into the human mode.

manifold forms of life and begin to contemplate the history of its development. Still we are struck by the extent to which (to express the facts roughly) God leaves things to work out their own perfection by the slow, as it were tentative, method of 'natural selection,' through which advance has in fact been made.

And this respect of God for His creatures is seen most of all in His relation to man. He never indeed allows human freedom to disturb the main course of the world's development; to tolerate that would be to abandon the providential government of the world [1]. But within such an area as allows man to exercise a real, though limited, freedom—to such a degree as at least may involve considerable disturbance in the divine order for the sake of the value of free, as distinct from mechanical, service—God stands aloof and respects that free nature which He has created, that image of His own freedom which He has, as it were, planted out in the heart of the physical creation. God respects His creature man His power refrains itself But is there, in order to leave room for man's freedom of choice, a limitation, not only of God's power, but of His foreknowledge? Is the old controversy as regards human freedom and divine foreknowledge to be solved in part by the suggestion that a limitation of divine foreknowing accompanies the very act of creating free agents? The idea has commended itself to some very thoughtful minds.

[1] Lotze, *Microcosmus* (Eng trans Clark, 1887) 1 pp 258 f 'Do we not as we actually are, free or not, as a matter of fact interfere—to disturb or destroy—with the nature around us, leaving behind many distinct traces of our wayward energy, while yet we cannot on a large scale shake the order of things?'

to Origen, as has already incidentally appeared in this discussion, and to Dr Martineau in modern times [1]. The accurate examination of the meaning assigned to divine 'foreknowledge' in the Bible tends to shake the traditional belief that God is there revealed as knowing absolutely beforehand how each individual will act Nevertheless, it is at least as difficult to reject this belief as to admit it. But, whatever be our relation to it, at least we must admit that the method of God in history, like the method of God in nature, is to an astonishing degree self-restraining, gradual, we are almost driven to say, tentative And all this line of thought—all this way of conceiving of God's self-restraining power and wisdom—at least prepares our mind for that supreme act of respect and love for His creatures by which the Son of God took into Himself human nature to redeem it, and in taking it limited both His power and His knowledge so that He could verily live through all the stages of a perfectly human experience and restore our nature from within by a contact so gentle that it gave life to every faculty without paralyzing or destroying any

Such considerations as these prevent our reason, or even—what is so different—our imagination, from falling back simply baffled before the facts, in the way of limitation of divine knowledge, presented by the Incarnation of the Son of God. But the main purpose of this dissertation has been simply to establish the facts and

---

[1] For Origen see above, p 116 For Dr Martineau see *A Study of Religion*, bk III ch II § 4 (Oxford, 1888, II. pp. 278 f) The Rev T B Strong (*Manual of Theology*, Black, 1892, pp 235-6) contemplates the idea as just possible

to show cause for believing that, in spite of the somewhat scanty recognition which they have hitherto obtained from orthodox theologians, we have to-day both liberty as Catholics, and positive obligation as interpreters of Scripture, to give them a franker and more full-faced acknowledgement.

DISSERTATION III

TRANSUBSTANTIATION AND NIHILIANISM.

THE object of this paper is—

I. To describe the theological process by which Transubstantiation became a dogma of the Roman Church.

II. To indicate the metaphysical difficulties in which the dogma is involved; and to show how it violates the accepted analogy of the Incarnation, and the philosophical principle which is involved in the Incarnation, viz. that the supernatural and divine does not annihilate the natural and material substance in which it manifests and communicates itself.

III. To answer the question—Why then did not the analogy of the Incarnation doctrine, dogmatically expressed as it was in the decrees which emphasized the permanent reality of our Lord's manhood, bar the way to the dogma of transubstantiation?

I

The growth of the doctrine of transubstantiation.

In the theological period, which is measured by the Council of Chalcedon on one side and on the other by the second Council of Nicaea in the east and the age of Charles the Great in the west — roughly A D 450–800, we find two tendencies in eucharistic doctrine.

There is the tendency from the doctrine of a real presence of the flesh and blood of Christ in and with the elements of bread and wine towards a doctrine of transubstantiation, i. e. a doctrine which regards the supernatural presence as annihilating its natural vehicle except in mere appearance. This tendency is more apparent during this period in the east than in the west, and it reaches distinct expression (c. A D. 750) in John of Damascus' systematized treatise *de Fide Orthodoxa* (IV. 13). John's theory may fairly be called a theory of transubstantiation, not because he uses the word 'transform' of the action of the Holy Spirit upon the elements, for that expression is used by writers who certainly do not hold any doctrine of transubstantiation [1],

---

[1] e g by the author of the *de Sacramentis*, ascribed to St Ambrose, who freely uses the phrases *convertere, mutare*, and asserts, as strongly as possible, the real presence of the flesh and blood of Christ in the eucharistic elements in virtue of consecration, but still writes (IV. 4) 'Si ergo tanta vis est in sermone domini Iesu ut inciperent esse quae non erant [i e in the original creation of the world], quanto magis operatorius est [i e in the eucharistic elements] ut sint quae erant et in aliud commutentur.' In some of the copies of this work in Lanfranc's time this reading had been altered

but because (1) adopting a suggestion of Gregory of Nyssa, he expressly speaks of the consecrated bread as by the supernatural and incomprehensible power of the Spirit transformed into the holy body, just as by the natural process of digestion bread is transformed, losing of course its own nature, into the substance of our bodies. and because (2) he accordingly repudiates the phrase 'symbols' (ἀντίτυπα) as applied to the elements of bread and wine *after* consecration—a phrase which his predecessors, believing that these elements remained in existence after consecration and retained with their nature their natural symbolism, had not shrunk from using[1].

(see his *de Corp et Sang Dom* 9), but it is undoubtedly original The author goes on to compare the change in the elements to that in the regenerate person.

Gregory of Nyssa in the same way describes the man who is ordained priest as μεταμορφωθεὶς πρὸς τὸ βέλτιον (*in Bapt Christi*, *P G* xlvi p 584 a), cf also his language about the 'transmutation' in the regenerate (*Orat Cat* c 40, *P G* xlv p 101 b, c), where it is carefully explained that the essence of manhood is unchanged by the transforming gift, and only its bad qualities obliterated The argument from Gregory's laxer use of these expressions, μετάστασις, μεταβολή, μεταστοιχείωσις, ἀναστοιχείωσις, μεταποίησις, μεταμόρφωσις, is unaffected by the fact that Gregory appears to suggest a doctrine of real transubstantiation in regard to the eucharist

St Cyril of Alexandria (*in Ioann* 11. 1, *P G* lxxiii p 245, quoted by Mason, *Relation of Confirmation to Baptism*, p 299) applies the term 'transelementation' (ἀναστοιχειοῦται) with apparent exactness to the water of baptism under the influence of consecration by the Spirit Cf also Cyril of Jerusalem's language (*Cat Myst* iii 3) about the chrism Yet these elements were not believed by these writers to cease to exist

[1] Thus the phrase is used as late as after the middle of the sixth century by Eutychius of Constantinople (*Sermo de Paschate et S Euch P. G* lxxxvi p 2391) ἐμμίξας ἑαυτὸν τῷ ἀντιτύπῳ τὸ σῶμα καὶ αἷμα τοῦ κυρίου τοῖς ἀντιτύποις ἐντιθέμενον διὰ τῶν ἱερουργιῶν. Epiphanius the deacon repeats John's repudiation of the phrase at the second council of Nicaea (act. 6, tom 3 ad fin) and, like John, denies that apostles or fathers ever used it of the elements after consecration—πρὸ τοῦ ἁγιασθῆναι ἐκλήθη ἀντίτυπα,

There are not wanting traces of a similar mode of explaining the real presence of Christ in the holy sacrament also in the west; but there the influence of Augustine was dominant, and, somewhat obscure as his view of the eucharist undoubtedly is, it is at any rate certain that he did not believe in transubstantiation. This is certain for two reasons (1) He speaks of the consecrated elements in the eucharist as in themselves only 'signs' of the body and blood of Christ: signs which, if they are themselves called the body and blood of Christ, are so called only on the principle that signs are called by the name of the things they signify. (2) He draws a marked distinction between the physical manducation of the sacrament which is possible to all and the manducation of the flesh and blood of Christ which he sometimes plainly declares to be possible only to the believing and spiritually minded, or to those who hold the unity of the Church, 'the body of Christ,' in love. Augustine's language is certainly as a whole susceptible of being interpreted in the sense of an 'objective' spiritual presence in the elements, after such a manner as does not interfere with the permanence of the bread and wine, such a presence as faith only can either recognize or appropriate; or it may fairly be interpreted on a receptionist theory like Hooker's—it is in fact probably somewhat inconsistent — but it is not susceptible of an interpretation in accordance with the doctrine of transubstantiation. And so long as Augustine's influence was dominant in eucharistic doctrine,

μετὰ δὲ τὸν ἁγιασμὸν σῶμα κυρίως καὶ αἷμα Χριστοῦ λέγονται καί εἰσιν καὶ πιστεύονται This, however, does not truly represent the facts

the language of western writers is mostly anti-transubstantiationist[1].

[1] Augustine's doctrine of the eucharist may be summarized under three heads (1) *The consecrated elements are signs of the body and blood, and not in themselves the things they signify* See *Ep* 98 9 *ad Bonifacium* 'Si autem sacramenta quandam similitudinem earum rerum quarum sacramenta sunt non haberent, omnino sacramenta non essent Ex hac autem similitudine plerumque etiam ipsarum rerum nomina accipiunt. Sicut ergo secundum quendam modum sacramentum corporis Christi corpus Christi est, sacramentum sanguinis Christi sanguis Christi est, ita sacramentum fidei fides est' (1 e baptism which represents the faith of the infant who is baptized is that faith), cf 'non enim Dominus dubitavit dicere *hoc est corpus meum* cum signum daret corporis sui' (*con Adim Manich.* 12). This passage, with others, must interpret his words when he comments thus *in Psalm* xxxiii (title) *Enarr.* 1. 10. '*Ferebatur* enim Christus *in manibus suis* quando commendans ipsum corpus suum ait *hoc est corpus meum*. Ferebat enim illud corpus in manibus suis.' . . 'accepit in manus suas quod norunt fideles et ipse se portabat quodam modo cum diceret *hoc est corpus meum* (11 2)' Roman Catholic controversialists generally omit to notice the *quodam modo* which corresponds to the *secundum quendam modum* above. The bread and wine then considered in themselves represent, and are not, the body and blood of Christ. In the same way the bread, because composed of many grains, represents the 'mystical body' of Christ, the Church, and this mystical body is sometimes spoken of as the *res sacramenti*, e.g. *Ep* 185 50 *ad Bonifacium* 'rem ipsam non tenent intus [Donatistae] cuius est illud sacramentum' (1. e. ecclesiam); cf *in Ioan. Tract.* xxvi. 17

(2) *But the spiritual gift of the eucharist is really the flesh and blood of Christ, the same flesh and blood in which He lived on earth, but raised to a new spiritual power, become 'spirit and life'* See *in Ps* xcviii. 9 'In ipsa carne hic ambulavit et ipsam carnem nobis manducandam ad salutem dedit, nemo autem illam carnem manducat nisi prius adoraverit' This 'flesh' in its glorified condition has become 'spirit' and 'life', so Augustine interprets St. John vi 63, see *Tract* xxvii 5 and app note C. He appears sometimes to distinguish the 'flesh' and the 'body,' e g *in Ps* xcviii after saying that the flesh of the eucharist is the same as the flesh of our Lord's mortal life, he goes on to say the body is not the same. 'Non hoc corpus quod videtis manducaturi estis et bibituri illum sanguinem quem fusuri sunt qui me crucifigent. Sacramentum aliquod vobis commendavi, spiritualiter intellectum vivificabit vos. Etsi necesse est visibiliter celebrari, oportet tamen invisibiliter intelligi.' Perhaps at times he thought of the spiritual essence of Christ's humanity, the 'flesh,' as receiving a new symbolical 'body' in the bread and wine, this spiritual essence of Christ's humanity

Dissertations.

In the great theological revival which marked the empire of Charles the Great and his first successors the doctrine of the holy eucharist became for the first time an explicit subject of controversy. The theologians of the beginning of this period mostly follow Augustine on the subject Thus Alcuin (Albinus Flaccus) repeats in his commentary on St John, the 'receptionist' language of Augustine [1]. So Amalarius of Metz (c. A D. 820), while

becoming also the spiritual essence of the Church , so that the sacramental 'body' represents equally Christ and the Church

(3) *This gift of the flesh and blood of Christ Augustine sometimes speaks of as given to all, good and bad, alike* See *de Bapt con Donat* v 9 'Sicut enim Iudas cui buccellam [i e the 'sop'] tradidit Dominus non malum accipiendo sed male accipiendo locum in se diabolo praebuit, sic indigne quisque sumens dominicum sacramentum non efficit ut quia ipse malus est malum sit, aut quia non ad salutem accipit nihil acceperit Corpus enim Domini et sanguis nihilominus erat etiam illis quibus dicebat apostolus, *qui manducat indigne iudicium sibi manducat et bibit* ' Cf *Serm* 71 17 *(de verbis Matt* xii 32) where he distinguishes the different modes in which the good and bad eat the flesh of Christ and drink His blood But at other times he identifies ' eating the flesh of Christ' quite explicitly with 'abiding in Christ' and with a living faith See esp *in Ioan Tract* xxvi and xxvii, e g xxvii 18 'Per hoc qui non manet in Christo et in quo non manet Christus procul dubio nec manducat [spiritualiter] carnem eius nec bibit eius sanguinem [licet carnaliter et visibiliter premat dentibus sacramentum corporis et sanguinis Christi], sed magis tantae rei sacramentum ad iudicium sibi manducat et bibit [quia immundus praesumpsit ad Christi accedere sacramenta]' (The words in brackets are an interpolation) Cf *de Civit* xxi 25 There is a great deal of this sort of language which makes it impossible to deny a strongly 'receptiorist' view in Augustine He does not seem to distinguish the *res* from the *virtus* in the eucharist

The above of course does not profess to be a complete treatment of St Augustine's eucharistic doctrine in any respect, nor even to touch upon his views of the sacrifice

[1] lib iii 15, 16 (*P L* c p 832) The *de Divinis Officiis* is acknowledged to be not by Alcuin It is, I think, not less plain that the *Confessio Fidei P L* ci pp 1027 ff) is not his But even here occurs the sentence 'tanta est virtus huius sacrificii ut solis iustis [non] peccatoribus corpus sit et sanguis Christi '

I say that the *Confessio Fidei* is, in spite of Mabillon's argument, plainly

Transubstantiation and Nihilianism. 235

he asserts a real spiritual change in the elements in virtue of consecration, interprets the language of St John vi, about 'eating the flesh' of Christ, of belief in His death and fellowship in His passion[1].

Again Florus the deacon, who wrote in an exceedingly edifying manner *de Expositione Missae* (c. A. D. 840) uses language which certainly implies the permanence after consecration of the outward elements[2]

not by Alcuin. Mabillon has not noticed that part iv 1-7 is a patchwork made up from the *de Expositione Missae* of Florus of Lyons (*P L* cxix p 15 : see cc 6, 17, 58-60, 62-3, 66-7) It appears plainly that Florus' work is the original, and not *vice versa* Also it will be noticed that Florus gives his authorities (c 1) and Alcuin is not among them, while the author of the *Confessio* does not give his The *Confessio* further shows acquaintance with the hymn *Pange lingua* (p 111 c 19), and the second half of part 111 (cc 23-42) is largely based upon [Boetius'] *de Fide Catholica*, incorporating lines 1-12, 24-30, 51-61, 84-90, 224-230, 244-252

[1] See *de Eccl Off* iii 24, 25 (*P L* cv pp 1141-2) 'Hic [at the consecration] credimus naturam simplicem panis et vini mixti verti in naturam rationabilem [spiritual], scilicet corporis et sanguinis Christi' 'Credit [ecclesia] namque corpus et sanguinem Domini esse ac hoc morsu caelesti benedictione impleri animas sumentium' *Ep* 4 *ad Rantgar* (p. 1334) '*Nisi manducaveritis carnem filii hominis, etc*, hoc est, nisi participes fueritis meae passionis et credideritis me mortuum pro vestra salute, non habebitis vitam in vobis' On the precedents for such an interpretation (not Augustine's) see appended note C

[2] For his *de Expos Missae* see also Hurter's *SS Patr Opusc Selecta*, vol xxxix His doctrine of the real presence in virtue of the invocation of the Holy Ghost on the elements and the use of the words of Christ's institution (§§ 81-84) is very clear In his *Opuscula adv Amalarium* i 9 (*P L* cxix pp 77, 78) he writes 'Prorsus panis ille sacrosanctae oblationis corpus est Christi, non materie vel specie visibili sed virtute et potentia spirituali Simplex e frugibus panis conficitur, simplex e botris vinum liquatur, accedit ad haec offerentis ecclesiae fides, accedit mysticae precis consecratio, accedit divinae virtutis infusio, sicque mire et ineffabili modo, quod est naturaliter ex germine terreno panis et vinum, efficitur spiritualiter corpus Christi, id est vitae et salutis nostrae mysterium, in quo aliud oculis corporis, aliud fidei videmus obtentu nec id tantum quod ore percipimus, sed quod mente credimus, libamus Mentis ergo est cibus ille, non ventris, non corrumpitur, sed manet in vitam aeternam, quoniam pie sumentibus confert

A landmark in the history of eucharistic doctrine is the work of Paschasius Radbert[1], *de Corpore et Sanguine Domini*, written about A.D. 831 when he was a simple monk of the older monastery of Corbey, and later, when he had become abbot of Corbey, about A.D 844, presented by him to Charles the Bald. Paschasius appears beyond all reasonable question to teach a doctrine of transubstantiation—that is, he teaches that the elements of bread and wine in the eucharist are at the moment when the priest pronounces the words of institution, by the power of Jesus Christ Himself and the operation of His Spirit, wholly and substantially converted into the true body and blood of Christ, so that what exists upon the altar is henceforth only the body and blood though it remains under the 'figure,' appearance, and sensible attributes of bread and wine. This appearance and these attributes remain to test faith and to avoid the scandal and horror which would result from the consecrated elements appearing what they are. The conversion of the elements is thus not an open one: it is a mystery, not a manifest miracle. But the body is the very same as was born of Mary and was crucified and buried: and the truth of this is driven home by the record of a number

vitam aeternam   Pie autem sumit qui spiritu fidei illuminatus in illo cibo et potu visibili virtutem intelligibilis gratiae esurit ac sitit   . Corpus igitur Christi, ut praedictum est, non est in specie visibili sed in virtute spirituali, nec inquinari potest faece corporea quod et animarum et corporum vitia mundare consuevit'

[1] There is, I think, some evidence for an influence of John of Damascus' theology of the eucharist (*de Fide Orthodoxa* iv. 13, Lequien i. p 368) both upon the Ambrosian treatise *de Sacramentis* and upon Paschasius' work But the matter is complicated by the relation of the *de Sacramentis* to the *de Mysteriis* also ascribed to St Ambrose.

Transubstantiation and Nihilianism.

of materialistic miracles, in which the hidden reality was made to appear in the form of the divine infant or as a bleeding limb of flesh. As against all rationalistic objections Paschasius exults in the divine power which can do all it will, the originative power which can produce this new creation, according to the plain word and promise of the very Truth Himself, Jesus Christ. So far Paschasius speaks the language of transubstantiation in its full force, but he still regards the body and blood of the eucharist as purely spiritual, and thus—unlike the later opponents of Berengar and some of his own contemporaries [1]— repudiates any attempt to bring it into connexion with the physical process of digestion, though it is uncertain whether he regards the bread and wine as retaining enough physical reality to admit of their being digested moreover, he is still so far under the influence of Augustine as to use hesitating language on the question whether the wicked receive the spiritual realities in the holy communion.

The following passages will illustrate the above statement (*de Corp. et Sang. Domini, Patr. Lat* cxx. p. 1269):

' Patet igitur quod nihil extra vel contra Dei voluntatem potest, sed cedunt illi omnia omnino. Et ideo nullus moveatur de hoc corpore Christi et sanguine, quod in mysterio vera sit caro et verus sit sanguis, dum sic voluit ille qui creavit; *omnia* enim *quaecunque voluit fecit in caelo et*

---

[1] E g Rabanus Maurus (*Ep ad Heribald Episc Antissiodor* 33 apud Mabillon, *Vetera Analecta*, Paris 1723, p 17, *P L* cx p 192, Gieseler, *l c* ii. p 285 n 5) replies to the inquiry, ' utrum eucharistia, postquam consumitur et in secessum emittitur more aliorum ciborum, iterum redeat in naturam pristinam quam habuerat antequam in altari consecraretur?' Cf Paschasius' own reference to the 'apocryphal book' quoted above.

in terra; et quia voluit, licet in figura panis et vini maneat, haec sic esse omnino nihilque aliud quam caro Christi et sanguis post consecrationem credenda sunt; unde ipsa veritas ad discipulos, *haec*, inquit, *caro est mea pro mundi vita*, et, ut mirabilius loquar, non alia plane quam quae nata est de Maria et passa in cruce et resurrexit de sepulchro.' . . .

'Veritas autem Deus est, et si Deus veritas est, quicquid Christus promisit in hoc mysterio utique verum est. Et ideo vera Christi caro et sanguis, quam qui manducat et bibit digne habet vitam aeternam in se manentem; sed visu corporeo et gustu propterea non demutantur, quatenus fides exerceatur ad iustitiam et ob meritum fidei merces in eo iustitiae consequatur' (i. 2, 5).

That after consecration there is 'nihil aliud quam corpus et sanguis Domini' is often repeated[1], and expressions are used such as 'corpus Christi et sanguis virtute Spiritus in verbo ipsius ex panis vinique substantia efficitur' (iv 1). After consecration the bread and wine may only typically be so called as Christ is the Bread of Life (xvi) The act of consecration is regarded as a new creative act of God (xv. 1), of which the priest is only the minister. The reasons for the 'figura' of bread and wine remaining are stated as above, and also (x. 1) because otherwise 'durius esset contra consuetudinem humanam licet carnem salutis tamen carnem hominis Christi in speciem et colorem ipsius mutatam et vinum in cruorem conversum accipere'; cf. xiii 2 'si carnis species in his visibilis appareret, iam non fides esset aut mysterium sed fieret miraculum, quo aut fides nobis daretur, aut a perfidis exsecratio communi-

---
[1] See ii 6, viii 2, xi. 2, xii 1, xvi, xx. 3

Transubstantiation and Nihilianism. 239

cantibus importunior grassaretur.' The record of miracles follows in ch. xiv. Of Paschasius' more spiritual language the following is an example · ' Frivolum est ergo, sicut in eodem apocrypho libro legitur, in hoc mysterio cogitare de stercore, ne commisceatur in digestione alterius cibi. Denique ubi spiritualis esca et potus sumitur ... quid commistionis habere poterit ' (xx. 3). On the reception by the wicked see vi 2 [1].

But Paschasius' doctrine met with decided opposition. Rabanus Maurus, writing in 853, emphatically denies that the body of the eucharist is the same body as that in which Christ lived and died [2]. He himself asserts an objective spiritual transformation [3] in the elements in

---

[1] Paschasius' language about the relation of the eucharistic act to Christ's sacrifice is well worth study, cap xi But we are not here concerned with the doctrine of the eucharistic sacrifice

[2] *Ep ad Heribald l c* ' Nam quidam nuper de ipso sacramento corporis et sanguinis Domini non rite sentientes dixerunt, hoc ipsum esse corpus et sanguinem Domini quod de Maria virgine natum est et in quo ipse Dominus passus est in cruce et resurrexit de sepulchro Cui errori quantum potuimus ad Eigilum abbatem scribentes, de corpore ipso quid vere credendum sit aperuimus ' (This letter is possibly that in Migne, *P L* cxii p 1510, see c 2) The opinion that the ' body ' of the eucharist is different from Christ's mortal body we shall see to have been held by Ratramn also

Among older fathers cf the language of Clem Alex *Paed* ii 2 19 διττὸν δὲ τὸ αἷμα τοῦ κυρίου τὸ μὲν γάρ ἐστιν αὐτοῦ σαρκικὸν ᾧ τῆς φθορᾶς λελυτρώμεθα, τὸ δὲ πνευματικόν, τουτέστιν ᾧ κεχρίσμεθα καὶ τοῦτ' ἔστι πιεῖν τὸ αἷμα τοῦ Ἰησοῦ τῆς κυριακῆς μεταλαβεῖν ἀφθαρσίας ἰσχὺς δὲ τοῦ λόγου τὸ πνεῦμα, ὡς αἷμα σαρκός Jerome *in Ephes* i 7 (ed Vallars vii p 553) · Dupliciter vero sanguis Christi et caro intelligitur vel spiritualis illa atque divina de qua ipse dixit *caro mea vere est cibus et sanguis meus vere est potus, et nisi manducaveritis carnem meam et sanguinem meam biberitis non habebitis vitam aeternam* , vel caro et sanguis quae ciucifixa est et qui militis effusus est lancea. Iuxta hanc divisionem et in sanctis eius diversitas sanguinis et carnis accipitur, ut alia sit caro quae visura est salutare Dei, alia caro et sanguis quae regnum Dei non queant possidere '

[3] *Liber de Sacris Ordinibus etc* (*P L* cxii p 1185) ' Quis unquam crederet quod panis in carnem potuisset converti vel vinum in sanguinem,

virtue of consecration, so that they become the body and blood of Christ in a true and real sense: but he does not appear to distinguish between the *res* and the *virtus sacramenti*[1]; and, in a word, he is still under the dominant influence of Augustine, whose words he repeats

But the main opponent of Paschasius' doctrine was Ratramn, a monk of his own convent. The emperor Charles had addressed two questions to Ratramn, presumably in common with other theologians[2]: (1) Whether

nisi ipse Salvator diceret, qui panem et vinum creavit et omnia ex nihilo fecit' Dr Hebert in his *Lord's Supper uninspired teaching* (Seeley & Co, 1879) 1 p 614, quotes from Rabanus as follows—'panem communem accepit [Christus], sed benedicendo in longe aliud quam fuerat transmutat ut veraciter diceret sic, *hoc est corpus meum* ' but his reference is, as so often, wrong and I cannot discover the passage

[1] *De Instit Cler* 1. 31 (*P L*. cvii. p. 317) 'Huius rei sacramentum, id est veritas corporis et sanguinis Christi, de mensa dominica assumitur quibusdam ad vitam, quibusdam ad exitium res vero ipsa omni homini ad vitam, nulli ad exitium quia aliud est sacramentum, aliud virtus sacramenti' Again Dr Herbert quotes ' neque indignitas [indigne sumentis] dignitatem tantae consecrationis evacuare poterit sed rem sacramenti non attingit [indignus] . idcirco nec effectus consequitur eiusdem sacramenti ' But I cannot verify the reference

[2] It has been supposed that John Scotus Erigena was consulted and wrote a work on the eucharist But this does not appear to be the case The work ascribed to him by Berengar and the men of his period is in fact Ratramn's work see *Praefatio* of H J Floss in *P L* cxxii p xxi Adrevaldus indeed, a contemporary, wrote a treatise (of which a fragment remains) *de Corpore et Sanguine Christi contra ineptias Ioannis Scoti*, but this is sufficiently accounted for by what is still to be found in Erigena's writings and what must have been found in the commentary on St John vi, when it was entire

Erigena held that Christ in heaven was still man, in the sense that in His one substance He still possessed the *natura* and *ratio* of humanity, but transmuted into the Godhead and with it *ubiquitous* Under these circumstances he might have anticipated the Lutheran doctrine of the eucharist and held that, in whatever sense He has a body at all, He is present with the same body in the eucharist But in fact he held a very 'symbolical' view of the eucharist, cf *Expos super Hierarch Cael S Dionys*. 1 3, where he inveighs against those 'qui visibilem eucharistiam

Transubstantiation and Nihilianism.

the body and blood are present in the eucharist *in veritate* or *in mysterio*? that is, as Ratramn explains it, whether there is in the eucharist a reality apparent only to faith, hidden under earthly veils, or whether the divine reality is there without veils? (2) Whether the sacramental body is the very body born of Mary and now in heaven? It does not appear whether these questions were addressed to theologians as a result of the presentation of Paschasius' treatise or no. Certainly the first question is not suggested by his position. But Ratramn's own view, as distinct from Paschasius', becomes quite plain in the process of his answer to both questions. He replies, like Paschasius, that the body and blood of Christ are present in the sacrament 'in mystery,' not 'in truth,' i e. under veils of sense, not in unveiled manifestation. But, unlike Paschasius, he argues from this in a sense opposed to transubstantiation. The elements by consecration are 'changed for the better'; they become what they were not, the veils of the body and blood. But this spiritual transformation does not affect their physical reality. In that respect they are not changed; they remain what they were. They symbolize in their natural reality the heavenly gift which they contain. The same

nihil aliud significare praeter se ipsam volunt assereie [i e presumably those who said the consecrated elements were really the body and blood in themselves and not typical of something else] dum clarissime praefata tuba [sc. Dionysius] clamat non illa sacramenta visibilia colenda neque pro veritate amplexanda quia significativa veritatis sunt '

His doctrine of Christ's humanity can be found stated with great clearness in *de Div Nat.* ii 11, v. 38. He held that there underlies each man's earthly body a secret *ratio* (or essence) of his corporeity which is to be his 'spiritual body' like that of the angels.

R

Dissertations.

object or substance (*res*) is both physically one thing and spiritually another. The following citations from his *Liber de Corpore et Sanguine Domini*[1] will make his position apparent

c. 9 'Ille panis qui per sacerdotis ministerium Christi corpus conficitur aliud exterius humanis sensibus ostendit et aliud interius fidelium mentibus clamat Exterius quidem panis quod ante fuerat forma praetenditur, color ostenditur, sapor accipitur · sed interius longe aliud multo pretiosius multoque excellentius intimatur, quia caeleste, quia divinum, id est Christi corpus, ostenditur quod non sensibus carnis sed animi fidelis contuitu vel aspicitur vel accipitur vel comeditur.'

But this involves no kind of change in what appears to the senses, no kind of physical change at all.

cc. 12–15 'Nulla permutatio facta esse cognoscitur,' i e. 'secundum veritatem species creaturae quae fuerat ante permansisse cognoscitur . .   nihil est hic permutatum . . . si nihil permutationis pertulerint nihil aliud exsistunt quam quod prius fuere . . . corporaliter namque nihil in eis cernitur esse permutatum Fatebuntur igitur necesse est aut mutata esse secundum aliud quam secundum corpus . . . aut si hoc profiteri noluerint, compelluntur negare corpus esse sanguinemque Christi [i. e. that any change has been made at all] quod nefas est non solum dicere verum etiam cogitare².'

Then comes the conclusion .

c 16 'At quia confitentur et corpus et sanguinem Dei

[1] *P L* cxxi p 126 f

[2] Ratramn clearly draws no distinction between accidents apparent to the senses and substance not to be changed sensibly is not to be changed corporally or in reality at all

Transubstantiation and Nihilianism. 243

esse, nec hoc esse potuisse nisi facta in melius commutatione, neque iste commutatio corporaliter sed spiritualiter facta sit, necesse est iam ut figurate facta esse dicatur : quoniam sub velamento corporei panis corporeique vini spirituale corpus spiritualisque sanguis exsistit : non quod duarum sint exsistentiae rerum inter se diversarum, corporis videlicet et spiritus, verum una eademque res secundum aliud species panis et vini consistit, secundum aliud autem corpus est et sanguis Christi.'

Ratramn (like earlier writers) compares what occurs to the eucharistic elements with what occurs to the element of water in baptism in virtue of the consecration of the priest (c. 17) 'Accessit sancti Spiritus per sacerdotis consecrationem virtus et efficax facta est non solum corpora verum etiam animas diluere et spirituales sordes spirituali potentia dimovere'

He goes on to make a stronger comparison. Feeling forced by St. Paul's words (1 Cor x. 1-4) to suppose that the Jews had sacraments as full of spiritual reality as the Christians, he ascribes to the sea and the cloud, to the water from the rock and the manna, a real spiritual potency [1]. He even declares that the Jews in the wilderness ate the flesh of Christ and drank His blood, and that Christ by His divine power changed the manna into His body and the water into His blood with the same reality as in the eucharist of the Church, and he sees in this an anticipation only earlier than that which occurred when our Lord, before His actual sacrifice, 'was able to turn the substance of bread and the creature of wine into the body and blood' of His

---

[1] Paschasius argues to the contrary effect (c v)

sacrifice (21–28). Curiously enough, it is at this point where the analogy of baptism and the Jewish sacraments might suggest that the only change in the eucharistic elements consists in their being endued with a spiritual significance and power, that Ratramn (for once) uses language suggestive of transubstantiation. By spiritual power and in a mystery we are to 'understand that the bread and wine are really converted into the substance of Christ's body and blood, to be received by the believers' (30). But this language is shown to go beyond his real mind by superabundant explanations under two heads

(1) That there is no change in the elements. 'nam secundum creaturarum substantiam quod fuerunt ante consecrationem hoc et postea consistunt' (54); 'in illo vel potu vel pane nihil corporaliter opinari sed totum spiritualiter sentire' (58) The truth is not 'ille panis et illud vinum Christus est,' but 'in illo sacramento Christus est' (59). The wine is no more changed into the blood of Christ corporally than the mingled water which represents the people is changed into the people: 'at videmus in aqua secundum corpus nihil esse conversum' (75)

(2) He distinguishes between the historical actual visible body of Christ, which is now in heaven—the 'veritas carnis quam sumpserat de virgine'—and the sacramental body—the 'sacramentum carnis'—and that in the most emphatic way (57). In this connexion he seems to speak as if the presence in the sacrament were only a presence of the divine Spirit, or the Word of God: and as if the sacrament were only called the body of Christ because the bread and wine make

Transubstantiation and Nihilianism. 245

a new body for the divine Spirit or Word to operate through 'Corpus Christi corpus est divini Spiritus.' 'Patenter ostendit [Ambrosius] secundum quod habeatur corpus Christi, videlicet secundum id quod sit in eo Spiritus Christi, i.e. divini potentia Verbi, quae non solum animam pascit verum etiam purgat[1]' (61, 64, 72). Again he speaks as if the bread were in no other sense Christ's natural heavenly body than it is the mystical body, that is the Christian people, which it also represents (73–74).

This is the only really doubtful question in Ratramn's doctrine: Is the unseen part in the sacrament merely the presence of the pure Spirit of God, or Word of God, as it were incarnating Himself in the bread to impart spiritual life to His people? or is it a presence of the incarnate and glorified Christ after a spiritual and heavenly manner? On this point St. Augustine leaves us in no doubt[2]. The 'inner part' of the sacrament is the flesh and blood which have become 'spirit' and 'life.' But Ratramn's language leaves us in doubt as to what he held and taught on this point. He ends his treatise however with language stronger than that of the sections we have just been discussing, for he quotes and comments on words of the liturgy which

---

[1] There would be some support for this view in the language of Tertullian, see appended note D, in that of Clement (above, p 239 n. 2) and Macarius Magnes (below, p 304). It is generally associated with the misunderstanding of St John vi 63, as if that were intended to explain away what Christ had been saying just before, and to imply that 'eating the flesh' of Christ and 'drinking His blood' was only a metaphor for receiving His words, or that only His spirit, not His humanity, could be communicated to men. On the patristic interpretation of this passage see appended note C.

[2] See above, p 233 n.

seem to assume that what we receive in the sacrament is the same as what we shall enjoy in heaven, only now under a veil and in a mystery, then unveiled and in manifest participation—'*pignus aeternae vitae capientes humiliter imploramus ut quod in imagine contingimus sacramenti manifesta participatione sumamus* (85 f), and he concludes with the language of a true faith—

'Nec ideo, quoniam ista dicimus, putetur in mysterio sacramenti corpus Domini vel sanguinem ipsius non a fidelibus sumi quando fides non quod oculus videt sed quod credit accipit quoniam spiritualis est esca et spiritualis potus, spiritualiter animam pascens et aeternae satietatis vitam tribuens; sicut ipse Salvator mysterium hoc commendans loquitur: *Spiritus est qui vivificat, nam caro nihil prodest.*'

Paschasius Radbert was at pains to insist upon the identity of the sacramental and the real body of Christ, against those who, like Ratramn, would 'weaken the force of Christ's own words[1],' and his side of the controversy was taken by Hincmar of Rheims[2] and Haimo, bishop of Halberstadt[3]. The statement of transubstantiation by the latter is very explicit. He denies that the consecrated elements can be called *signs* of the natural

---

[1] See *Expos in Matt* xii, in xxvi 26 (*P L* cxx p 890) 'Audiant qui volunt extenuare hoc verbum corporis'

[2] *de Cav Vitiis et Virt Exerc ad Carol Calv* c 10 (*P L* cxxv p 926) It is worth notice that he retains a doctrine of Fulgentius (*P L* lxv p 391) and declares it to be beyond question that there is a participation of Christ's body and blood in *baptism* also—'nulli est aliquatenus ambigendum', so that baptized infants who die do not fall into the condemnation of John vi (p 925)

[3] *P L* cxviii p 817

Transubstantiation and Nihilianism.

body of Christ, though they are signs of the mystical body, and he writes thus of the consecration

'Substantiam ergo panis et vini, quae super altare ponitur, fieri corpus Christi et sanguinem per mysterium sacerdotis et gratiarum actionem, Deo hoc operante divina gratia secreta potestate, nefandissimae dementiae est fidelibus mentibus dubitare. . . . Commutat ergo invisibilis sacerdos suas visibiles creaturas in substantiam suae carnis et sanguinis secreta potestate In quo quidem Christi corpore et sanguine propter sumentium horrorem sapor panis et vini remanet et figura, substantiarum natura in corpus Christi et sanguinem omnino conversa, sed aliud renuntiant sensus carnis, aliud renuntiat fides mentis Sensus carnis nihil aliud renuntiare possunt quam sentiunt; intellectus autem mentis et fides veram Christi carnem et sanguinem renuntiat et confitetur, ut tanto magis coronam suae fidei recipiat et meritum, quanto magis credit ex integro quod omnino remotum est a sensibus carnis . . . . Nullum signum est illud cuius est signum; nec res aliqua sui ipsius dicitur signum sed alterius'

And at this point the controversy remained till it was rekindled two centuries later in connexion with Berengar We need not concern ourselves with the somewhat intricate details of the Berengarian controversy in the eleventh century. It is enough for us to know that Berengar's teaching and 'the book of John Scotus' on which it was based—i. e in fact Ratramn's work, which was both by Berengar and his opponents ascribed to Scotus—were repeatedly condemned, and that the doctrine of transubstantiation became accepted as a dogma of the Church which it was heresy to deny, though the actual word transubstantiation does not occur in any ecclesiastical decision till it was decreed by the Lateran Council in 1215

Nor again are we concerned with the task of passing moral judgements on the actors in the controversy Berengar was not of the stuff of which martyrs are made, and more than once sought safety from his ecclesiastical opponents by repudiating his own beliefs On the first of these occasions he accepted, if he did not subscribe to, a horribly materialistic formula of Cardinal Humbert's, which will be noticed later on [1]. On the other hand, it must be admitted that he met with nothing like fair treatment from his opponents This at least we may safely say ; and without entering further into the moral question, we may pass on to attempt to describe exactly what Berengar's position was—judging of this chiefly from the recovered portion of his treatise *de Sacra Coena* [2]—and what the position of his opponents.

On the whole Berengar reproduces, and with consciousness of his obligation [3], the view of the book which he ascribed to John the Scot, and which was in fact the

---

[1] Lanfranc says that he subscribed to it (*de Corp et Sang Domini* 2, *P L.* cl) 'Tu vero acquiescens accepisti, legisti, confessus te ita credere iureiurando confirmasti, tandem manu propria subscripsisti' He himself denies that he subscribed to it or assented positively to it, but admits that he accepted it in silence (*de S Coena*, pp 25-6) ' Manu quod mendaciter ad te pervenit non subscripsi nam ut de consensu pronuntiarem meo nullus exegit, tantum timore praesentis iam mortis scriptum illud absque ulla conscientia mea iam factum manibus accepi' cf p 74 'a protestatione veritatis et defensione mea obmutui '

[2] My references are to the edition of A. F and F. Th Vischer, Berlin 1834 In this book we have Berengar's mature view, which as he says (p 44) was only gradually reached, through the discipline of persecution and prolonged study   [3] *de S. Coena,* p 36

work of Ratramn. But his work differs markedly from Ratramn's. He is much more controversial—being mainly occupied in repudiating transubstantiation rather than in elaborating a positive theory; and he is a thorough scholastic, full of the methods and terms of the new dialectic His book indeed is important, as for other reasons, so for its place in scholasticism. The Church had not yet made up its mind to adopt the rising philosophy of the time. There was a great tendency on the part of ecclesiastics to glorify simple belief and to deprecate the attempt to understand Christian doctrines, or to meet all mental difficulties with a simple appeal to divine omnipotence [1]. Berengar contends then against his opponent Lanfranc for the legitimacy of dialectic. He had been accused of 'deserting authorities and taking refuge in dialectic[2]'; and he is not slow to reply that 'to take refuge in dialectic through all obstacles is the mark of the best judgement; because to take refuge in dialectic is to take refuge in reason, and he who does not take refuge there, seeing that it is in virtue of the possession of reason that man is made in the image of God, has deserted his own honour and cannot be renewed from day to day in the image of God.' And he justifies this appeal to logic by the example of Augustine [3].

Connected with the appeal to logic, as against authority pure and simple, is Berengar's depreciation of majorities.

---

[1] See Hugh of Langres, *de Corp et Sang Christi contra Berengar* (*P L* cxlii) at the beginning, and Witmund (below, pp 261-2), and references to Lanfranc in the following note

[2] p 99, cf p 164 'Et primo illud non tacendum quod persuadere conaris quod ad mensam dominicam pertineat posse utiliter credi, non posse utiliter inquiri'   [3] p 101.

He loves to recall the fact that in the African controversy about re-baptism in the third century [1], and in the Arian controversy in the fourth [2], the majority went wrong and the maintainers of what proved to be the truth were but the few. Thus when he is confronted with the argument that the great majority held against him on the matter of the sacrament, and that this was a sign that he was in error, he replies that exactly the same argument from common belief would substantiate the doctrine that man is in the image of God in virtue of his physical shape, 'because all but a very few Christians both hold this and have no doubt that it is to be held as a matter of Christian faith.' Indeed, he confidently maintains that the people who hold with him about the eucharist are not fewer than those who hold the truth against Anthropomorphism [3].

Berengar then stands stiffly for the right of reason and against the mere force of majorities in religion; but he certainly is not behindhand in his appeal to 'authentic scriptures'—a phrase which in those days covered all authoritative writings, both the bible and the fathers [4]. On the whole he is critical and successful in his treatment of authorities · notably he argues with very damaging force against the doctrine of transubstantiation from the language of the Canon of the Mass and other ancient prayers to be found in his day in what

---

[1] pp 27, 34, 39, 44, 58   [2] p 55

[3] pp 54, 55. On the current Anthropomorphism see references in Gieseler, *Eccl Hist* ii p 391, especially the report which Ratherius, bishop of Verona, gives of its prevalence in the dioceses of Vicenza and Verona

[4] p 277 The appeal behind fathers to Scripture as the ultimate criterion seems not at this period to have occurred to any one.

Transubstantiation and Nihilianism. 251

he calls the 'book of the Lord's table' (*liber mensalis*)[1]. In his discussion of the meaning of patristic passages, there is one specially interesting passage in which he calls attention to a use of negatives which prevails not only in the fathers, but in Scripture and common speech[2]. A thing is said absolutely *not* to be that which from the present point of view is not of importance in comparison with something else of much more importance which it is or has become and which it is desirable to emphasize. A certain Gerald, he instances, has become a bishop, and is yet conducting himself improperly. What could be more in accordance with custom than to reprimand him by reminding him that he is 'no longer Gerald, but a bishop'? He multiplies instances of a similar mode of speech from the bible and the fathers, on other topics than the eucharist. 'I am a worm and *no man*', 'my doctrine is *not* mine'; 'who were born *not* of blood, nor of the will of man'; 'it is *no longer* I that live'; 'he is *not* a Jew, which is one

---

[1] See p 277 He quotes, p 283, a collect for Christmas Day (still in use in the Roman Mass) *Munera nostra nativitatis hodiernae misteriis apta proveniant, ut, sicut homo genitus idem refulsit Deus, sic nobis haec terrena substantia conferat quod divinum est*, a collect which certainly suggests that the *terrena substantia* in the eucharist is as real as the *homo* in the Incarnation P 285, he quotes another prayer, the force of which is still more unmistakeable, and which is not, as far as I know, in present use *Gratias exhibemus tibi, Domine, quod etiam temporalem ac mutabilem creaturam, panem atque vinum, quae de mensa tua secundum corpus accipimus, ad salutem nobis animae valere instituisti, praesta ut qui sacramenta accipimus, quod minus est (minus est enim signato signum omne), beneficia potiora, sacramentorum res, in homine interiore sumamus, qui per sacramenta, quod minus est, in corpore reficimur, per res sacramentorum, quod potius est, mente reficiamur.*

[2] p 177 'Non desunt in communi oratione, non desunt in scripturis dicta quae merito conferantur istis beati Ambrosii dictis'

outwardly.' It is not then, he argues, fair to conclude that whenever a father says 'the bread and wine after consecration are not bread and wine, but the body and blood of Christ,' he is maintaining the doctrine of transubstantiation:—the less fair when similar phrases are used about the water in baptism which no one supposes to cease to exist, and when there are other passages where the permanence of the bread and wine are plainly stated [1]. This argument really shows a thorough grasp of the situation.

Philosophically Berengar's denial of transubstantiation is a denial that accidents can subsist apart from their substance or subject, or attributes apart from that of which they are attributes. Nothing can be this or that ('just' or 'white') when it has ceased itself to be. Logically indeed we distinguish substances from attributes or accidents, but this is merely notional. We can have no reason to believe that there is a substance which is separable from the qualities in which it consists [2]. You say, he argues, that after consecration the subject or substance of bread is annihilated and another subject

[1] pp 177 ff, p 172

[2] p 81 'nullo modo Socrates iustus erit, si Socratem esse non contingeret,' 92, 93, 171 'constat nulla ratione colorem videri, nisi contingat etiam coloratum [a coloured substance] videri,' 182 'causa videndi coloris vel cuiuscunque quod in subiecto est, subiecti ipsius visio est, apud ipsam, quae Deus est, veritatem subiecti et eius quod in subiecto est, non sensu sed intellectu solo separabilium compactricem,' 195 'impossibile est secundum hanc ut dixi mutationem, corrupto subiecto, non corrumpi quod erat in subiecto,' 211 'quod secundum subiectum non sit, minime posse secundum accidens esse'

The commentary of Alexander of Hales on this argumentation is curious, see pars iv qu x memb. v art iii *de consecratione* § 1 'minuit utilitatem meriti quia ponendo quod accidentia non possunt esse sine subiecto, innitendo rationibus humanis, meritum fidei minuitur.'

Transubstantiation and Nihilianism. 253

generated, viz the body of Christ; but that this is invisible, so that you cannot see the body of Christ. Yes, he replies, you can, if the substance is that. You can see it as much as you could ever see the old substance. What could you ever see of the bread except its visible qualities: and if you say the body of Christ now subsists under visible qualities, it is present, like the bread, visibly, tangibly, &c[1] It is just as visible as a white man would be were he to paint his face like a negro[2].

From this point of view, he presses his opponents with the materialism of their doctrine. 'While you think to thrust me,' he says to Lanfranc, 'into the Mincio (of heresy); you yourself are rushing into the Po (of materialism)[3].' If the body of Christ is, as you affirm, —and as he himself had been made to declare by Cardinal Humbert—*corporally* present in the eucharist, what must be there is not the whole body, but a portion of the body. For what is corporally present is locally present; and if the body is locally present, whole and undivided, and is so consumed, on one altar, it cannot be locally present on a million other altars and in heaven[4]. (Indeed he again and again affirms what, as we shall see, is not antecedently improbable—that Cardinal Humbert, and even Lanfranc, held the view that what was present in the sacrament was a *portiuncula carnis*[5].) But such a view is untenable. for

---

[1] pp. 127, 134-5, 202.
[2] p 127 'quia si supervestiatur facies tua colore Aethiopis necesse est faciem tuam videri, si colorem constiterit videri'
[3] p. 119, cf p 43   [4] p 198 f
[5] p 81 'Humbertus ille tuus   qui in sacrificio ecclesiae nihil aliud quam portiunculam carnis sensualiter et sanguinis post consecrationem superesse

the body of Christ is indivisible and does not admit of partition¹. Nor is it conceivable that (as Humbert's formula expressly asserted) the body of Christ, incorruptible and immortal, can be broken by the hand of the priest or pressed by the teeth of the communicants². Once more, he inveighs against the idea that in the consecration of the eucharist there is a production of a substance (*generatio subiecti*), i e of the body of Christ. For that body already exists, one and indivisible, and how can what already exists be produced³?

On the whole, in view of the then current doctrine of transubstantiation, Berengar's logic is, if pitiless, morally as justifiable and successful as his appeal to authority.

As has been said, Berengar is mainly occupied, in

confirmat'; cf p 200 'scribis [i e Lanfranc] fieri in altari portiunculam carnis per generationem subiecti'

¹ p 158

² pp 118, 199 'Constabit nihilominus eum qui opinetur Christi corpus caelo devocatum adesse sensualiter in altari ipsum se deicere quod recordium est, dum confirmat se manu frangere, dente atterere Christi corpus, quod tamen ipsum negare non possit impassibile esse et incorruptibile'

³ p 163 'Non quia corpus Christi et sanguis possint vel in toto vel in parte nunc esse incipere secundum generationem subiecti, quia Christi corpus per mille annos iam exsistens nullo modo nunc esse incipere, nullo modo potest nunc generari' This 'creationist' language about the miracle of transubstantiation is still used by Alger, *de Sacr Corp et Sang. Dom* i. 16 112, and others There is, however, another kind of language by which the bread and wine are said to be 'transposed into' or 'pass into' the body of Christ. Thus 'si creaturas quas de nihilo potuit creare, has ipsas multo magis valeat in excellentioris naturae dignitatem convertere et in sui corporis substantiam *transfundere*' (Fulbert of Chartres, *P L* cxli p 204) A later scholastic controversy arose, and still subsists, as between these theories of an *actio productiva* and an *actio adductiva*, see Lessius *de Perfect. Divin* xii 16 §§ 114-119 He decides for the former, 'verius igitur mihi semper visum, Christi corpus poni sub speciebus per actionem productivam, quam replicationem vel reproductionem vel collationem eiusdem esse substantialis appellare possumus'

Transubstantiation and Nihilianism. 255

the portion of his late controversial work which remains to us, in controversial negations. His own positive view is not elaborated Certainly however he appears—like Ratramn—to have held to the doctrine of a real objective, but spiritual, presence in the elements in virtue of consecration. Thus he distinguishes different kinds of 'conversion' or change, and affirms of the elements a conversion which while it leaves them what they were makes them something they were not[1]. This he constantly affirms is the character of divine benediction—not to destroy but to raise to a higher power[2]. Again, if he asserts that the bread and wine after consecration are still signs, he expressly distinguishes kinds of signs[3]. The bread and wine, he says, are signs of an existing reality, and not only existing but actually present with the signs, for the *res sacramenti* necessarily attends the *sacramentum*[4]. Like others however he certainly denies that the wicked receive the body and blood of Christ[5], he assimilates, again like others, the eucharistic gift to that of baptism[6]; and at times he seems to pass from a 'spiritual' to a merely 'memorial' view of

[1] p 161

[2] p. 163 'per consecrationem, inquam, quod nemo interpretari poterit per subiecti corruptionem,' p 116 'omne quod sacretur necessario in melius provehi, minime absumi per corruptionem subiecti'

[3] p 43 'Non interesse nihil inter figuram vel signum rei quae nunquam fuit, rei nondum exhibitae pronunciatoriam, et figuram vel signum rei exsistentis, rei iam exhibitae commonefactoriam'

[4] p. 43 'Constat enim, ubi fit sacramentum, nulla posse non esse ratione rem quoque sacramenti.'

[5] p 89 thus he glosses 1 Cor. xi. 29 'not discerning the body' as 'not discerning the *sacrament* of the body'; and (p 278) he lays stress on the phrase of the invocation—that the bread and wine may become '*to us*' the body and the blood of Christ.

[6] p. 128 'per omnia comparabili.'

the eucharistic elements[1]. It must be remembered that in the language of the day *intellectualis* and *spiritualis* were synonyms. A 'spiritual' presence would also be called 'intellectual'; and that could easily mean a presence only in the intelligence or memory[2].

On the whole however, I repeat, his language is plain for the real presence; for example:

'Hic ego inquio: certissimum habete dicere me, panem atque vinum altaris post consecrationem Christi esse revera corpus et sanguinem[3].'

'Panis autem et vinum, attestante hoc omni scriptura, per consecrationem convertuntur in Christi carnem et sanguinem, constatque omne quod consecretur, omne cui a Deo benedicatur, non absumi, non auferri, non destrui, sed manere et in melius quam erat necessario provehi[4].'

But Berengar's opponents would not be conciliated by any belief in the real presence, however distinct, that was combined with a belief in the permanence of the outward substances of bread and wine. Transubstantiation was held at that time in the Church both fanatically

---

[1] p 222 'Exigit ut ipsum eundem Christi sanguinem semper in memoria habens in eo, quasi in viatico ad conficiendum vitae huius iter, interioris tui vitam constituas sicut exterioris tui vitam in exterioribus constituis cibis et potibus'

[2] See for this transition of thought one of Berengar's earliest opponents, Hugh of Langres, *de Corp et Sang Chr con Berengar* (*P. L* cxlii. p 1327) 'Corpus quod dixeras crucifixum intellectuale constituis In quo evidentissime patet quod incorporeum confiteris Qua in re universalem ecclesiam scandalizas . . . si quod adiunctum est sola fit intellectus potentia revera non capitur quomodo, vel unde, vel idem sit quod adhuc non subsistit Est enim intellectus essentiarum discussor non opifex, iudex non institutor Et quamvis rerum vel monstret vel figuret imagines, nullum corpus materiali producit exordio'

[3] p. 51. [4] p 248; cf below, p. 259 n 2.

Transubstantiation and Nihilianism.

and materialistically. The plainest witness to this is the confession of faith already referred to, which was drawn up by Cardinal Humbert and forced upon Berengar at Rome, in the presence of Pope Nicholas and other bishops, in the year 1059 This, first negatively by way of recantation and then positively by way of affirmation, asserts under anathema that 'The bread and wine after consecration are not only a sacrament but also the true body and blood of our Lord Jesus Christ and are sensibly, not only in a sacrament but in truth, touched and broken by the hands of the priests and pressed by the teeth of the faithful.' The sense of the passage as a whole leaves no doubt that it is the body and blood which are declared to be the subject of the physical acts mentioned.

This appalling decree is as follows [1]:

'Ego Berengarius, indignus diaconus ecclesiae sancti Mauricii Andegavensis, cognoscens veram catholicam et apostolicam fidem, anathematizo omnem haeresim, praecipue eam de qua hactenus infamatus sum, quae astruere conatur panem et vinum, quae in altari ponuntur, post consecrationem solummodo sacramentum et non verum corpus et sanguinem domini nostri Iesu Christi esse, nec posse sensualiter nisi in solo sacramento manibus sacerdotum tractari vel frangi aut fidelium dentibus atteri. Consentio autem sanctae Romanae et apostolicae sedi, et ore et corde profiteor de sacramento dominicae mensae eam fidem tenere, quam

---

[1] See Lanfranc, *de Corp et Sang Dom* 2 Mansi, *Concil* xix p 900 At a later date (1078) Berengar signed a profession which went no further than affirming the substantial conversion of the elements into the true flesh and blood But this was when Hildebrand (Gregory VII) was pope, who, first as papal legate at Tours (1054) and all along had gone as far as he could venture in support of Berengar

dominus et venerabilis papa Nicolaus et haec sancta synodus auctoritate evangelica et apostolica tenendam tradidit mihique firmavit: scilicet panem et vinum, quae in altari ponuntur, post consecrationem non solum sacramentum sed etiam verum corpus et sanguinem domini nostri Iesu Christi esse, et sensualiter non solum sacramento sed in veritate manibus sacerdotum tractari et frangi et fidelium dentibus atteri: iurans per sanctam et homoousion Trinitatem et per haec sacrosancta Christi evangelia. Eos vero qui contra hanc fidem venerint cum dogmatibus et sectatoribus suis aeterno anathemate dignos esse pronuntio. Quod si ego ipse aliquando aliquid contra haec sentire ac praedicare praesumpsero, subiaceam canonum severitati. Lecto et perlecto sponte subscripsi.'

It is very noticeable that both Lanfranc and Hugh of Langres, who wrote against Berengar, while on the one hand they misinterpret Berengar as asserting a bare memorial of Christ in the holy eucharist [1], on the other defend implicitly such language as that of the decree, affirming that the body and blood of Christ are physically eaten by the communicant, though they are not thereby subject to corruption and diminution [2].

The most considerable theological effort against Berengar is the treatise *de Corporis et Sanguinis Christi*

---

[1] See Lanfranc, *l. c* cap. 22, and Hugh, as cited above

[2] Hugh, *l c* 'putas non bene intelligens attrita quaeque consequenter corrumpi' Lanfranc (*l c* c 2) quotes with the highest expression of approval Humbert's decree, cf also c 17· the announced faith and teaching of the Church is 'carnem et sanguinem domini nostri Iesu Christi et ore corporis et ore cordis, hoc est corporaliter ac spiritualiter manducari et bibi' Both Hugh and Lanfranc meet the argument that what is continually eaten must diminish by an appeal to the physical miracle of the widow of Zarephath's oil, and demand an act of faith, without reasoning, in the inscrutable action of divine power.

Veritate, by Witmund (Guitmundus) a Norman, who, after declining to accept an English bishopric under William the Conqueror, was afterwards made archbishop of Aversa in Italy. This treatise, written apparently in Normandy between the years 1060 and 1078, is our fullest source of information for the theological feeling of the majority of the Church during the Berengarian controversy [1]. Witmund begins by recognizing two distinct beliefs among the Berengarians [2]. some of them holding a merely symbolical view of the eucharist, others a doctrine of the real presence of the body and blood in the substances of bread and wine—which latter view he calls *impanatio* and *invinatio*. Both views alike however fall under condemnation for denying the doctrine of transubstantiation, and to this therefore he first applies himself. He conceives the change in the elements to be such as causes them to become in physical reality the body and blood of Christ, only under the remaining accidents of bread and wine. He does not shrink from the idea that Christ's body is pressed by the teeth of communicants [3], or even of animals [4], for it lay in the

---

[1] It has been recently reprinted (with approbation) in *SS. Patr. Opusc Sel.* vol xxxviii, from which I quote it

[2] l. 8 'Berengariani omnes in hoc conveniunt quia panis et vinum essentialiter non mutantur, sed ut extorquere a quibusdam potui multum in hoc differunt, quod alii nihil omnino de corpore et sanguine Domini sacramentis istis inesse, sed tantummodo umbras haec et figuras esse dicunt. Alii vero rectis ecclesiae rationibus cedentes, nec tamen a stultitia recedentes, ut quasi aliquo modo nobiscum esse videantur, dicunt ibi corpus et sanguinem Domini revera sed latenter contineri et ut sumi possint quodammodo, ut ita dixerim, impanari. Et hanc ipsius Berengarii subtiliorem esse sententiam aiunt'

[3] l. 10 'Quare non possit dentibus premi, qui manibus Thomae et post resurrectionem potuit attrectari?'

[4] ll. 7, 8 Or (as a prior alternative) angels may have carried off the

tomb and after the resurrection it both trode the earth and was touched by the hand of Thomas. Indeed nothing physical can defile it. Nor does he shrink from holding it possible that Christ may divide His body and blood in portions to the faithful[1], though it may also remain undivided and entire in every particle of every host[2]. But he does deny that the flesh and blood of Christ are liable to violence or corruption[3]: that is (so physical is his conception of transubstantiation) he denies that the consecrated elements are liable to natural putrefaction[4]. They may seem so to the eye of the disobedient and unbelieving, who have misused them for purposes of incredulous inquiry; but the senses are delusive, and allowed to be delusive for the punishment of presumption, unless indeed they can be turned to account to win the merit of a faith contrary to their evidence[5]. He denies that the elements are the subjects of the ordinary

---

sacramental realities, and they may have been only in appearance devoured by animals, 'a muribus corrodi vel consumi' This appears to have been a frequent occurrence, see Abelard, *P L.* clxxviii pp 1743-4 'De hoc quod negligentia ministrorum evenire solet, quod scilicet mures videntur rodere et in ore portare corpus illud, quaeri solet· sed dicimus quod Deus illud non dimittit ibi ut a tam turpi animali tractetur, sed tamen remanet ibi forma ad negligentiam ministrorum corrigendam.' Cf Peter Lombard, quoted below, p 268 n 1 Cf. among the Greeks, Pseudo-John Damasc *de Corp. et Sang Chr.* cap. 5 (Lequien, 1. p 659)

[1] 1 15 'Ut corpus suum per partes ipse dividere possit, .. quis impossibile hoc audeat aestimare?'

[2] 1 16-18   [3] 1 15

[4] 11 2 'Nobis enim panis ille Dei caelestis, illa eucharistia, divinum illud manna, quod immaculati agni carnem impassibilem factam de sacris altaribus sumimus, per quod et vivimus et a corruptione sanamur, nunquam putrescit'

[5] 11 3 'Aut certe fidei eius soliditas copiosius remuneranda comprobetur, quod contra id etiam quod oculus cernit de rebus ac potentia Domini sui et communi ecclesiae fide non dubitarit.'

Transubstantiation and Nihilianism. 261

processes of digestion : 'cibum incorruptibilem, quod est corpus Domini, cum a mortalibus editur, secessus necessitatem pati, nefas est arbitrari[1]' If any priest has been so wicked or simple as to consecrate bread in quantities to allow of its relation to nourishment and digestion being tested, either his unbelief may have made his consecration invalid[2], or some other food may have been substituted at the moment of reception, whether by angels to protect the sacred things or by devils to deceive the sinner[3].

Again if it is said that according to some ecclesiastical canons the consecrated hosts are in certain cases to be committed to the flames—if this be done in fact, we must believe that they are allowed to appear to be consumed as far as the remaining accidents of the previous substance are concerned, while the thing itself is only 'committed to the pure element to be concealed and straightway restored to the heavenly seats[4].'

Witmund seeks physical analogies for the miracle of transubstantiation so far as to suggest that bread and wine become our own flesh and blood[5]; that our voice, the vesture of our thought, imparts itself undivided to all hearers; that our 'anima' is undivided in all parts of our body[6]. But he dwells more on the obligation to believe mysteries. All creatures of God are in fact inexplicable miracles[7]; the senses are fallible, and

[1] ii 13.
[2] ii 18 'Non enim nisi apud eos, qui verba Christi per virtutem divinam tantae rei operatoria esse credunt, panem et vinum in carnem et sanguinem Domini transire necessario credimus' In this belief, however, Witmund stands alone.
[3] ii. 18   [4] ii. 10   [5] i 9   [6] i 19.
[7] i. 20 'omnes creaturae Dei miracula nobis inexplicabilia sunt'; iii. 22

simple faith in the omnipotence and word of God is a duty [1].

Then he proceeds to argue with the *umbratici*—so he calls the Berengarians—on the matter of authority. Doing violence to manifold statements of the fathers he is inclined to deny that the consecrated elements are ever called the 'sacraments [2]' (*signa*) of the body and blood, though, if they are, he insists that a sign can be also that of which it is a sign. But on the whole he is very unsatisfactory in this part of his subject [3]. Nor is he more satisfactory when he proceeds to discuss the theory which he calls *impanatio* and *invinatio* [4]. He explains away what is against him or ignores it—for instance the statement of Ambrose 'ut sint quae erant et in aliud commutentur [5]', and he makes much of the catholic character of his doctrine as against the local character of the Berengarian view [6]. The Catholic Church is the kingdom of heaven which has succeeded to the empire of Rome, according to Daniel's prophecy,—for a visible proof of which the Church of the Lateran has taken the place of the palace of the Caesars—and this Church with its pontiffs has condemned Berengar [7]. He ends up his treatise with a discussion of two curious views which he had mentioned at the beginning as existing among opponents of Berengar, who still found offence in the doctrine that the wicked receive the body and blood of Christ [8]. The first view is that by divine providence it is secured that

'nulla omnino res sine miraculo fit.' This fact (by a vague use of the word miracle) is used to justify belief in 'miracles of the host'

[1] i 9, 22, 28, &c.   [2] ii 37   [3] ii 22 ff
[4] iii 27   [5] iii 32   [6] iii 40.
[7] iii. 42.   [8] i 8.

Transubstantiation and Nihilianism. 263

those hosts which the wicked are to receive shall not be transubstantiated; the second, that when unworthy communicants approach the altar, the hosts they are to receive are re-transubstantiated into bread and wine. Against both these theories Witmund holds decisively that the wicked do eat corporally, though not spiritually, the body and blood of Christ [1].

Opinions similar to those of Witmund appear in the contemporary—perhaps slightly earlier—tract of Durandus, the first abbot of the monastery of St. Martin of Troarn in the diocese of Bayeux. Writing against the Berengarians [2]—whom he calls the 'moderni dogmatistae responsalesque Satanae'—he regards the belief in the physical corruption and digestion of the sacramental elements as a mere result of their heresy [3]. He himself argues from the language of our Lord—'He that eateth my flesh and drinketh my blood *dwelleth in me and I in him*'—that the sacramental gift is permanent and not transitory; and this means to his mind that the sacramental elements cease at their consecration to retain their material properties and at their reception also their material appearances: 'ubi,' he says (i.e. in the words of Christ just referred to), 'ut cunctis sanum sapientibus patenter liquet, non digestionis obscenitas sed divinae per sacramentum mansionis repromittitur negotium fidelibus: ac proinde divinum mysterium

---

[1] iii 49 ff.
[2] *Liber de Corp et Sang Christi, P L* cxlix p. 1375 Durandus does not exhibit so accurate a knowledge of the opinions of the Berengarians as Witmund He regards them as simply affirming a figurative interpretation of the eucharist
[3] *l c* p. 1377 c 'quodque consequitur eorumdem sacramentorum corruptela'

fideliter atque competenter acceptum, et in id quod iam ex parte erat ab eo quod adhuc visui subiacebat exteriori divinitus ex toto transformatum, sumentium quoque animas mentesque sanctificat[1].'

These discussions are very disagreeable; but I have thought it worth while to describe these tracts at some length, because, taken with the other writings against Berengar which remain to us from the eleventh century, they force us to bear in mind that, however much later scholastics may have refined the doctrine of transubstantiation, in its original form as held and pressed upon the 'heretics' it was of a plainly materialistic and superstitious character.

The influence of Berengar's teaching did not rapidly pass away[2]. The writers of the earlier part of the twelfth century are still occupying themselves with the doctrine of transubstantiation. Thus Alger, a canon and scholastic of Liege who died about 1130, wrote a work *de Sacramentis Corporis et Sanguinis Dominici* [3], which obtained so great a reputation that it was said by Peter the Venerable 'to leave nothing for even the most scrupulous reader even to desire.' It is closely akin to Witmund's work. The doctrine of transubstantiation is so fully held as a physical miracle[4], producing a local[5] presence of Christ, that that which is on the altar can only be called a *sacra-*

---

[1] *l c* p 1379 b, cf 1382 a 'nimis videtur absurdum et a re ipsa decernitur alienum ut, ubi Christus percipitur, de stercore cogitetur'

[2] See the quotation from Zacharias, perhaps of Besançon, c 1157, in Gieseler, *Eccl. Hist* iii p 313

[3] Recently reprinted in *SS Patr Opusc Sel* vol xxiii; see p 55.

[4] 1. 8 (50) 'non solum pro sacramento sed et pro miraculo'

[5] *Prol.* (3).

Transubstantiation and Nihilianism. 265

ment of Christ, in the sense that Christ there hidden under the accidents of a vanished substance is a sacrament of Christ unveiled in heaven [1]. Like Witmund, he denies that the consecrated species are corruptible or the subjects of digestion, and thinks that the consideration that only *moral* evil is in God's sight impure, coupled with the consideration of possible angelic interpositions, prevents a Catholic from feeling a difficulty about the accidents which may befal the sacred species in being devoured by animals [2].

Perhaps a few years later Gregory of Bergamo, under the stress of a revival of Berengarianism, wrote his *Tractatus de Veritate Corporis Christi* [3]. This little book is interesting because in it we have what appears to be the first explicit enumeration of the sacraments as seven. Hitherto the sacraments had been commonly reckoned as three, viz. baptism, chrism, and the eucharist. These now rank as chief, and among them baptism and the eucharist are pre-eminent as ordained by Christ Himself,

---

[1] 1 18 (122-6)

[2] See 11 1 (4) 'Sed et cum de ceteris sacramentalibus speciebus, columba scilicet et igne in quibus sanctus Spiritus apparuit, Augustinus contra Maximinum dicat quia corporales illae species, peracto significationis officio, transierunt et esse ulterius destiterunt, nihil indignius de his corporalibus speciebus quae Christi contegunt corpus est sentiendum.' (14) 'Non solum corpori Christi sed et ipsi sacramento visibili eadem causa mucorem negamus et putredinem, qua superius digestionem, quia cum illae species sine panis et vini substantia sint, quomodo mucescere et putrescere magis quam digeri possint, non facilis patet causa' (15) 'Cum enim praeter peccatum creatori, qui ubique est, omnia munda sint, quomodo videtur immundius esse in ventre muris quam in ventre adulteri impoenitentis?' (13) 'Sic est alia multa in hoc spirituali sacramento invisibiliter fieri credenda sunt angelico ministerio'

[3] This tract, printed for the first time in 1877, is to be found in *SS. Patr. Opusc Sel* xxxix.

while four other 'older' sacraments are added to the list, viz. ordination, marriage, holy Scripture, and the taking an oath[1]. Again Gregory emphasizes the distinction of the *res* from the *virtus sacramenti* in baptism no less than in the eucharist, the *res* being the 'thing signified,' i e in baptism the death, burial, and resurrection of Jesus Christ When he comes to apply this to the eucharist, significantly enough he makes the outward part, or *sacramentum*, to be the body and blood of Christ present in virtue of transubstantiation and the *res* to be the mystical body the Church[2]. In the *Brevis Tractatus* of Hildebert (finally Metropolitan of Tours) *de Sacramento Altaris*[3] of about the same date the doctrine of transubstantiation is scholastically defined, but—possibly because he had been at one time Berengar's pupil—the effort after spirituality of conception is much more noticeable. The eucharist is said to be 'the food of the inner man ; not human, but divine, entering spiritually and divinely into the spirit , not converting

[1] c 13 'haec numero adimplentur septenario' 14 'Tria siquidem in ecclesia gerimus sacramenta quae sacramentis aliis putantur non immerito digniora, scilicet baptismum, chrisma, corpus et sanguis Domini Quorum trium primum et ultimum ex ipsius Redemptoris institutione percepimus, ex apostolica vero traditione illud quod medium posuimus Sunt praeterea quaedam alia quae videntur velut antiquiora sacramenta, videlicet sacerdotis ordinatio, legitimum coniugium, sacramenta quandoque dicuntur scripturarum et iusiurandi sacramentum.'

[2] c 18 'Apparet ergo corpus et sanguinem Salvatoris sacramentum rite exsistere, non tantum per id solum quod interius veraciter esse creditur, sed per exteriorem panis vinique speciem quae cernentium oculis repraesentantur'

[3] *SS Patr Opusc Sel.* xxxix p 274 f. He is perhaps the first to affirm that the entire Christ is in either *species* taken by itself *de Coena Dom P L* clxxi p 535 'in acceptione sanguinis totum Christum, verum Deum et hominem, et in acceptione corporis similiter totum ' Cf. Anselm, *Epp* iv. 107, *P. L.* clix. p 255

itself into spirit, but feeding the spirit in a spiritual and divine manner, entering spiritually, operating spiritually, coming by a spiritual way from heaven and by a spiritual way returning thither [1].' The body of Christ is 'in one place only after a bodily manner, in many places after a spiritual manner. For it is not of a body to be in many places at once [2].'

The same tendency to shrink from the more materialistic statement of transubstantiation is apparent in the great work—the *Books of the Sentences* of Peter Lombard, dating from about the middle of the twelfth century. He repudiates the actual fraction of the body of Christ in the sacrament, as asserted in Berengar's confession and admitted by Witmund and other opponents of his doctrine. Nor will he admit, with Abelard, a fraction which is in appearance only and not in reality. He decides that the more probable opinion is that there is a real fraction of the species of bread, i.e. in other words, he attributes more reality to the bread, at least so much substantiality as admits of its being broken without the heavenly substance being involved in it [3]. This is the doctrine which prevails in later theology [4]. Again, Peter Lombard refuses to decide whether the

[1] c 1   [2] c 2
[3] lib iv dist 12. So St. Anselm before him had said (*l c* p 256) 'Secundum speciem remanentem quaedam ibi fiunt quae nullo modo secundum hoc quod est possunt fieri, scilicet quod attentur, quod uno loco concluditur et a soricibus roditur et in ventrem traicitur'
[4] See St Thomas Aquinas, *Summa*, p. iii qu 77 art 7 He also holds that the species can be corrupted (art 4), and can nourish (art 6) : and this is the Tridentine doctrine See the *Catechism* of the Council, part ii, de Eucharistia, qu. 64, where one reason given for withholding the chalice from the laity is that the *species* of wine, if reserved for the sick, might go sour.

conversion of the elements into the body and blood of Christ is 'substantial' or of some other kind [1]. In both these respects and in his avoidance of other disagreeable decisions [2] he exhibits an appreciable withdrawal from the extreme materialism of the older writers.

Beyond this point the matter shall not be pursued. The fourth Lateran Council of 1215—reckoned the twelfth ecumenical—defined the dogma in regard to the eucharist as follows:

'Una vero est fidelium universalis ecclesia, extra quam nullus omnino salvatur In qua idem ipse sacerdos et sacrificium Iesus Christus · cuius corpus et sanguis in sacramento altaris sub speciebus panis et vini veraciter continentur; transubstantiatis [3] pane in corpus et vino in sanguinem potestate divina, ut ad perficiendum mysterium unitatis accipiamus ipsi de suo quod accipit ipse de nostro Et hoc utique sacramentum nemo potest conficere nisi sacerdos, qui rite fuerit ordinatus secundum claves ecclesiae, quas ipse concessit apostolis et eorum successoribus Iesus Christus [4].'

[1] *l c* dist. 11.

[2] 'Illud etiam sane dici potest quod a brutis animalibus corpus Christi non sumitur, etsi videatur. Quid ergo sumit mus vel quid manducat? Deus novit hoc' (dist 13)

[3] The word 'transubstantiare' is first, apparently, found in Stephen of Autun (c A D 1112-1139) *Tract de Sacr Altaris*, c 14 (*P L.* clxxii p 1293)

[4] Mansi, *Concil* xxii p 982.

II

The metaphysical theory and philosophical principle involved.

We have traced the history of the development of the dogma of transubstantiation. Taking it in its more refined form as now accepted in the Roman Church, it is open to three overwhelming objections·

1. There is nothing to justify it, as distinguished from any other doctrine of the real presence, in the original Christian tradition or in the New Testament.

2. It is involved in tremendous metaphysical difficulties.

3 It is contrary to the principle of the Incarnation—that is, to the principle of Christian theology.

1. The first objection is supremely important. To state the case mildly—there is no idea or doctrine of the New Testament or of original Christianity, which requires the dogma of the annihilation of the natural *species* in the eucharist in order to protect it And this fact at once distinguishes this dogma from such a dogma as that of the *homoousion*. On the other hand there is language in the New Testament—such as the repeated use of the term 'bread' of the consecrated element in 1 Cor. xi. 26-28—which is repugnant to it. But without

here trespassing further upon the consideration of New Testament doctrine, I propose somewhat to develop the two last specified objections to the dogma of transubstantiation

2. Metaphysically it is involved in tremendous difficulties Let us take it as it is stated by a Roman writer of deserved repute in his own communion, the Jesuit Lessius, in his celebrated work *de Perfectionibus Moribusque Divinis*[1]. He finds that it involves twelve special 'miracles,' using the word in its proper sense, for he says 'quantum fieri potest, Deus causis utitur iam constitutis et ad miracula quasi invitus descendit' Of these the first is the destruction of the natural substances of bread and wine: the second is the reproduction and restoration of the same substances at the moment when, the process of digestion beginning, the divine presence is withdrawn and the former substances recur, though now in a condition of being digested the third is the existence, in the interval during which the divine presence exists, of accidents inhering in no substance. Other miracles are found in the fact that these substance-less accidents can be acted upon and act physically as if they were really existent bread and wine Enough what an appalling burden of irrational metaphysics to lay upon the Christian conscience!

Lessius glories in these miracles; other Roman Catholic writers may withdraw them into the background. But none can get rid of the fact that the doctrine of transubstantiation (i) postulates the existence of a 'substance' in each object distinct from all the

[1] lib xii c 16

Transubstantiation and Nihilianism. 271

qualities by which it can make itself known—an hypothesis of which there could be no proof short of divine revelation, and which human thought has quite outgrown (ii) postulates the annihilation of these unknowable substances of bread and wine at a specified moment —again altogether without evidence as the annihilation is not supposed to make any ascertainable difference in the objects · (iii) granted the existence of substances as distinct from attributes, postulates a series of gratuitous miracles in the relations of the one to the other.

And I must notice in passing that the materialistic conception of the sacrament, involved at best in the transubstantiation idea, has resulted in the doctrine, mentioned by Lessius and apparently universally accepted in the Roman Church [1], that the divine gift given in this sacrament is only *temporary*. It is withdrawn as soon as the species begins to be digested It is not a gift of permanent and spiritual divine inhabitation but a brief divine visit. 'This day' (so it is expressed devotionally) my Lord

> 'Came to my lowly tenement
> And stayed *a while* with me'

This doctrine is the direct result of the materialism involved in transubstantiation, and is contrary to the original and Christian idea that he that eateth Christ s flesh and drinketh His blood has life in himself,' 'eternal

---

[1] Cf. J. Perrone, S J, *Praelectiones Theologicae* (Turin, 1866), de Euchar § 151, vol viii p 146 ' Etenim cum species eo devenerint ut corpus sive materia dissolvi seu corrumpi deberet, cessante reali corporis Christi praesentia, Deus omnipotentia sua iterum pioducit materialem panis aut vini substantiam in eo statu quo naturaliter inveniretur si conversio nulla praecessisset '

life,' 'abides' in Christ and Christ in him, 'lives for ever' on account of the life of Christ the 'living bread[1].'

Moreover, it cannot be too emphatically stated that the dogma of transubstantiation involves the Church in the acceptance of a particular metaphysical theory in a sense in which the *homoousion* dogma does not. The word *ousia* ('substance,' 'essence,' or 'being') may be said to be metaphysical, but it represents an idea necessarily common to all metaphysical, and indeed to all human, thought. You must have some word to express that in virtue of which anything is called what it is called, or is what it is—its 'being.' And the *homoousion* dogma says no more than that the 'being' of the Son is identical with the being of the Father, that in whatever sense the Father is God the Son is also God. We could not express it better to-day. Such phrases as 'being' and 'person' may be called metaphysical, but they belong to universal metaphysics. On the other hand, when you distinguish 'substance' or 'being' from 'accidents' or 'qualities' in each object, and postulate a separation of the two elements, you are using the terms of a particular metaphysical theory alien to common thought and transitory even in the metaphysical schools. All men at all times recognize the fact of grades and kinds of being. Only a few philosophers at special periods have imagined that the being of a thing is something distinct from the sum of its qualities, and they could hardly get a hearing in the philosophical world to-day.

3. But it is an even more important objection that

[1] St John vi. 53-59 [R V].

Transubstantiation and Nihilianism. 273

this theory violates a central principle of Christian theology, viz. that the supernatural does not annihilate the natural.

This principle received full attention when Gnosticism, in different forms, frankly repudiated it Gnostic teachers could accept no incarnation, because they could not allow the thought that the Supreme could actually be united to a material and natural body. In different ways, for a similar reason, they repudiated the material ordinances of Christianity as vehicles of grace. Irenaeus says of some of them [1] that 'in deprecation of all these [sacramental ordinances] they say that the mystery of the ineffable and invisible power ought not to be accomplished through visible and corruptible creatures and (the mystery) of the inconceivable and incorporeal through sensible and corporeal things ; but that perfect redemption is simply the knowledge of the ineffable Greatness'

In opposition to Gnosticism Irenaeus emphasizes the Christian principle that all things are of one substance · that there is no antagonism between the spiritual and the material or 'the supernatural' (as we call it) and the natural. Christ took a real human body just as He gives us His grace through real material substances.

'Our opinion is consonant with the eucharist and the eucharist confirms our opinion For we offer to Him what are His own creatures, announcing harmoniously

---

[1] *con Haer.* 1 21. 4 ἄλλοι δὲ ταῦτα πάντα παραιτησάμενοι φάσκουσι μὴ δεῖν τὸ τῆς ἀρρήτου καὶ ἀοράτου δυνάμεως μυστήριον δι' ὁρατῶν καὶ φθαρτῶν ἐπιτελεῖσθαι κτισμάτων, καὶ τῶν ἀνεννοήτων καὶ ἀσωμάτων δι' αἰσθητῶν καὶ σωματικῶν εἶναι δὲ τελείαν ἀπολύτρωσιν αὐτὴν τὴν ἐπίγνωσιν τοῦ ἀρρήτου μεγέθους

T

the fellowship and unity, and confessing [as a consequence] the resurrection, of flesh and of spirit. For as bread of the earth receiving upon it the evocation of God is no longer common bread but eucharist, made up of two things, an earthly and a heavenly; so also our bodies receiving the eucharist are no longer corruptible, having the hope of the eternal resurrection [1].'

The same principle was again in evidence at the period of controversy with the different forms of Monophysitism from Chalcedon downwards. Again and again in that controversy the doctrine of the Incarnation, the doctrine that the divine (or supernatural) does not destroy or absorb the human (or natural), was, so to speak, proved by the eucharist, the earthly elements of bread and wine being dignified, but not annihilated, by the spiritual presence of which they are made the vehicle. This argument is used by the author, said to be St. Chrysostom, of the letter to Caesarius [2],

---

[1] *con Haer* iv 18 5 προσφέρομεν δὲ αὐτῷ τὰ ἴδια, ἐμμελῶς κοινωνίαν καὶ ἕνωσιν ἀπαγγέλλοντες καὶ ὁμολογοῦντες σαρκὸς καὶ πνεύματος ἔγερσιν. ὡς γὰρ ἀπὸ γῆς ἄρτος προσλαμβανόμενος τὴν ἔκκλησιν τοῦ θεοῦ οὐκέτι κοινὸς ἄρτος ἐστίν, ἀλλ' εὐχαριστία, ἐκ δύο πραγμάτων συνεστηκυῖα, ἐπιγείου τε καὶ οὐρανίου οὕτως καὶ τὰ σώματα ἡμῶν μεταλαμβάνοντα τῆς εὐχαριστίας, μηκέτι εἶναι φθαρτά, τὴν ἐλπίδα τῆς εἰς αἰῶνας ἀναστάσεως ἔχοντα The same principle was, as is well known, emphasized by Tertullian both as regards Christ's person and the sacraments cf appended note D

[2] ap Routh, *Script Eccl Opusc.* (Oxford, 1858) ii. p 127 'Unus Filius, unus Dominus, idem ipse proculdubio unitarum naturarum unam dominationem, unam potestatem possidens, etiamsi non consubstantiales exsistunt, et unaquaeque incommixtam [incommixta *Petrus Martyr*] proprietatis conservat agnitionem, propter hoc quod inconfusa sunt duo Sicut enim antequam sanctificetur panis, panem nominamus, divina autem illum sanctificante gratia mediante sacerdote liberatus est quidem appellatione panis, dignus autem habitus est dominici corporis appellatione, etiamsi natura panis in ipso permansit, et non duo corpora, sed unum corpus Filii praedicatur.' The fragment (the history of which is given in *Dict. of Chr.*

Transubstantiation and Nihilianism. 275

by Theodoret[1], by Gelasius[2], by Augustine as represented in a 'sentence' of Prosper[3], by Ephraim, bishop

Biog s v. CAESARIUS) belongs, we can hardly doubt, to the *Epistle to Caesarius* (of uncertain authorship) of which another part is given in Migne, *Chrysost Opera*, P G lxiv p 494 There can be little doubt that the reason why some strong patristic passages against transubstantiation have but little ms. evidence for their genuineness is because mediaeval copyists did their best to obliterate them As we have seen an Ambrosian passage had been altered before Lanfranc's time (see p 230 n.). Such passages are not at all likely to have been forged in mediaeval times.

[1] *Dial* ii *Inconfusus*, p. 126 (ed Schultze, see also in Routh, *l c* p 132) ERANISTES ὥσπερ τοίνυν τὰ σύμβολα τοῦ δεσποτικοῦ σώματός τε καὶ αἵματος, ἄλλα μέν εἰσι πρὸ τῆς ἱερατικῆς ἐπικλήσεως, μετὰ δέ γε τὴν ἐπίκλησιν μεταβάλλεται καὶ ἕτερα γίνεται οὕτω τὸ δεσποτικὸν σῶμα μετὰ τὴν ἀνάληψιν εἰς τὴν οὐσίαν μετεβλήθη τὴν θείαν ORTHODOXUS ἑάλως αἷς ὕφηνες ἄρκυσιν οὐδὲ γὰρ μετὰ τὸν ἁγιασμὸν τὰ μυστικὰ σύμβολα τῆς οἰκείας ἐξίσταται φύσεως μένει γὰρ ἐπὶ τῆς προτέρας οὐσίας καὶ τοῦ σχήματος καὶ τοῦ εἴδους, καὶ ὁρατά ἐστι καὶ ἁπτά, οἷα καὶ πρότερον ἦν, νοεῖται δὲ ἅπερ ἐγένετο καὶ πιστεύεται καὶ προσκυνεῖται, ὡς ἐκεῖνα ὄντα ἅπερ πιστεύεται παράθες τοίνυν τῷ ἀρχετύπῳ τὴν εἰκόνα, καὶ ὄψει τὴν ὁμοιότητα χρὴ γὰρ ἐοικέναι τῇ ἀληθείᾳ τὸν τύπον καὶ γὰρ ἐκεῖνο τὸ σῶμα τὸ μὲν πρότερον εἶδος ἔχει καὶ σχῆμα καὶ περιγραφὴν καί, ἁπαξαπλῶς εἰπεῖν, τὴν τοῦ σώματος οὐσίαν ἀθάνατον δὲ μετὰ τὴν ἀνάστασιν γέγονε καὶ κρεῖττον φθορᾶς καὶ τῆς ἐκ δεξιῶν ἠξιώθη καθέδρας καὶ παρὰ πάσης προσκυνεῖται τῆς κτίσεως, ἅτε δὴ σῶμα χρηματίζον τοῦ δεσπότου τῆς φύσεως

[2] Gelasius, *de Duab Nat in Chr adv Eutych et Nest* 'Certe sacramenta quae sumimus corporis et sanguinis Christi divina res est, propter quod et per eadem divinae efficimur consortes naturae, et tamen esse non desinit substantia vel natura panis et vini Et certe imago et similitudo corporis et sanguinis Christi in actione mysteriorum celebrantur Satis ergo nobis evidenter ostenditur, hoc nobis in ipso Christo domino sentiendum quod in eius imagine profitemur, celebramus, et sumimus, ut, sicut in hanc scilicet in divinam transeunt sancto Spiritu perficiente substantiam, permanente [? permanentia] tamen in suae proprietate naturae, sic illud ipsum mysterium principale, cuius nobis efficientiam virtutemque veraciter repraesentant ex [? his ex] quibus constat proprie permanentibus, unum Christum, quia integrum verumque, permanere demonstrant' (Routh, *l c* p 139) On the authenticity of this passage see *Dict of Ch Biog* ii p 620, s v GELASIUS.

[3] Quoted in Alger, *de Sacr Corp et Sang Dominici* (see above, p 264) i 6 as a 'similitudo beati Augustini in libro sententiarum Prosperi' 'sacrificium ecclesiae duobus confici duobusque constare, sicut persona Christi constat et conficitur ex Deo et homine.' It does not exist in our copies of Prosper's sentences, but may well be genuine.

of 'Theopolis' (Antioch)[1], and as nearly as he dared —so nearly that Bellarmine called him heretical—by Rupert of Deutz[2]. These writers (with the possible exception of the last) unmistakeably declare that the 'nature' or 'substance' of the bread and wine remain after consecration.

The principle which this theology both of the Incarnation and of the eucharist illustrates is admirably stated by the best theologian of the sixth century, Leontius of Byzantium[3].

---

[1] Quoted in Photius, *Bibliotheca* cod 229 (*P G* cii p 980), from his work against Nestorius and Eutyches He argues for the unconfused reality of Christ's manhood and continues οὕτω καὶ τὸ παρὰ τῶν πιστῶν λαμβανόμενον σῶμα Χριστοῦ καὶ τῆς αἰσθητῆς οὐσίας οὐκ ἐξίσταται καὶ τῆς νοητῆς ἀδιαίρετον μένει χάριτος καὶ τὸ βάπτισμα δὲ πνευματικόν, ὅλον γενόμενον καὶ ἐν ὑπάρχον, καὶ τὸ ἴδιον τῆς αἰσθητῆς οὐσίας, τοῦ ὕδατος λέγω, διασώζει, καὶ ὃ γέγονεν, οὐκ ἀπώλεσεν. See also in Routh *l c.* p. 143

[2] Quoted in Gieseler, *Eccl Hist* iii 314 Totum attribuetis operationi Spiritus sancti, cuius effectus non est destruere vel corrumpere substantiam, cuiuscumque suos in usus assumit, sed substantiae bono permanenti quod erat invisibiliter adicere quod non erat Sicut naturam humanam non destruxit, cum illam operatione sua ex utero virginis Deus Verbo in unitatem personae coniunxit sic substantiam panis et vini, secundum exteriorem speciem quinque sensibus subiectam, non mutat aut destruit, cum eidem Verbo in unitatem corporis eiusdem, quod in cruce pependit, et sanguinis eiusdem, quem de latere suo fudit, ista coniungit Item quomodo Verbum a summo demissum caro factum est, non mutatum in carnem, sed assumendo carnem sic panis et vinum, utrumque ab imo sublevatum, fit corpus Christi et sanguis, non mutatum in carnis saporem sive in sanguinis horrorem sed assumendo invisibiliter utriusque, divinae scilicet et humanae, quae in Christo est immortalis substantiae veritatem' (*P.L* clxvii p 617-8)

[3] *con. Nest et Eut.* ii (*P G* lxxxvi p 1333) καὶ τοῦτο δὲ μὴ καταλείψωμεν ἀπαρασήμαντον, ὅτι τριῶν αἰτιῶν θεωρουμένων, ἐξ ὧν πᾶσα ἀποτελεῖται ἐνέργεια ἡ μὲν γάρ ἐστιν ἐκ φυσικῆς δυνάμεως, ἡ δὲ ἐκ παρατροπῆς τῆς κατὰ φύσιν ἕξεως, ἡ δὲ ἑτέρα θεωρεῖται κατὰ τὴν πρὸς τὸ κρεῖττον ἀνάβασίν τε καὶ πρόοδον τούτων ἡ μὲν φυσική, ἡ δὲ παρὰ φύσιν, ἡ δὲ ὑπὲρ φύσιν ἐστὶ καὶ ὀνομάζεται ἡ μὲν οὖν παρὰ φύσιν, κατ' αὐτό γε τὸ ὄνομα, ἀποπτωσίς τις οὖσα τῶν φυσικῶν ἕξεων καὶ δυνάμεων, λυμαίνεται τῇ τε οὐσίᾳ αὐτῇ καὶ ταῖς ταύτης φυσικαῖς ἐνεργείαις ἡ δὲ φυσικὴ ἐκ τῆς ἀπαραποδίστου καὶ κατὰ φύσιν

'Let us not,' he says, 'leave it unnoticed that every sort of energy results from one of three distinguishable causes one sort of energy proceeds from natural power; another from the perversion of the natural habit; the third represents an elevation or advance of the nature towards what is higher. Of these the first is and is called natural, the second unnatural; the third supernatural. Now the unnatural, as its name implies, being a falling away from natural habits and powers, injures both the substance itself and its natural energies The natural proceeds from the unimpeded and naturally cogent cause. But the supernatural leads up and elevates the natural energy and empowers it for actions of a more perfect order, which it would not have been able to accomplish so long as it remained within the limits of its own nature. The supernatural therefore does not destroy the natural, but educes and stimulates it both to do its own business and to acquire the power for what is above it.' He exemplifies this principle by the way in which art, without destroying its natural material, elevates it, whether in music or mechanics, to higher 'supernatural' uses. And he applies it to our Lord's humanity to emphasize that its natural laws remained unimpeded and unaltered by its supernatural union with the Godhead. 'The supernatural,' he concludes, 'implies the permanence of the natural. The very possibility of a miracle is gone if the natural is overthrown by what

ἐρηρεισμένης ἀποτελεῖται αἰτίας ἡ δὲ ὑπὲρ φύσιν ἀνάγει τε καὶ ὑψοῖ καὶ πρὸς τὰ τελειότερα δυναμοῖ καὶ ἅπερ οὐκ ἂν ἴσχυσεν ἐνεργεῖν τοῖς κατὰ φύσιν ἐναπομείνασα οὐκ ἔστιν οὖν τὰ ὑπὲρ φύσιν τῶν κατὰ φύσιν ἀναιρετικά, ἀλλα παράγωγα καὶ παρορμητικά, εἰς τὸ κἀκεῖνά τε δυνηθῆναι καὶ τὴν πρὸς τὰ ὑπὲρ ταῦτα δύναμιν προσλαβεῖν. . οὐδὲ γὰρ τὰ ὑπὲρ φύσιν ἔχει χώραν, μὴ τῆς φύσεως ἐχούσης κατὰ φύσιν ἀφῄρηται δὲ καὶ τὸ εἶναι θαῦμα, τῷ ὑπὲρ φύσιν· τῆς φύσεως μεταστάσης, καὶ γίνεται ὕβρις ἡ φιλοτιμία τυραννήσασα τὴν ἀλήθειαν

is supernatural, and pride when it tyrannizes over the truth of nature deserves the name of insolence.'

This great Christian principle the transubstantiation dogma fundamentally violates. Its supporters have (as has appeared above) often exulted in declaring that the eucharistic miracle is against nature, and, both in ancient and modern times, they have been driven to admit implicitly or explicitly, that the analogy of the Incarnation and the sacrament in one important respect—that in which the fathers of Chalcedon made so much of it—fails to maintain itself[1]. Thus Lessius[2], for example, in drawing out seven analogies of the eucharist with the Incarnation, significantly leaves out that one of which the fathers made chief mention. But the sacraments are the 'extension of the Incarnation': they exhibit the same principles of divine action. And it is an argument of the most serious weight against a theory which is intended to explain one of the sacraments, that it has against it all the analogy of its great prototype.

[1] Thus in mediaeval times Georgius Scholarius (quoted in Lequien's edition of John of Damascus, 1 p 270) says that the eucharist is the greatest of all miracles, because while in Christ's person the higher nature does not destroy the lower, here it does. Hugo a S Victore, *de Sacr* ii 8, 9 (*P. L.* clxxvi p 468), writes 'conversio ipsa non secundum unionem sed secundum transitionem credenda est'

[2] *l c* § 129 Perrone also deals most unsatisfactorily with the matter see *l c.* §§ 143-5.

III.

Nihilianism the background of the theory of transubstantiation.

We now approach the question why the analogy of the incarnation doctrine—embodied as it was in dogmas which guarded the substantial reality and permanence of our Lord s manhood—did not prove a bar to the development and establishment of the doctrine of transubstantiation. The answer to the question is not far to seek Throughout the period during which the doctrine of transubstantiation was in controversy, the reality of our Lord's manhood, and the principle of the Incarnation which its reality expresses, were very inadequately held The dogmas were indeed retained but their meaning was little considered. What has been already described as nihilianism was the current mode of conceiving the Incarnation . that is to say, the manhood of Christ was regarded almost exclusively as the veil of Godhead or as the channel of its communication. These are indeed the only points of view from which the Incarnation need be regarded in order to supply a background for the authority of revealed doctrine and the reality of sacramental grace. But the aspect of the manhood of Christ on which stress is laid in the Gospels—the reality of His human example, human temptation, human struggles, human limitations — this was very little considered.

As a consequence, the principle which this aspect of the Incarnation brings into relief—the principle that the divine and the supernatural does not overthrow or obliterate the human and the natural—was little emphasized, and it failed accordingly to present the obstacle which it should have presented to the development of the dogma of transubstantiation

The prevalence of nihilianism (as explained above) in the early mediaeval period is not disputable. We have already[1] traced its influence in the west from its source in Apollinarius' teaching through the quasi-monophysitism of 'Dionysius' and his translator, Scotus Erigena. It unfortunately found support in a passage of Augustine himself, who was the accepted standard of orthodoxy. Augustine, commenting on the Latin of Phil. ii. 7 *habitu inventus est ut homo*, had, as has already appeared, glossed the passage with the words 'habendo hominem inventus est ut homo non sibi sed eis quibus in homine apparuit'—thus apparently making the humanity not something into the experience of which the Son really entered, but a mere mode of manifestation This quotation from Augustine became a commonplace and coalesced with Monophysite influences. Thus it appears in Albinus Flaccus[2] and Rabanus Maurus[3], and we have already seen how it was quoted by the Master of the Sentences. To appreciate the extent to

---

[1] See above, pp 171-9

[2] *adv Felicem*, ii 12 (*P L.* ci p 156) Alcuin is also responsible for such perilous phrases as 'homo *transivit* in Deum' (*de Fid S Trin* iii 9, p 44), 'persona *perit* hominis non natura' (*adv. Felic* ii. 12, p 156)

[3] *P L* cxii p 489 It is a stock quotation in commentaries on the Philippians.

Transubstantiation and Nihilianism. 281

which nihilianism prevailed, it is necessary to look through the theology of the period more or less in bulk. Such a simple phrase as this of Gregory of Bergamo—true but manifestly one-sided—expresses the current way of thinking about Christ, 'Caro videbatur et Deus credebatur [1].'

The connexion of this phase of thought with transubstantiation is not hard to see. Apollinarius' doctrine was in fact transubstantiation in regard to the manhood of Christ. He loved to speak not of the 'hypostatic' but of the 'substantial' unity of the humanity with the Godhead, that is, its unity in one substance or nature [2]. Scotus Erigena protests against the phraseology of popular orthodoxy in speaking of 'two substances' in Christ. He is two natures, no doubt, but in *one substance* [3] 'Christus in unitate humanae et divinae sub-

---

[1] *l c.* § 11
[2] See quotations in Leontius, *l c*, *P G* lxxxvi 1964 d ζωοποιεῖ δὲ ἡμᾶς ἡ σὰρξ αὐτοῦ διὰ τὴν συνουσιωμένην αὐτῇ θεότητα τὸ δὲ ζωοποιὸν θεικόν θεικὴ ἄρα σάρξ, ὅτι θεῷ συνήφθη ὁμοούσιον αὐτῷ . οὐκ ἄρα ὁμοούσιον ἀνθρωπίνῳ τὸ θεῖον p 1957 a φύσις γὰρ καὶ οὐσία ταυτόν ἐστιν Cf the famous phrase adopted by Cyril from Apollinarius μία φύσις τοῦ θεοῦ λόγου σεσαρκωμένη (vid supr p 153)
[3] Joh Scotus, *de Div Nat P L* cxxii p 1018 Commenting on St Matt vii 21-2 *Domine, Domine,* he suggests that this 'geminatio dominici nominis' may be intended to represent the state of the indolently orthodox who speak of 'two substances' in Christ: 'vel certo simplicium fidelium minus catholicae fidei altitudinem considerantium ignaviam significat, putantes Dominum nostrum Iesum Christum duabus substantiis esse compositum, dum sit una substantia in duabus naturis Quanti sunt qui Dominum Iesum Christum ita segregant, ut neque divinitatem illius humanitati neque humanitatem divinitati in unitatem substantiae, seu ut latini usitatius dicunt in unitatem personae adunatam vel credant vel intelligant, cum ipsius humanitas et divinitas unum et inseparabile unum sint, salva utriusque naturae ipsius ratione' The 'ratio' of the humanity remains though the humanity itself is frequently spoken of as 'translata' or 'transmutata in Deum', cf pp. 539 b, c, and 1015 c, d

stantiae ultra omne quod sensu sentitur corporeo super omne quod virtute percipitur intelligentiae Deus invisibilis in utraque sua natura.' Phrases of a Monophysite colour, like the 'divine and human substance' or the 'divine humanity and human divinity,' appear also in Florus and Witmund[1] Paschasius Radbert, even when retaining the orthodox language of two substances, speaks of the humanity of Christ (misinterpreting Heb. 1.3 *figura*, vel *character, substantiae eius*) as the figure or the character, that is letter of the alphabet, significative of the divine substance, and justifies thereby the position that the eucharistic bread may be called a figure of a divine reality and yet be itself really that of which it is a figure, as the manhood is no other thing than the divine person who assumed it[2].

Some of the writers who use this language are not adherents of transubstantiation. But in Paschasius Radbert, in Witmund, in Gregory of Bergamo, this way of regarding the Incarnation is in definite connexion with the theory of transubstantiation. Later on the affinity of the two theories is apparent in the pages of scholastic commentaries on the *Sentences* of Peter Lombard Nihilianism, as stated by Peter, had been already

---

[1] See Witmund, *l. c* ii 32 (*P L* cxlix p 1458) 'ex divina consistens et humana substantia' (I am not sure that he does not mean 'consist of the divine substance and of the human' But the subsequent sections are nihilianist in tone. See especially cc 38, 39) Florus *de Expos Miss* 34 (*P L.* cxix p 33) 'sed inter solam divinitatem et humanitatem solam mediatrix est humana divinitas et divina humanitas Christi'

[2] *l c* iv 2 (*P L* cxx p 1279) 'sic ex humanitate Christi ad divinitatem Patris pervenitur· et ideo iure figura vel character substantiae illius vocatur
verumtamen neque Christus homo falsitas dici potest neque aliud quam Deus licet figura id est character substantiae divinitatis iure dicatur'

Transubstantiation and Nihilianism.

condemned[1], but it is none the less commented upon, and it is treated as a view according to which the humanity is reduced to an accident of the divine substance. Thus Thomas Aquinas describes it in these words. 'Tertia opinio dicit animam et carnem accidentaliter personae Verbi advenire ut homini vestimentum.' Again, '[Tertia opinio ponit quod homo] praedicatur de Christo accidentaliter ... cum habitus sit genus accidentis, videtur quod Deus fuerit homini accidentaliter unitus.' This opinion is rejected on grounds of authority—Pope Alexander's condemnation —and of reason, but it is allowed, on the ground of the supposed comparison of the humanity to a robe in Phil ii. 7, that it 'habet aliquam similitudinem cum accidente ... unde antiqui dixerunt quod vergit in accidens; et quidam propter hoc addiderunt quod degenerat in accidens, quod tamen non ita proprie dicitur, quia natura humana in Christo non degenerat, imo magis nobilitatur[2].' A later Dominican schoolman, Durandus a S. Portiano (c 1318), concludes against nihilianism in these words: 'Relinquitur ergo quod sicut natura humana non transit in naturam accidentis sic non advenit accidentaliter per inhaerentiam personae divinae[3].'

It may now be said to have been sufficiently shown that transubstantiation in eucharistic doctrine is the analogue of nihilianism with regard to the Incarnation. The existing dogmas, so strongly guarding the substantiality of the manhood, stopped the progress of the

[1] See above, p. 177
[2] See Thom Aquin *in Quat Libr Sententt* lib iii dist vi exposition, and art 4
[3] *in Quat Libr Sententt* lib iii. dist vi art. 4

latter view, but there were no similar dogmas in the case of the former. Even before nihilianism was condemned the theory of transubstantiation had reached a position of acceptance, and it became a dogmatically required term very shortly after the condemnation of the theory which may be described as its elder sister.

But it may be said: Granted all this, yet if transubstantiation is a dogmatic term of the Latin Church, which has also been accepted by the Orthodox and Russian Churches of the east [1], and if the Latin schoolmen have abandoned the grossness of its original use, may we not in the interests of unity accept the phrase? To this pleading I should reply that it is quite true that it is possible to minimize the meaning of transubstantiation till it becomes practically compatible with an acceptance of the permanence of the natural elements in the ordinary sense of these terms, coupled with a denial of their permanence in a laboured metaphysical sense which is no longer in use among philosophical writers other than Roman Catholics Thus Cardinal Franzelin says: 'It is demonstrable, as well from the reason of the sacrament as from the clear teaching of the fathers, that that which in the most holy sacrament is the immediate object of the senses is something objectively real [2]:' and this sort of language may be pressed till transubstantiation is made to

---

[1] Macarius, *Théologie Dogmatique Orthodoxe* (Paris, 1860) §§ 215, 216. Cf *Transubstantiation and the Church of England*, by J B Wainewright (Mowbray, 1895), pp 22 ff Denny and Lacey, *de Hierarchia Anglicana* (Cambridge, 1895) §§ 185–6

[2] *Tract de SS. Euch Sacram et Sacrif*, thesis xvi 11. 9 1, p 273, as quoted by Wainewright, *l c* Cf. Einig, *Tract de SS Euch Myst* (Trier,

mean almost practically nothing. But as was indicated above, the mere fact that it must be concluded from the doctrine that the heavenly substances vanish when digestion begins and the old substances recur, is a sign that the real force of the doctrine cannot be finally evaded. Further, it can never be a satisfactory settlement to accept a phrase in a sense so unreal that you are not prepared to apply it anywhere else. Finally, to accept the phrase in regard to the eucharist is to abandon a great principle which runs through all theology—the principle that the supernatural does not annihilate and supersede the natural. This, as has been shown at length, is the principle of the Incarnation, and it was only the weakened hold of the principle in the sphere of Christology which accounts for its being denied in the sphere of the sacrament. This is the principle which the development of biblical criticism is forcing us to reassert in the region of the doctrine of inspiration, where it means that the supernatural action of the Holy Ghost does not destroy the natural action of human faculties or overthrow the natural processes of literary development. In the application again of Christianity to the sanctifying of human character we are for ever bound to insist that the human character in its most fundamental nature is meant to be developed, not overthrown by supernatural grace. Finally, all that science has gone to teach us about the divine action in creation compels us to emphasize the same principle: the respect which God

1888) p. 47 'species panis et vini sunt aliquid obiectivum reale.' This appears to go even beyond the language of Anselm, see p. 267 n. 3, for he continues after the passage there quoted 'ideo autem quod non est apparet et quod est celatur, quia si quod est videretur animus humanus abhorreret.'

286 *Dissertations.*

pays to the natural substances which express His own will in creation and are sustained by His own immanence. In every department of inquiry we are bound to use the phraseology which best expresses the principle which Leontius asserts for us, that 'the supernatural does not destroy the natural ¹.'

¹ See above, p 277.

ADDENDA

To pp. 19–21. When these pages were written I was ignorant of a paper by Dr. Theo. Zahn on *die Syrische Statthalterschaft und die Schatzung des Quirinius* (*Neue kirchliche Zeitschrift*, 1893, 8, pp. 633–654). It is now too late to discuss its somewhat surprising results. But it is desirable to call the attention of scholars to it Dr. Zahn impugns the trustworthiness of Josephus, denies the *later* governorship of Quirinius, asserts that he was governor of Syria only B.C 4 (3) to 2 (1), and at the beginning of this period, after not before the death of Herod, took the only census that was taken; and maintains that this census is referred to by St. Luke both in Luke ii 2, and Acts v. 37, though he antedates it by about a year.

To Dissertation II. At the last moment I cannot resist the temptation to insert the following illustration of the contrast between Origen's doctrine and Augustine's with regard to the reality of the *kenosis*. Both writers are, in view of St. Paul's language in Eph. v 22–23, interpreting of Christ's incarnation the words, 'A man shall leave his father and mother, &c' Origen writes thus (*in Matth.* tom xv. 17): καὶ καταλέλοιπέ γε διὰ τὴν ἐκκλησίαν κύριος ὁ ἀνὴρ πατέρα ὃν ἑώρα ὅτε ἐν μορφῇ θεοῦ ὑπῆρχεν. Augustine writes (see Prosper, *Sentent. lib.* 330; *P. L.* li. p 478) 'Reliquit Christus Patrem . . . non quia deseruit et recessit a Patre, sed quia non in ea forma apparuit hominibus in quo aequalis est Patri.'

APPENDED NOTES

A.

SUPPOSED JEWISH EXPECTATION OF THE VIRGIN BIRTH

IT was stated above (p. 35) that it does not appear that there was any Jewish expectation that Christ should be born of a virgin. This has been for many years an accepted position among scholars (see Stanton's *Jewish and Christian Messiah*, p. 377), but in the *Academy* of June 8, 1895, Mr Badham attempts to traverse it. He gives a list of Rabbinical passages in which this expectation is supposed to appear. But his quotations have a history. All those which have any real bearing on the subject are from Martini's *Pugio Fidei* (c. A.D. 1280) or from Vincenti's *Messia Venuto* (A.D. 1659). If we have not read these works we have read the quotations, or the most important of them, in the notes to Pearson *On the Creed* (Oxford 1877, p. 306) and elsewhere. They surprised us no doubt when we first read them, but we soon learnt, perhaps from a more recent editor of Pearson's work, that there is nothing corresponding to them in any existing printed texts or mss. of the Talmud. This Mr Badham admits in his letter. But what then is the use of quoting them? They may or may not be forgeries, but at least they cannot be quoted, for they are contrary to all that we know from other sources about Jewish beliefs. The passages to be quoted or referred to immediately from Justin, Tertullian and Jerome prove that the contemporary Jews interpreted *'almah* in Isaiah vii 14 as 'young woman,' that there was no existing expectation among them that the Christ should be born of a virgin, and no evidence of their ever having thought differently. Had there been any such evidence the Christians would have been eager to charge the Jews with having changed their minds. The lxx translates *'almah* as παρθένος in Isaiah vii as in Genesis xxiv. 43[1], but the word does not appear to have made any impression till it was read in the light of events by the early Christians.

The passages referred to are as follows Justin Martyr, *Dial.* 43. after citing Is. vii continues: ὅτι μὲν οὖν ἐν τῷ γένει τῷ κατὰ σάρκα τοῦ Ἀβραὰμ οὐδεὶς οὐδέποτε ἀπὸ παρθένου γεγέννηται οὐδὲ λέλεκται γεγεννημένος ἀλλ' ἢ οὗτος ὁ ἡμέτερος Χριστός, πᾶσι φανερόν ἐστιν. ἐπεὶ δὲ ὑμεῖς καὶ οἱ διδάσκαλοι ὑμῶν τολμᾶτε λέγειν μηδὲ εἰρῆσθαι ἐν τῇ προφητείᾳ τοῦ Ἡσαΐου Ἰδοὺ ἡ παρθένος ἐν γαστρὶ ἕξει, ἀλλ' Ἰδοὺ ἡ νεᾶνις ἐν γαστρὶ λήψεται καὶ τέξεται υἱόν, καὶ ἐξηγεῖσθε τὴν προφητείαν ὡς εἰς Ἐζεκίαν, τὸν γενόμενον ὑμῶν βασιλέα, πειράσομοι καὶ ἐν τούτῳ καθ' ὑμῶν βραχέα ἐξηγήσασθαι καὶ ἀποδεῖξαι εἰς τοῦτον εἰρῆσθαι τὸν ὁμολογούμενον ὑφ' ἡμῶν Χριστόν. This is repeated in cc. 66–7. Similar statements as to Jewish interpretation are to be found in Tertullian, *adv Jud.* 9 'mentiri audetis, quasi non virginem sed iuvenculam concepturam et parituram scriptura contineat,' cp. *adv Marcion.* iii 13; and Jerome, *adv Helvid.* 5, ii. p 209 (ed. Vallarsi).

Mr. F C Conybeare does not appear to have read Mr Badham's letter with much care. Writing in the *Academy* of June 15 he describes it as a 'letter on the prevalence among the ancient Jews of the belief that the Messiah was to be born of a virgin,' and alludes to the 'Rabbinic analogies' to pagan beliefs 'brought to light by Mr. Badham.' He clearly has not realized the antecedents of Mr. Badham's quotations Otherwise it is not the orthodox Christians whom he would have impugned so vigorously for 'special pleading' and refusal 'to look facts in the face' As it is he suggests that the belief among the Jews came 'through the Greeks and Egyptians,' and specially insists upon the parallel to the virgin birth of our Lord afforded by the Greek legend of the birth of Plato I have alluded to a similar belief in the case of Augustus (p. 55). It is to

---

[1] In two places in the *Song of Solomon* it is translated νεᾶνις

be noted, however, that none of the pagan authors cited by Mr. Conybeare refers to Plato as born of a virgin It is only Jerome who does this as in the similar case of the Buddha (see above, p. 58, note 2). The Greek legend represents Plato as born of the union of his mother Perictione with the phantasm of the god Apollo, the god appearing in a vision and a voice forbidding Ariston, her husband, to exercise his marital rights till the child was born. The following are the versions of Diogenes Laertius, Apuleius, and Jerome, referred to by Mr Conybeare·

Diogenes Laertius Σπεύσιππος δ' ἐν τῷ ἐπιγραφομένῳ Πλάτωνος περὶ δείπνου καὶ Κλέαρχος ἐν τῷ Πλάτωνος ἐγκωμίῳ καὶ 'Αναξιλίδης ἐν τῷ δευτέρῳ περὶ φιλοσόφων φασίν, ὡς 'Αθήνησιν ἦν λόγος ὡραίαν οὖσαν τὴν Περικτιόνην βιάζεσθαι τὸν 'Αρίστωνα, καὶ μὴ τυγχάνειν. παυόμενόν τε τῆς βίας ἰδεῖν τὴν τοῦ 'Απόλλωνος ὄψιν. ὅθεν καθαρὰν γάμου φυλάξαι, ἕως τῆς ἀποκυήσεως (*de vit phil* iii 2, p. 164, ed 1692).

Apuleius. 'Sunt qui Platonem augustiore conceptu prosatum, dicunt, cum quaedam Apollinis figuratio Perictione se miscuisset' (*de dogm Plat* 1. 1, ed Hildebrand ii. p. 173).

Jerome 'Speusippus quoque sororis Platonis filius et Clearchus in laude Platonis et Anaxilides in secundo libro philosophiae Perictionem, matrem Platonis, phantasmate Apollinis oppressam ferunt, et sapientiae principem non aliter arbitrantur nisi de partu virginis editum' (*adv. Jovin.* i. 42, Vall. ii. p 309)

I am sure that this conception of heroes as born from the union of gods and women is wholly alien to Jewish beliefs, and that there is no reason to believe that it exercised any influence on the Jews. Such a legendary conception had been introduced into Jewish literature only to be once for all put to death, see Gen. vi. 1–8.

That Jerome and Origen (see *con. Cels.* i 37) should have used these legends as an *argumentum ad hominem* with the heathen, and have even assimilated them to the Christian history, is by no means surprising.

B.

THE READINGS OF CODEX SINAITICUS.

THE *Codex Sinaiticus* referred to on p. 61 is the Syriac palimpsest of the four Gospels discovered by Mrs. Lewis in the Convent of St Catharine on Mount Sinai in February, 1892[1], and which has excited so much interest as giving us another and almost complete text of the *Syr Vet.*, which had hitherto lain before us only in the Curetonian fragments. The new Syriac text was published in Oct 1894 by the Cambridge University Press[2], and was followed in December of the same year by '*A Translation of the Four Gospels from the Syriac of the Sinaitic Palimpsest,* by Agnes Smith Lewis, M R A S '

This Codex is connected with the subject of Dissertation I by its new and interesting readings in St. Matt 1, as will appear if we extract the passage from Mrs. Lewis' translation.

St. Matt. i 16 *Jacob begat Joseph · Joseph, to whom was betrothed Mary the Virgin, begat Jesus, who is called the Christ. . .*

18 *And the birth of the Christ was on this wise · When Mary his mother was espoused to Joseph, when they had not come near one to the other, she was found with child of the Holy Ghost*

19 *Then Joseph her husband, because he was just, did not wish to*

20 *expose Mary, and was minded quietly to repudiate her. But while he thought on these things, the angel of the Lord appeared*

---

[1] See *How the Codex was found*, by Margaret Dunlop Gibson (Macmillan, 1893)

[2] *The Four Gospels in Syriac*. Transcribed from the Syriac palimpsest by the late Robert L Bensly, M A, and by J Rendel Harris, M.A., and by F Crawford Burkitt, M A. With an introduction by Agnes Smith Lewis. Cambridge, at the University Press, 1894.

Appended Notes. B. 293

to him in a vision and said unto him, Joseph, son of David, fear not to take Mary thy wife: for that which is begotten from
21 her is of the Holy Ghost   And she shall bear to thee a son, and thou[a] shalt call his name Jesus   for he shall save his people
22 from their sins   Now this which happened was that it might be fulfilled which was spoken of the Lord by Isaia the prophet,
23 who said, Behold a virgin shall be with child, and shall bring forth a son, and they shall call his name Emmanuel, which being
24 interpreted is, God with us   When Joseph arose from his sleep, he did as the angel of the Lord had commanded him, and
25 took his wife · and she bore to him a son, and he called his name Jesus

[a] Or she shall call

For the sake of fuller illustration it will be useful to subjoin the more significant variations of the Peshitta and Curetonian Syriac :—

	CUR.	PESH.
ver 16	Joseph, he to whom was espoused Mary the Virgin, she who bare Jesus the Christ	Joseph the husband of Mary from whom was begotten Jesus, who is called the Christ
19	Joseph (om. her husband)	Joseph her husband
20	Mary thy espoused	Mary thy wife
21	shall bear to thee	shall bear a son
	and his name shall be called	and thou shalt call his name
23	and his name shall be called	and they shall call his name
24	and took his wife	and took Mary
25	and lived purely with her until she bare the son and she called	and knew her not till she bare her firstborn son and she called.

The Greek text (W. H and Tisch) agrees with Pesh. except in ver 24 *his wife* (cur.) and 25 *a son* (for *her firstborn son*): ἐκάλεσεν in ver. 25 might possibly be ambiguous

In this passage the statements which arrest our attention, and which have in fact already given rise to a controversy in the

Academy[1], are these. *Joseph begat Jesus, she shall bear to thee a son, and he took his wife and she bore to him a son.* What are we to say of them? In endeavouring to discuss their meaning it will be very essential to distinguish between two questions

(i) What is their meaning in relation to our Lord's virgin birth, taken as they stand? and (ii)—a question really prior in fact—What is the value of the text of Cod. Sin., and of these readings in particular?

i.

At the first sight, the readings in question seem to give a naturalistic account of our Lord's birth, as if Joseph had been His father after the ordinary manner. But the scribe of Cod Sin. certainly did not hold such a view himself. For these readings are in juxtaposition with, or rather embedded in, a miraculous account of the birth, which agrees in all respects with the text we are familiar with. *Joseph begat Jesus*, but it was in an unusual sense, which the writer goes on to explain—*And* (=*But*, δέ) *the birth of the Christ was on this wise.* In St. Luke i there is a lacuna where the account of the annunciation should occur, and several words are obliterated at the beginning of the second chapter, but enough remains to show that there also the account of the birth is in practical agreement with the Greek text Further, significant phrases such as *the child with Mary his mother* (St. Matt. ii. 11, no mention being made of the father), and *take the child and his mother* (St Matt. ii. 13, 20, said to Joseph[2]) are left unaltered: while in St. Luke iii 23 we read *And Jesus, when he was about thirty years old, as he was called the son of Joseph*

---

[1] The letters began with one from Mr F C Conybeare on Nov 17, 1894.
[2] Not *take thy child*, or *thy wife and child*

Appended Notes. B.

In fact, apart from categoric statements about our Lord's birth, there are not wanting indications that our scribe held virginity in high esteem, and would lay proportionate stress on Mary's virginity. So

(a) He speaks of her as *Mary the Virgin* He does not write *to whom was betrothed a virgin, Mary* (like our Bible in St Luke 1 27, *to a virgin betrothed to a man ... and the virgin's name was Mary*), but *Mary the Virgin*, '*the* Virgin' as it were κατ' ἐξοχήν. Mr Conybeare [1], recognizing the expression as a kind of permanent title, supposes it to = 'the widow'; but a much more obvious explanation is to see in it the hand of one who held that Mary remained ever a virgin.

(β) The same theory, of belief in the perpetual virginity of Mary, also accounts most naturally for the omission of *knew her not until* in ver 25—the scribe shrinking from the ambiguity of the *until*.

(γ) He gives a solution of a difficulty which the fact of the virgin birth might raise If our Lord was not literally begotten of Joseph, and it is Joseph's genealogy which is given in Matt 1, how do we know that our Lord was in fact descended from David? Our scribe answers by writing in Luke 11. 5 *because they were both* [i. e Mary as well as Joseph] *of the house of David* [2]

---

[1] In the *Academy* of Nov 17, p 401
[2] According to Mr Burkitt (in the *Guardian*, Oct 31, 1894, p 1707) this reading is also that of Tatian's *Diatessaron*, it being one of the 'remarkable coincidences' between it and Cod Sin But it is not the reading of the Arabic version (Hamlyn Hill's trans, p 47). Ephraim, it is true, writes *alio loco eadem scriptura dixit utrumque, Iosephum et Mariam, esse ex domo David* (*Evang Concord Expos* ed Moesinger, p 16), but as it occurs in his comments on the annunciation, the *eadem* may justify Moesinger in referring it to 1 27, instead of 11. 4 It might indeed be Ephraim's own inference from the different utterances of scripture, as he is occupied in meeting the difficulty mentioned above. It is at times hard to know what is Tatian and what is Ephraim Thus on p 1708 Mr. Burkitt assumes that Tatian read *and cast him down* in St Luke iv 29. Ephraim certainly believed that the men of Nazareth did cast him down, for *insurrexerunt contra eum et apprehen-*

(δ) In St. Luke ii. 33 where he follows the Greek text he also has *his father and his mother*, but in ver 39 where he paraphrases *they*, he says *Joseph and Mary*.

(ε) His high estimation of virginity is shown by the substitution of *days* for *years* in the description of *Hanna the prophetess*, who *was [aged] many days, and seven days only was she with her husband after her virginity* (St. Luke ii. 36)

The result however of this juxtaposition of phrases is to leave us with an inconsistency But is it not an inconsistency with which we are familiar and which is indeed inevitable? It has been shown in Dissertation I (§ 2)—and proof is hardly needed —that the fact of the virgin birth must have remained a secret, 'kept and pondered on' in the hearts of Joseph and Mary alone, certainly during our Lord's own life. Jesus must have passed among his fellow-countrymen for the son of Joseph; Joseph must have been reckoned his father. This must have led to a use of language, which could not have been wholly discarded, even when the narrative of the virgin birth itself was made public in the Gospels. Thus on the pages of our English bibles still remain expressions such as these—*Joseph the husband of Mary, Joseph her husband, Mary thy wife, his wife* (St. Matt. i. 16, 19, 20, 24), *the parents, his parents, thy father and I* (St. Luke ii. 27, 41, 48, also *his father and his mother*, ver 33 R.V.), *Is not this the carpenter's son? Is not this Jesus the son of Joseph?* (St Matt xiii. 55, St. John vi 42), *Jesus of Nazareth, the son of Joseph*[1] (St. John i. 45). These readings present no difficulty to us because of our familiarity with them, and the new readings of Cod Sin. may well be but an extension of the same phenomenon. They all occur in that part of the Gospel which is evidently based on Aramaic documents, documents, that is, written for a Jewish public. But it was just to the

dentes eduxerunt et detruserunt eum (Moes pp 130–1); but it may have been his own inference or exegesis, as in the Arabic version we read *that they might cast him from its summit* (H. Hill, p 113)

[1] These are the words of Philip of Bethsaida, as the preceding questions were asked by the Jews and Galilaeans.

Jews that at the beginning our Lord would pass, externally, as the son of Joseph. The most decisive expression is found at the end of the genealogy. But again it was just the contemporary Jews who would require genealogical proof that our Lord was of 'the house of David.' Thus we could readily imagine that the earliest genealogies of *Jesus the Christ*, whether drawn up for public evidence of His Davidic descent or for the private satisfaction of his relatives, would very likely end with the words *and Joseph begat Jesus the Christ*: and remembering the putative use allowed by the Jews in genealogical reckonings, according to which under certain circumstances a man would be reckoned the 'son' of his father's brother[1], one who does believe in the virgin birth need not find in such an expression a harder saying than, e g the words *Joram begat Ozias* (ver 8). But later, when the immediate need of proof of the Davidic descent passed away, and Gentile converts not familiar with Jewish genealogizing might mistake the meaning of the phrase, the Evangelist would naturally recast it. And that the form of the text in Cod Sin is not that in which it left the Evangelist's hands we shall have reason to see from our examination of the prior problem—What is the value of the new text?

ii.

At first sight the peculiar readings of Cod Sin. seem to be relics or survivals of the primitive or original history of the nativity, which as presenting a simply naturalistic account has on dogmatic grounds been so altered that it would have wholly disappeared, but for the discovery of these as it were 'fragments of an earlier world' in Cod Sin, which thus reveals a stage in the process of correction But on an examination of the readings in detail they lose their primitive character. We have seen

---

[1] Cf St Matt xxii. 23-28

that original documents of the genealogy may well have ended with some such phrase as *Joseph begat Jesus* but that the readings of Cod Sin. represent the original text of the Gospel seems highly improbable.

Taking them in the reverse order (1) the omission of *knew her not until* in ver. 25 is without support, if we accept cod bobiensis (*k*) But this agreement, if not accidental, is to be ascribed to the same, and most obvious, *motif* in each case, viz a desire of the scribe to safeguard the (perpetual) virginity of Mary as mentioned above On this ground, and still more on external grounds (the Philonian use of the phrase), Mr. Conybeare[1] thinks the omission is not original. Indeed it would be hard to find a reason for the interpolation of the missing phrase, if not original.

(2) The next variation to consider would be the datives *to thee, to him* in vers 21, 25. Cur. has *to thee* in ver. 21, otherwise they are also without support, and the addition of such datives seems to be a characteristic of the version, at least in the next two chapters we have *to them* (11. 7), *to them* (12), *unto him* (13), *to him* (16), *to him* (20), *his* (*garner*, 111. 12) *unto him* (14), *to him* (17) In relation to the virgin birth they are not really significant. for such ethical datives would be amply satisfied by the position of Joseph as foster-father

(3) The case seems different with ver. 16. The Greek text of Tischendorf and Westcott and Hort runs thus Ἰακὼβ δὲ ἐγέννησεν τὸν Ἰωσὴφ τὸν ἄνδρα Μαρίας, ἐξ ἧς ἐγεννήθη Ἰησοῦς ὁ λεγόμενος Χριστός, but Cod Sin has *and Joseph to whom was betrothed Mary the Virgin begat Jesus who is called the Christ*. and for this reading there is a certain amount of attestation[2], viz. among the versions (a) and Greek cursives of the Ferrar group (b).

---

[1] *Academy*, Dec 8, 1894, p 474 For the question about Philo, see Diss I, pp 61–63

[2] For the Latin readings I am indebted to the conspectus of Rev W. C Allen in *Academy*, Dec 15; his account of the Greek cursives must be corrected by Dr Rahlfs' information given in *Academy*, Jan 26, 1895

Appended Notes. B.

(a)

Syr Cur.   he to whom was espoused Mary the Virgin, she who bare Jesus the Messiah.

Lat. vet.

a (cod vercell. s. iv)   cui desponsata virgo Maria genuit Iesum qui dicitur Christus

b (cod. veron s. v)   cui desponsata erat virgo Maria, virgo autem Maria genuit Iesum Christum

c (cod. colbert s. xii)   cui desponsata virgo Maria, Maria autem genuit Iesum qui dicitur Christus.

d (cod. bezae s. vi)   cui desponsata virgo Maria peperit Christum Iesum.

g_1 (cod. sangerm. 1 s. viii)   cui desponsata virgo Maria genuit Iesum qui vocatur Christus

k (cod bobiens. s. v)   cui desponsata virgo Maria genuit Iesum Christum

q (cod monac. s. vi)   cui desponsata Maria genuit Iesum qui vocatur Christus

Arm   'cui desponsata virgo Maria genuit, similiter .. aim' (Tisch. ed. viii^va)

(b)

codd 346, 556 scr (= 543 greg)[1] ᾧ μνηστευθῆσα [sic] παρθένος Μαριὰμ ἐγέννησεν Ἰησοῦν τὸν λεγόμενον Χριστόν.

Here there is some attestation, but we see at once that the support is given, not to the part of the reading which bears the appearance of originality (as shown above), *Joseph begat Jesus* —but to that part which makes us suspect its secondary character, *to whom was espoused Mary the virgin*. Why was

[1] The beginning of St Matthew is wanting in codd 13, 69, while 124 has the usual reading (Rahlfs)

espoused here—especially when in Luke ii. 5 against the Greek mss (*his espoused*) our writer has *Mary his wife*? Compared with *was espoused* (ἐμνηστεύθη) the Greek reading τὸν ἄνδρα Μαρίας is much more primitive from its very boldness It would have been difficult to find a scribe to substitute the latter, had he found ἐμνηστεύθη in his text. Again why *the virgin*? In the Greek Gospels Mary is only spoken of as *a virgin*, referring to her condition at the time; nowhere does she bear the name of *the virgin* as a title. Taken with the omission of *knew her not* (ver. 25), it can but be ascribed to the tendency mentioned above—the high emphasis on virginity and *a fortiori* of Mary's virginity.

On the other hand the internal evidence really supports the priority of the Greek reading. The symmetry of the threefold division of the genealogy leads us to expect an expansion or fuller phrase at the end of the third as at the end of the first and second divisions, while in particular τὸν Ἰωσὴφ τὸν ἄνδρα Μαρίας is quite analogous to τὸν Δαυεὶδ τὸν βασιλέα. Again the mention of Tamar, Rahab, Ruth, Bathsheba, leads the way for the mention of Mary But why should Mary be mentioned unless there was something special in her case as in theirs? and if she was to be mentioned and it was an ordinary case of paternity, as we had ἐγέννησεν ἐκ τῆς Θάμαρ, ἐκ τῆς Ῥαχάβ, ἐκ τῆς Ῥούθ, ἐκ τῆς τοῦ Οὐρίου, why did our scribe not give the Syriac for Ἰωσὴφ ἐγέννησεν Ἰησοῦν ἐκ τῆς Μαρίας? Instead he interpolates a phrase which verbally stands in no connexion with the birth—*to whom was espoused Mary the virgin*, while the Greek text retains the ἐκ which we expected, and the connexion of Mary with the child—ἐξ ἧς ἐγεννήθη. We must remember the freedom of translation in the early versions[1], and the particular phrase we

---

[1] In the case both of Cur. and Cod. Sin this character of the translation is well brought out by Fr M.-J. Lagrange in the *Revue Biblique* of July, 1895 'Cur et Sin traduisent par à peu près, ne se souciant que du sens qu'ils atteignent en général directement, sans chercher le moins du monde à serrer le texte. . . Il en résulte qu'ils ne s'efforcent point de rendre un passif par un passif, de traduire les mots qui n'importent pas au sens, lors même

Appended Notes. B.

are discussing is found also in the Cur. Syr. and early Lat versions without, as far as I know, any special claim for it to be original having hitherto been made. To repeat, as it stands in Cod Sin., the sentence *to whom was espoused Mary the Virgin*, without the supposition that Mary fulfilled some special or unique rôle in relation to the birth, is quite meaningless.

On these grounds then, internal as well as external, we feel no hesitation in accepting the Greek as the original text and that of Cod Sin as secondary And to this conclusion Dr Sanday apparently inclines at the end of an investigation he writes[1]: 'But having got back so near to the text of the Greek mss, it would be natural to ask whether we ought ever to have left them As a rule, where there is paraphrase it is the western text which paraphrases So that at the present moment I lean to the opinion that the traditional text need not be altered'

This examination of the readings in detail has rendered unnecessary a discussion of what is really the first question of all—What is the value of the version given by Cod Sin and of its text as a whole? But indeed such discussion must be left to Syriac specialists, and it is altogether too premature to look for any certain or unanimous conclusions at present We must be content to wait.

There is however a point on which something can be said at once. It has been suggested that the codex was written by a scribe who was a heretic or at least of heretical tendencies. The argument has been most fully put together in an article in the *Church Quarterly Review* of April, 1895 (pp 113, 114), but the writer cannot be considered to have proved his point. It is true that the ms. has undergone violent treatment It was

que la tournure est plus sémitique que grecque. *Il répondit* (prit la parole) *et dit*, est simplement rendu *il dit*. A plus forte raison ne tiennent-ils pas des particules grecques, comme δέ, qui est, ou passé sous silence, ou traduit par la copule .. Liberté, négligence, vulgarité du style sont des caractères trop accuses pour laisser place au doute' (pp. 402, 3)

[1] *Academy*, Jan 5, 1895.

'pulled to pieces¹' in one place there are signs of erasure by a knife², and seventeen leaves are missing³. But the treatment does not suggest anything more than would have been suffered by any ms in the course of being used for a palimpsest: and the fact that the version was rough and free, and had for some centuries been superseded by an exacter version (the Peshitta) —in a word the fact that it was not 'a work of high repute,' would have been a sufficient excuse for John the Recluse to make use of it for his own literary purposes in A.D. 778. It is however in the presentation of the internal evidence that the reviewer is most inconclusive One of his instances, St. Luke IX. 35 *my son the chosen*, occurs in the text of our R V.; and can there be any difference between *the son of Joseph* and *the carpenter's son* (St. Matt. XIII 55), between *as he was called* and *as was supposed* (St. Luke III. 23), between *my Son and my beloved* and *my beloved Son* (St. Matt. III 17, St Luke III. 22, St Mark IX 7)? Some of his omissions are mentioned in the margin of the R V as having authority, e.g in St. Luke XXIV. 51, St. Mark XVI. 9–20, and St Matt XXIV 36 In the last instance not only was the absence of *neither the Son* a reading favoured by certain catholic fathers⁴, but it is neutralized by the presence of the words in St. Mark XIII 32. Other readings have support in the old Latin versions —St Luke II 5, St. John I. 34, or in the Curetonian—St. John VI. 47. That after our Lord's baptism the Holy Spirit *abode upon him* (St. Matt III. 16) is surely orthodox doctrine, being that of St. John (1 32). The only passages left are St. John III. 13 *which is from heaven*, VIII 58 *I have been*, III. 18 *only son* (omitting *only begotten*), and St. Matt. XXVII. 50 *his spirit went up*. From this evidence it is surely not possible to find our scribe guilty of 'heresy.'

¹ Mrs Lewis, *Translation*, introd p. xix ² *Ib* p. 13
³ In fact 11 sheets (= 22 leaves) are missing, but as 2 sheets were taken from the beginning and 3 from the end of the Gospel, 5 leaves would be without any of the Gospel text This looks as if the objectionable matter (if such there was) was outside the Gospels But would it not have seemed the most obvious way to get rid of such matter by writing over it?
⁴ See pp 128, 135.

C

ON THE PATRISTIC INTERPRETATION OF ST JOHN vi 63 τὸ πνεῦμά ἐςτιν τὸ ζωοποιοῦν, ἡ ςὰρξ οὐκ ὠφελεῖ οὐδέν· τὰ ῥήματα ἃ ἐγὼ λελάληκα ὑμῖν πνεῦμά ἐςτιν καὶ ζωή ἐςτιν. ἀλλὰ εἰςὶν ἐξ ὑμῶν τινὲς οἳ οὐ πιςτεύουςιν

i.

It is possible to interpret these words as explaining away the previous discourse—as meaning that what is to profit is not really the flesh and blood of our Lord but simply His spiritual, life-giving utterances received and interpreted by faith. The following patristic passages appear to favour this view·

Tertullian, *de Res Carn* 37. He is arguing against gnostics who pleaded the words 'the flesh profiteth nothing' as a ground for disparaging the flesh of Christ. The flesh, replies Tertullian, is only disparaged from one point of view, that is as a source of life. It is spirit, says our Lord, not flesh, that gives life. 'Exsequitur etiam, quid velit intelligi spiritum *verba, quae locutus sum vobis, spiritus sunt*, sicut et supra· *qui audit sermones meos, et credit in eum qui me misit, habet vitam aeternam et in iudicium non veniet, sed transiet de morte ad vitam.* Itaque sermonem constituens vivificatorem, quia spiritus et vita sermo, eundem etiam carnem suam dixit, quia et sermo caro erat factus, proinde in causam vitae appetendus et devorandus auditu et ruminandus intellectu et fide digerendus.'

Eusebius of Caesarea, *de Eccl Theol* iii 12. He is arguing against Marcellus who urged the passage of St. John as carrying with it the conclusion that the 'unprofitable' flesh of Christ would not be eternally permanent, and he interprets thus: δι' ὧν ἐπαίδευεν αὐτοὺς πνευματικῶς ἀκούειν τῶν περὶ τῆς σαρκὸς καὶ τοῦ αἵματος αὐτοῦ λελεγμένων· μὴ γὰρ τὴν σάρκα ἣν περίκειμαι νομίσητέ με λέγειν, ὡς δέον αὐτὴν ἐσθίειν, μηδὲ τὸ αἰσθητὸν καὶ σωματικὸν αἷμα πίνειν ὑπολαμβάνετέ με προστάττειν, ἀλλ' εὖ ἴστε ὅτι τὰ ῥήματά μου ἃ λελάληκα ὑμῖν πνεῦμά ἐστι καὶ ζωή ἐστιν· ὥστε αὐτὰ εἶναι τὰ ῥήματα καὶ τοὺς λόγους αὐτοῦ τὴν σάρκα καὶ τὸ αἷμα, ὧν ὁ μετέχων ἀεί, ὡσανεὶ ἄρτῳ οὐρανίῳ τρεφόμενος, τῆς οὐρανίου μεθέξει ζωῆς.

Macarius Magnes, *Apocriticus* iii. 23 (p 105) σάρκες οὖν καὶ αἷμα τοῦ Χριστοῦ ἤτοι τῆς σοφίας (ταυτὸν γὰρ καὶ ὁ Χριστὸς καὶ ἡ σοφία) οἱ τῆς καινῆς καὶ παλαιᾶς διαθήκης ἀλληγορικῶς λελαλημένοι λόγοι, οὓς χρὴ τρώγειν μελέτῃ καὶ πέττειν ἐν τῇ γνώμῃ διαμνημονεύοντας καὶ ζωὴν ἐξ αὐτῶν οὐ πρόσκαιρον ἀλλ' ἔχειν αἰώνιον. οὕτως Ἰερεμίας εἰς τὸ στόμα τοὺς λόγους ἐκ τῆς χειρὸς τῆς σοφίας δεξάμενος ἔφαγε καὶ φαγὼν ἔσχε ζωήν· οὕτως Ἰεζεκιὴλ κεφαλίδα λόγων φαγὼν ἐγλυκαίνετο καὶ τὸ πικρὸν τῆς παρούσης ζωῆς ἀπεβάλλετο οὕτως ὁ καθ' ἕνα τῶν ἁγίων καί ποτε καὶ πάλαι καὶ αὖθις καὶ μετέπειτα τὴν σάρκα τῆς σοφίας τρώγων καὶ τὸ αἷμα καὶ πίνων, τουτέστι τὴν γνῶσιν αὐτῆς καὶ τὴν ἀποκάλυψιν ἐν ἑαυτῷ δεχόμενος, ἔζησε τὸν αἰῶνα καὶ ζῶν οὐ λήξει ποτέ. οὐ γὰρ μόνοις τοῖς μαθηταῖς ἐδίδου τὴν σάρκα φαγεῖν τὴν οἰκείαν ἑαυτοῦ καὶ πιεῖν ὁμοίως τὸ αἷμα (ἢ γὰρ ἂν ἠδίκει τοῦτο ποιῶν καιρίως τισὶ μὲν παρέχων, τισὶ δὲ οὐ πρυτανεύων τὴν αἰώνιον ζωὴν) ἀλλὰ πᾶσιν ὁμοίως ὁσίοις ἀνδράσι καὶ προφητικοῖς ὁμοῦ ταύτην ἀλληγορικῶς τὴν σιταρχίαν ἔδωκεν[1].

Amalarius of Metz has been cited above p 235, n. 1, as interpreting the eating Christ's flesh and drinking His blood to mean

---

[1] It may be mentioned (as this author is not easily accessible, not being included in Migne's *Patrology*) that the whole of the passage from which the above is quoted is paraphrased in *Dict of Chr Biog* iii 770, s v. MACARIUS

Appended Notes. C.

believing in His passion. This probably implies that he interpreted St. John vi. 63 to mean: 'what will profit you is not to eat my flesh but to believe my words.'

ii.

On the other hand the words may be interpreted in such a way as not to practically overthrow the whole previous discourse: they may be interpreted to mean that *mere* flesh profits nothing, but that 'the things of which I (Jesus) have been speaking'—the flesh and blood of the Son of Man, ascended and glorified (see ver. 62)—are not mere flesh, but spirit and (therefore) life. So St. Paul calls the ascended Christ 'life-giving spirit' in a passage where the permanence of His human body is strongly implied, 1 Cor. xv. 45–50. This interpretation is illustrated by the following passages:

Athanasius, *Ep. .v ad Serapion.* 19 (*P. G.* xxvi. p 665) καὶ ἐνταῦθα γὰρ ἀμφότερα περὶ ἑαυτοῦ εἴρηκε, σάρκα καὶ πνεῦμα· καὶ τὸ πνεῦμα πρὸς τὸ κατὰ σάρκα διέστειλεν, ἵνα μὴ μόνον τὸ φαινόμενον, ἀλλὰ καὶ τὸ ἀόρατον αὐτοῦ πιστεύσαντες μάθωσιν, ὅτι καὶ ἃ λέγει οὐκ ἔστι σαρκικά, ἀλλὰ πνευματικά· πόσοις γὰρ ἤρκει τὸ σῶμα πρὸς βρῶσιν, ἵνα καὶ τοῦ κόσμου παντὸς τοῦτο τροφὴ γένηται, ἀλλὰ διὰ τοῦτο τῆς εἰς οὐρανοὺς ἀναβάσεως ἐμνημόνευσε τοῦ υἱοῦ τοῦ ἀνθρώπου, ἵνα τῆς σωματικῆς ἐννοίας αὐτοὺς ἀφελκύσῃ καὶ λοιπὸν τὴν εἰρημένην σάρκα βρῶσιν ἄνωθεν οὐράνιον καὶ πνευματικὴν τροφὴν παρ' αὐτοῦ διδομένην μάθωσιν. ἃ γὰρ λελάληκα, φησίν, ὑμῖν πνεῦμά ἐστι καὶ ζωή. ἴσον τῷ εἰπεῖν· τὸ μὲν δεικνύμενον καὶ διδόμενον ὑπὲρ τῆς τοῦ κόσμου σωτηρίας ἐστὶν ἡ σὰρξ ἣν ἐγὼ φορῶ· ἀλλ' αὕτη ὑμῖν καὶ τὸ ταύτης αἷμα παρ' ἐμοῦ πνευματικῶς δοθήσεται τροφή· ὥστε πνευματικῶς ἐν ἑκάστῳ ταύτην ἀναδίδοσθαι καὶ γίνεσθαι πᾶσι φυλακτήριον εἰς ἀνάστασιν ζωῆς αἰωνίου.

Apollinarius quoted by Leontius Byzant. *adv. Fraud Apollinaristarum* (*P. G.* lxxxvi. p 1964) ζωοποιεῖ δὲ ἡμᾶς ἡ σὰρξ αὐτοῦ, διὰ τὴν συνουσιωμένην αὐτῇ θεότητα· τὸ δὲ ζωοποιὸν θεικόν· θεικὴ ἄρα σάρξ, ὅτι θεῷ συνήφθη· καὶ αὕτη μὲν σώζει, ἡμεῖς δὲ σωζόμεθα μετέχοντες αὐτῆς ὡσπερεὶ τροφῆς.

Cyril of Alexandria, *in Ioan.* vi. 64 (*P G.* lxxiii p. 601) οὐ σφόδρα, φησίν, ἀσυνέτως τὸ μὴ δύνασθαι ζωοποιεῖν περιτεθείκατε τῇ σαρκί. ὅταν γὰρ μόνη νοῆται καθ' ἑαυτὴν ἡ τῆς σαρκὸς φύσις πως, οὐκ ἔσται δηλονότι ζωοποιός· ζωογονήσει μὲν γάρ τι τῶν ὄντων οὐδαμῶς, δεῖται δὲ μᾶλλον αὐτὴ τοῦ ζωογονεῖν ἰσχύοντος. . . . ἐπειδὴ γὰρ ἥνωται τῷ ζωοποιοῦντι λόγῳ, γέγονεν ὅλη ζωοποιὸς πρὸς τὴν τοῦ βελτίονος ἀναδραμοῦσα δύναμιν, οὐκ αὐτὴ πρὸς τὴν ἰδίαν βιασαμένη φύσιν τὸν οὐδαμόθεν ἡττωμένον. κἂν ἀσθενῇ τοιγαροῦν ἡ τῆς σαρκὸς φύσις, ὅσον ἧκεν εἰς ἑαυτήν, εἰς τὸ δύνασθαι ζωοποιεῖν, ἀλλ' οὖν ἐνεργήσει τοῦτο τὸν ζωοποιὸν ἔχουσα λόγον καὶ ὅλην αὐτοῦ τὴν ἐνέργειαν ὠδίνουσα. σῶμα γάρ ἐστι τῆς κατὰ φύσιν ζωῆς καὶ οὐχ ἑνός τινος τῶν ἀπὸ τῆς γῆς, ἐφ' οὗπερ ἂν καὶ ἰσχῦσαι δικαίως τὸ **ἡ σὰρξ οὐκ ὠφελεῖ οὐδέν** οὐ γὰρ ἡ Παύλου τυχόν, ἀλλ' οὐδὲ ἡ Πέτρου, ἤγουν ἑτέρου τινὸς τοῦτο ἐν ἡμῖν ἐργάσεται· μόνη δὲ καὶ ἐξαιρέτως ἡ τοῦ σωτῆρος ἡμῶν Χριστοῦ, ἐν ᾧ κατῴκησε πᾶν τὸ πλήρωμα τῆς θεότητος σωματικῶς καὶ γὰρ ἂν εἴη τῶν ἀτοπωτάτων τὸ μὲν μέλι τοῖς οὐκ ἔχουσι κατὰ φύσιν τὸ γλυκὺ τὴν ἰδίαν ἐπιτιθέναι ποιότητα καὶ εἰς ἑαυτὸ μετασκευάζειν τὸ ὦπερ ἂν ἀναμίσγηται, τὴν δὲ τοῦ θεοῦ λόγου ζωοποιὸν φύσιν μὴ ἀνακομίζειν οἴεσθαι πρὸς τὸ ἴδιον ἀγαθὸν τὸ ἐν ᾧπερ ἐνῴκησε σῶμα. οὐκοῦν ἐπὶ μὲν τῶν ἄλλων ἁπάντων ἀληθὴς ἔσται λόγος ὅτι ἡ σὰρξ οὐκ ὠφελεῖ οὐδέν, ἀτονήσει δὲ ἐπὶ μόνου τοῦ Χριστοῦ, διὰ τὸ ἐν αὐτῇ κατοικῆσαι τὴν ζωήν, τοῦτ' ἔστι τὸν μονογενῆ.

Cyril's language in this passage appears to be influenced by that of Apollinarius.

Hilary, *de Trin* viii 14 'De veritate carnis et sanguinis non relictus est ambigendi locus. Nunc enim et ipsius Domini professione et fide nostra vere caro est et vere sanguis est Et haec accepta atque hausta id efficiunt, ut et nos in Christo et Christus in nobis sit. Anne hoc veritas non est?'

Augustine, *in Ioannis Evang. Tract.* xxvii. 5 'Quid est ergo quod adiungit. *Spiritus est qui vivificat, caro non prodest quid-*

Appended Notes. C.

quam? Dicamus ei (patitur enim nos non contradicentes, sed nosse cupientes): O Domine, magister bone, quomodo *caro non prodest quidquam*, cum tu dixeris. *nisi quis manducaverit carnem meam, et biberit sanguinem meum, non habebit in se vitam?* An vita non prodest quidquam? et propter quid sumus quod sumus, nisi ut habeamus vitam aeternam, quam tua carne promittis? Quid est ergo, *non prodest quidquam caro?* Non prodest quidquam, sed quomodo illi intellexerunt: carnem quippe sic intellexerunt, quomodo in cadavere dilaniatur aut in macello venditur, non quomodo spiritu vegetatur. Proinde sic dictum est *caro non prodest quidquam*, quomodo dictum est *scientia inflat* Iam ergo debemus odisse scientiam? absit. Et quid est, *scientia inflat?* sola, sine charitate. Ideo adiunxit: *charitas vero aedificat*. Adde ergo scientiae charitatem, et utilis erit scientia· non per se, sed per charitatem. Sic etiam nunc, *caro non prodest quidquam* sed sola caro: accedat spiritus ad carnem, quomodo accedit charitas ad scientiam, et prodest plurimum Nam si caro nihil prodesset, Verbum caro non fieret, ut inhabitaret in nobis. Si per carnem nobis multum profuit Christus, quomodo caro nihil prodest? Sed per carnem Spiritus aliquid pro salute nostra egit Caro vas fuit: quod habebat attende, non quod erat. Apostoli missi sunt, numquid caro ipsorum nobis nihil profuit? Si caro apostolorum nobis profuit, caro Domini potuit nihil prodesse? Unde enim ad nos sonus verbi, nisi per vocem carnis? unde stylus, unde conscriptio? Ista omnia opera carnis sunt, sed agitante spiritu tanquam organum suum. *Spiritus ergo est qui vivificat, caro autem non prodest quidquam·* sicut illi intellexerunt carnem, non sic ego do ad manducandum carnem meam'

But he goes on (after an interval) '*Verba quae ego locutus sum vobis, spiritus et vita sunt.* Quid est, *spiritus et vita sunt?* Spiritualiter intelligenda sunt. Intellexisti spiritualiter? *Spiritus et vita sunt.* Intellexisti carnaliter? Etiam sic illa *spiritus et vita sunt*, sed tibi non sunt.'

D.

TERTULLIAN'S DOCTRINE OF THE EUCHARIST.

THE above dissertation is only intended to cover a certain period of the history of eucharistic doctrine with which Tertullian has nothing to do But there is so little that appears to be trustworthy written about Tertullian's eucharistic doctrine, and it is at the same time so often controversially referred to, that I have thought I might be forgiven in summarizing his teaching.

Four preliminary propositions may be safely made as regards the teaching of Tertullian. He contends strongly—

(1) That Christ as He is now in heavenly glory is still in the flesh see *de Carne Christi* 24 'et videbunt et agnoscent qui eum confixerunt utique ipsam carnem in quam saevierunt, sine qua nec ipse esse poterit nec agnosci'

(2) That it is to the still human Christ thus glorified in the flesh that we Christians are united by His Spirit. Christ dwells in each individual Christian, and the Church as a whole is Christ: see *de Fuga* 10 'Christum indutus es siquidem in Christum tinctus es · [Christus] in te est.' *de Poenit.* 10 'in uno et altero ecclesia est: ecclesia vero Christus. ergo cum te ad fratrum genua protendis, Christum contrectas, Christum exoras.' *de Orat.* 6 'perpetuitatem postulamus in Christo et individuitatem a corpore eius.'

(3) That the link between Christ and his people is a bodily link (see *de Pudicit.* 6 corporis nexus). It is this because of the sacramental principle. A sacrament is a physical means of spiritual grace : because it is physical, it appeals to us through our bodies (and in this Tertullian finds a pledge for our bodily

resurrection). cp *de Res. Carnis* 8 'cum anima [in Christo] Deo allegitur ipsa [caro] est quae efficit ut anima allegi possit Scilicet caro abluitur ut anima emaculetur · caro ungitur ut anima consecretur : caro signatur ut et anima muniatur . caro manus impositione adumbratur ut et anima spiritu illuminetur · caro corpore et sanguine Christi vescitur ut et anima de Deo saginetur.' In this sacramental principle and its accompanying obligation Tertullian sees one special outcome of the Incarnation, 'vestimentum quodammodo fidei quae retro nuda erat. . . . obstrinxit fidem ad baptismi necessitatem' (*de Bapt* 13). And in the simplicity of the sacramental rites, which contrasts with the imposing apparatus of pagan mysteries, he sees a special evidence of the divine attributes of simplicity and power (*de Bapt* 2).

(4) That the sacraments of the Church are thus outward channels of spiritual grace, the spiritual grace of the risen and glorified Christ; see *de Bapt* 11, where it is stated that the baptism of Christ was only like John the Baptist's till after the resurrection—'nondum adimpleta gloria Domini nec instructa efficacia lavacri per passionem et resurrectionem.'

Coming now to the eucharist in particular, it is quite certain that Tertullian believed the consecrated bread and wine to be both channels and veils of a divine gift and presence ; channels through which we are 'fed with the fatness of God' (cf *de Res* 8 cited above), and also veils of the divine gift thus communicated to us. Thus the bread *is* the body of Christ, see *de Orat.* 14 'accepto corpore Domini et reservato.' It is believed by Christians to be something which the heathen do not believe it to be : *ad Uxor* ii. 5 'non sciet maritus quid secreto ante omnem cibum gustes ? et si sciverit panem non illum credit esse qui dicitur.' Thus they show great anxiety to prevent a crumb or drop of the sacred bread and wine falling to the ground, *de Cor. Militis* 3 'calicis aut panis etiam nostri aliquid decuti in terram anxie patimur' The body of Christ is 'given' and 'taken' as well as 'eaten,' see *de Idol.* 7 'manus admovere corpori Domini.' Thus inconsistent Christians still 'quotidie corpus eius lacessunt.'

Dissertations.

But in what sense are the bread and wine the body and blood of Christ? or in other words, what is the exact nature of the unseen spiritual presence in the eucharist? The obvious answer in accordance with Christian belief is that it is the body (or flesh) and blood of Christ, present after a spiritual and heavenly manner. So Tertullian speaks of our being fed 'opimitate dominici corporis, eucharistia scilicet' (*de Pudicit.* 9). Again he says (*adv. Marcion* i 14) that Christ 'makes his body present by means of bread (panem quo ipsum corpus suum repraesentat).' *Repraesentare* in Tertullian continually and constantly means *to make actually present over again* (on the force of *re-* see *adv. Marcion.* v. 9). Thus *adv. Marcion.* v 12 'repraesentatio corporum' is used of the last judgement; iii 7 Christ's second advent is the 'secunda repraesentatio', when on earth He effected a cure. He is said 'repraesentare curationem' (iv. 9). Cf. *adv Praxean* 24: the Son strictly cannot be said 'repraesentare Patrem,' i e. to make the Father actually present, for He is personally distinct from the Father: but He 'representat Deum,' i.e. makes God actually present, because He is God and is the 'vicarius' (or representative) of the Father Cf. also *adv. Marcion.* iii. 10, 24, iv 6, 13, 22, 23, 25.

On the other hand in *de Res. Carnis* 8 (already quoted), the body and blood of Christ were put in line with the outward parts in the other sacraments, while the inward gift was described as the 'fatness of God,' i e. the divine life. The question arises then: Does Tertullian regard the inward gift and presence of the eucharist as purely the gift and presence of the divine Spirit, the Spirit of Jesus finding Himself a new symbolical 'embodiment' in the bread and wine, which are hence *called* His body and blood? This would be borne out by a curious passage, *adv Marcion.* iv. 40. Marcion had apparently argued against the material reality of Christ's human body from the fact that He could call bread His body. No, replies Tertullian, the eucharistic body only witnesses to the real body as figure to substance—'acceptum panem et distributum discipulis corpus

Appended Notes. D.

suum illum fecit, *hoc est corpus meum* dicendo, id est, figura corporis mei : figura autem non fuisset nisi veritatis esset corpus.' He goes on to say that there is analogy for Christ calling bread His body in the fact that Jeremiah (according to the old Latin reading of Jer xi. 19) had prophesied of His body under the term bread, '*coniciamus lignum in panem eius,* scilicet crucem in corpus eius.' Then he proves the carnal reality of Christ's body from the fact that it is accompanied with blood, *This is my body* is followed by *This is my blood* 'Consistit probatio corporis de testimonio carnis, probatio carnis de testimonio sanguinis.' But again he seems to give a figurative meaning to the eucharistic blood, pointing out how wine in the Old Testament is several times called blood—'the blood of the grape,' &c There is a similar but briefer passage earlier in the same work, *adv. Marcion.* iii. 19.

These passages certainly suggest not that Tertullian believed in no real presence in the sacramental elements, for that would be contrary to so much that he says elsewhere, but that he believed the bread to be symbolically called the body of Christ because it 'embodied' a presence and gift of His Spirit And this view is not decisively contradicted by anything else in his writings[1]. In a somewhat different way the wine would be called symbolically Christ's blood, because it embodies a spiritual gift of divine life from Christ But it may still be said : the spiritual gift thus conveyed is not merely a gift consisting in the spirit of Christ, but a gift of Christ's spiritualized flesh and blood, that is a gift of His manhood and not barely of His Godhead. In this case the outward vehicles would still remain what they were, *symbols* of the inward reality which they convey. It is in this sense that the outward sacramental elements

---

[1] No argument, one way or another, can be founded on the expression, *de Orat* 6 'corpus eius in pane censetur · *hoc est corpus meum*' *Censeri* has at least no necessary idea of symbolism attaching to it cp *de Bapt* 5 ' similitudo [Dei] in aeternitate [hominis] censetur,' i. e the divine similitude is found (really existing) in man's immortality.

are continually called 'symbols' or 'signs' or 'figures' in Catholic theology—i e. *efficacia signa*, which effect or convey what they symbolize. The bread would symbolize Christ's body, because it 'embodies' the flesh or spiritual essence of His manhood, and the wine would embody, as well as symbolize, the spiritual blood, the 'blood which is the life.' We cannot bring ourselves to doubt that Tertullian, if confronted with this question, must have accepted it and not regarded the gifts of the eucharist as gifts independent of Christ's abiding manhood. But it has to be remembered on the other hand that he appears (as cited in app. note C, p. 303) to believe that in St. John vi Christ's 'flesh and blood' means no more than His life-giving words to be received in faith.

It is perhaps safest to assume that Tertullian was uncertain in his own mind as to the exact meaning which he assigned to the eucharistic language of the Church and the exact nature which he attributed to the eucharistic gifts. The tradition of the Church taught that the consecrated bread and wine are the body and blood of Christ: and different Church teachers did their best to interpret this doctrine.

INDICES

I

HOLY SCRIPTURE

Acts of the Apostles	14, 15, 52, 76, 161 (παῖς κυρίου)
Acts i. 7	84, 115-6, 136
angelic appearances	21-27
Apocalypse	9, 54
Apocryphal Gospels	56, 60
apostolic preaching	6, 11, 13
baptism of Christ	78, 113, 187, cf 309
body of Christ	
mystical	117, 132, 127, 136, 158, 233 n, 245, 266
sacramental	233 n, 239 n, 241, 244-5, 310-1
brethren (and relatives) of Christ	13, 29, 38
Chagigah	40 n
Colossians i 17	91
ii. 3	90, 133, 136
ii 9	90, 187
conversion	66
1 *Corinthians* x 1-4	243
xi 26-28	269
xi. 29	234 n, 255 n
xv 28	117, 126-7
xv. 47	11 n
2 *Corinthians* viii 9	89-90, 184
xii 2	125
Cyrenius	19
David, davidic	20, 34, 38, 78 n
diabolic agency	24-26
faith in Christ	82-3, 169
the FATHER giving the SON	91, 210
Galatians iv 22, 29	62
Genesis xi 5	129 n
xxi. 1, xxv 21, xxix 31	62
Ep to the Hebrews	53, 79, 82-3, 91-2, 102, 189
Hebrews i 3	91
iv. 15	79, 141
Heli	39
Herod	10, 20, 29-30
Hosea xi 1	33
infallibility (and impeccability) of Christ	73, 80, 96, 187, 208-9
Isaiah vii 14	35, 289-90
vii 15, 16	118
lx 3	34
St James	17, 54
Jeremiah i 6	118-9
iii. 4	62
xi 19	311
xxxi. 15	33
Jewish Christianity	49, 51, 53-4

Index.

St. John Baptist 4, 17, 58, 60, 78-9, 309
St. John Evangelist 7-10, 17, 76-7, 79, 84-87, 91, 102, 146, 203
St. John 1. 14 184, 191
   iii 3 66
   iii 13 85 n, 91, 302
   iii 34 85 n
   vi 53 f 235, 239 n, 246 n
   vi. 56 263, 271-2
   vi. 63 233 n, 245-6, 303 f
   vi. 64 81 n
   viii 40 165
   viii 58 187, 193, 302
   x 30 164-5
   xi 14 80
   xi 34 82, 126, 149, 155, 158, 162, 164, 165
   xii 27 139 n
   xiv 28 111, 164
   xvii 5 85, 147-8, 185, 193, 195
   xxi 22 84 n
Joseph 6 n, 13, 20, 22, 28, 39, 77, 292-302

kenosis (see *Phil* ii 5-11) 108, 118-9, 146, 147-9, 183 f, 189, 190, 200-1

Lightfoot, *Hor Hebr* 39 n
St Luke 13-18, 35, 37 n, 82
St. Luke's genealogy 39
St Luke i, ii 16-18, 52, 63, 294
   i. 41 f (Elisabeth) 22
   ii 2 (census) 19-21
   ii. 5 295
   ii 31-35 (Simeon) 17
   ii. 36 296
   ii 40 78
   ii. 48 7 n, 296
   ii 49 57, 77-8, 81, 186

St Luke ii. 52 78, 115, 118, 120, 123-4, 127-9, 136-7, 141, 150-2, 161, 167 n, 181

Magi 30-1, 34
St Mark 7
St Mark vi. 3 (and ||^s) 7
   ix 21 82
   x. 18 96 n, 114
B V Mary 6 n, 9, 13, 18, 20, 22, 28, 39, 48, 61, 77, 292-301
massacre of innocents 29-30, 55 n
St. Matthew's genealogy 37-39
   use of prophecy 31 f
St Matt i ii 29, 37, 63, 292 f
   xi. 27 115, 165
   xviii 3 66
   xxiv. 36 (St Mark xiii 32) 83-4, 111, 115-118, 123-133, 135-6, 141, 149-150, 155, 158-9, 162, 166 n, 185, 195, 198-200, 203
   xxvi 26 (*see* 'body') 233 n, 246, 311
   xxvi 38 128 n, 133 n, 141
   xxvii. 46 (St Mark xv. 34) 83, 105, 127, 132, 137, 141, 159, 197, 203
   xxviii. 18 192 n
   xxviii 20 193
Messiah, messianic 15-18, 31, 52-54, 76-7, 78 n
Micah v. 2 34-5
miracles of Christ 57, 79-80, 140, 142, 165-6, 185, 203
Moses 61

negatives in Scripture, a use of 251

O T. language about God 172, 220

St. Paul 10-11, 17, 53, 62, 76, 88-90, 91-2, 102, 189, 203, 305

II. Names and Terms. 317

St. Peter	7, 17, 54, 79	Satan	24–26, 79, 144
Philippians ii. 5–11 (see *kenosis*)		'Second Adam'	11, 65–7
	88–9, 143, 181, 184, 199, 200, 203	Synoptists	77–79
ii 7	176, 280	Talmud	39, 289
prayers of Christ	80, 82, 129, 133 n, 165, 185, 203	temptation of Christ	79, 109–10, 140, 141, 144, 187
prophecy	31–6, 57–8, 60	tradition in Scripture	42
prophetic attributes of Christ	80–1, 84, 185		
		Zacharias	22, 58
Samuel	60, 78	Zechariah	32

II
NAMES AND TERMS

Abelard (1079–1142)   176 n, 260 n, 267
Academy   61 n, 289, 290, 294, 298 n
actio adductiva, productiva   254 n
adoptionists   160 n, 161
Adrevaldus (c. 818–878, monk of Fleury)   240 n
Africanus, Julius (of Emmaus, s. iii init)   29, 38 n
Agnoetae   154–158, 161
Agobard (779–840, abp of Lyons 813)   162
Alcuin, Albinus Flaccus (c 735–804, at Charlemagne's court 782)   102 n, 167, 234, 235 n, 280
Alexander III (pope 1159–1181)   176 n, 177, 283
Alexander of Hales (doctor at Paris †1245)   252 n
Alger (canon of Liége c. 1101, † c. 1131)   254 n, 264–5, 275 n
Allen, Rev. W C.   298 n
Amalarius of Metz († c 837)   234–5, 304

Ambrose (bp of Milan 374, †397)   127–9, 132, 215 n, 230 n, 236 n, 245, 262
de Sacramentis   230 n, 236 n
de Mysteriis   236 n
Anastasius   104
Andrewes (1555–1626, bp of Winchester 1618)   197
Anglicanism   196 f 205, 213
Anselm (1033–1109, abp of Canterbury 1093)   266 n, 267 n, 285 n
anthropomorphism   250
ἀντίδοσις ἰδιωμάτων   182–3
ἀντίτυπα   231
Apollinarius (bp of Laodicea, Syria, † c. 390)   138–9, 141 n, 142, 145 n, 152–4, 175 n, 280–1, 305–6
Apuleius (fl 173)   291
Aquinas, Thomas (1225–1274, dominican 1243)   156 n, 160 n, 168, 169 n, 174 n, 177 n, 180, 183 n, 267 n, 283
Aristides (of Athens, s ii init.)   46

318 *Index.*

Arius (c 256–336), Arianism 122–3, 139, 159, 208–9, 250
Arnold, Sir Edwin   59
Asclepiades   55
Asita   56, 58
Athanasius (c 296–373, bp of Alexandria 326)   103–4, 123–6, 129, 130, 139, 140, 145, 153, 164, 171, 305
Atia   55
Augustine (354–430, bp of Hippo 395)   132, 136–8, 166, 176, 232, 233 n, 234, 237, 240, 249, 265 n, 275, 280, 306–7
Augustus (B C 63 — A D 14)   4, 20–1, 55–6, 290

Badham, Mr F P   289–290
Bar-cochba   45, 48 n
Basil (c. 329–379, abp of Caesarea 370)   123, 127, 130
Beal, Rev S   58 n
Bellarmine, Cardinal (1542–1621, Italian Jesuit)   276
Berengar (998–1088, archdeacon of Angers)   240 n, 247–258, 259, 262–5, 267
Bergmann   19
Bernard (1091–1153, founded Clairvaux 1115)   166 n
Beveridge (1638–1708, bp of St. Asaph 1704)   198
Bingham (1668–1723)   178
Boetius (c 470–524, consul 510)   111 n, 194, 235 n
Bright, Dr W.   104 n, 164, 199–201, 208 n
Bruce, Dr A B   4 n, 89 n, 150, 152, 179 n, 181 n, 182, 184 n, 188 n, 189 n
Buddha   4, 56–58, 291
Bull (1634–1710, bp of St Davids 1705)   112 n, 178, 198
Burkitt, Mr F. C   292 n, 295 n

Cabasilas, Nicolas (†1371, bp of Thessalonica)   172
Candidus   209 n
Carlyle   65
Carpenter, Dr E   55 n, 56 n
Caspari, Dr C P.   153
Cassian, John (c 360–c 450)   98
Cassiodorus (c 480–c 575, consul 514, monk c 550)   115 n, 167
Cerinthus (s 1)   8, 49–51
Charles the Bald (823–877, k of France 840)   236, 240
Charles the Great (742–814, king 768, emperor 800)   230
Chrysostom, John (c 347–407, bp of CP 398)   31 n, 102 n, 131, 274
Church, Dean   199, 200
Church Quarterly Review   48 n, 153, 222 n, 301
Clement of Alexandria (c 160—c 220)   47, 113–4, 121, 202, 239 n, 245 n
Clement of Rome (s 1)   106–7
Codex Sinaiticus   61 n, 84 n, 85 n, 292–302
Colet (†1519, dean of St Paul's 1505)   179, 180
communicatio idiomatum   182–3
Conybeare, Mr F. C   48 n, 55 n, 61 n, 290–1, 294 n, 295, 298
Copleston, Bp   56 n, 58, 59 n
Corderius, B (Jesuit, s xvii)   174 n
Councils—
   Nicaea (325)   42 n, 195, 208–9
   Ephesus (431)   155 n, 195
   Chalcedon (451)   153, 154–5, 162–3, 210–1, 230, 278
   Constantinople III (680)   154, 211
   Nicaea II (787)   230, 231 n
   Lateran IV (1215)   178, 248, 268
   Basle (1431–1438)   168 n
   Trent (1545–1563)   267 n
creationist language   254 n

II. Names and Terms. 319

creeds, confessions 42-47, 107-8, 170-1, 182 n, 212
Cyril of Alexandria (c 376-444, bp of A 412) 131, 145-6, 149-154, 163 n, 164-5, 201, 231 n, 281 n, 306
Cyril of Jerusalem (c 315-386, bp of J. 350) 231 n

Dale, Dr R W 23 n
Delitzsch, Dr F 38 n, 189
Denny and Lacey 284 n
depotentiation 152, 188
Didache 42 n, 53
Didymus of Alexandria (c 309- c. 394) 130-1
Diogenes Laertius 291
Dionysius of Alexandria (†265, bp of A 247) 122
Dionysius the Areopagite (s V-VI) 172-174, 175 n, 241 n, 280
divinity of Christ assumed 106-7
docetism 114, 146
dogma 170
Domitian (emp 81-96) 30 n, 38 n
Dorner, Dr J A 112 n, 154 n, 155 n, 172 n, 179 n, 181 n, 184, 193-5
double life of Christ 183, 192, 215
δοῦλος κυρίου 160-1
Draseke, Dr J 153
Durandus of St. Portian (†1334, domin. bp of Meaux 1326) 283
Durandus of Troarn (†1089, abbot of St. Martin, T 1059) 263

Ebionism 51-54
Edersheim, Dr A 19 n, 22 n, 35 n
Einig, Dr P 284 n
Eleutherus (pope between 170 and 190) 43
Enoch, Book of 17 n, 26 n
Ephraim of Antioch (†545, bp of A. 527) 275-6

Ephraim Syrus (†373, deacon of Edessa) 130, 295 n
Epiphanius, deacon 231 n
Erasmus (1467-1536) 179-180
Erigena, John Scotus (Irish monk, in France 846, † c 877) 174-5, 240 n, 247-8, 280-1
Eulogius (†607, bp of Alexandria 579) 126 n, 156-7, 158-9
Eusebius (c 260-339, bp of Caesarea c 313) 29 n, 38 n, 41 n, 43 n, 54 n, 100-103, 104, 304
Eutyches (c 378—c 454, abbot in CP) 143, 154
Eutychius (512-582, bp of CP 552) 231 n

Fairbairn, Dr A M 4 n, 60, 189-192
Farrar, Dr F W. 19 n
Fathers, the 213-4, 250
Felix of Urgel (bp of U. c 783, deposed 799) 162
Florus Diaconus (of Lyons, † c 860) 235, 282
Floss, H. J 240 n
Franzelin, Cardinal 284
Fulbert of Chartres (†1029, bp of C 1007) 254 n
Fulgentius (468-533, bp of Ruspe 508) 167, 246 n

Geikie, Dr C 19 n, 35 n
Gelasius (pope 492-496) 275
Georgius Scholarius (= Gennadius, bp of CP 1453-1458) 278 n
Gess, W F 184, 188
Gibson, Miss M D 292 n
Gieseler, Dr J C L 211 n, 237 n, 250 n, 264 n, 276 n
gnosticism 8, 50, 109, 111, 113, 273
Godet, Dr F. 14 n, 19 n, 39, 184-8, 191-2

Gregory of Bergamo (bp of B 1134) 265-6, 281, 282
Gregory the Great (pope 590-604) 157, 159, 167 n
Gregory Nazianzen (c 325-389, bp of Sasima 373, CP 379-381) 123, 126-7, 130, 137, 159, 183 n
Gregory Nyssen (c. 331-394, bp of Nyssa 372) 127, 139-44, 146 n, 183 n, 209 n, 231
Gregory Thaumaturgus (bp of Neocaesarea c 240) 153
Guardian 295 n
Guitmundus, *see* Witmund
Gwatkin, Dr H M. 122 n, 208 n, 209 n

Hadrian I (pope 772-795) 160 n
Haimo (778-853, bp of Halberstadt 840) 246-7
Harnack, Dr A. 3 n, 122 n
Harris, Mr Rendel 7 n, 46 n, 292 n
Hatch, Dr E 173 n
Hebert, Dr C 240 n
Hegesippus (s 11 fin.) 38 n, 41 n, 54
Hermas (s 11 med) 48 n, 107 n
Heurtley, Dr 42 n, 208
Hilary of Poitiers (†368, bp of P c. 353) 72, 74-5, 104 n, 111 n, 128 n, 132-5, 137, 145-9, 209 n, 306
Hildebert (1057-1133, abp of Tours 1125) 266-7
Hildebrand (= Gregory VII, pope 1073-1085) 257 n
Hill, Rev. J. Hamlyn 295 n
Hillel 38
Hincmar (†882, abp of Reims 845) 246
Hippolytus (of Rome, s iii init) 52 n
Holland, Rev. H. S. 25 n
homo 111 n, 115 n

homoousion 269, 272
Hooker, Richard (1553-1600) 143, 196-7
Huet, P. D. (1630-1721, bp of Avranches 1689) 115 n, 120 n
Hugh of Langres (†1051, bp of L. 1031) 249 n, 256 n, 258
Hugh of St. Victor (†1141) 278 n
Humbert, Cardinal (†1063, card. 1051) 248, 253-4, 257, 258 n
Hutton, Mr R H 192
Huxley, Prof T H. 217

Ignatius († c 115, bp of Antioch) 8, 34 n, 46, 48 n, 106-7
impanatio, invinatio 259, 262
intellectualis 256
Irenaeus (bp of Lyons 177) 8, 41 n, 43-4, 49, 50, 52, 93, 98-100, 107-112, 121, 171, 198, 273

Jerome(c 346-420,at Bethlehem 387) 58 n, 120, 128 n, 132, 135-6, 239 n, 289-291
Pseudo-Jerome 136 n
Jewish Quarterly Review 48 n
John Cassian, *see* Cassian
John Chrysostom, *see* Chrysostom
John of Cornwall (c. 1170) 176 n, 177 n
John Damascene (c 676—c. 760, monk of S Saba) 102 n, 126 n, 156 n, 160-1, 166, 183 n, 230-1, 236 n
Pseudo-John 260 n
John Scotus Erigena, *see* Erigena
Josephus (37—c 100) 19, 20 n, 26 n, 29 n, 30, 31 n, 38 n
Jovius 175 n
Julius (pope 337-352) 153
Julius Marathus 55
Justin Martyr († c 163) 45, 51, 289-290
Justinian (emperor 527-565) 145 n

II. Names and Terms.

Keim   19 n, 35
Kernel and the Husk, the   3 n, 58, 61, 63 n
Kohler, Dr   48 n

Lagrange, Fr M -J   300 n
Landriot, Mgr   177 n
Lanfranc (c 1005-1089, abp of Canterbury 1070)   230 n, 248 n, 249, 253, 257 n, 258, 275 n
Leo (pope 440-461)   163, 197, 211
Leontius of Byzantium (s vi)   132, 144, 153, 155 n, 156, 157-8, 160, 175 n, 182 n, 276-8, 281 n, 286, 305
Leporius   132, 137-8
Lequien (dominican, s xvii–xviii)   183 n, 278 n
Lessius (1554-1623, Jesuit of Louvain)   254 n, 270, 278
Lewis, Mrs   292, 302
Liddon, Dr H. P.   128 n, 155
Lightfoot, Bp   36 n, 88 n, 92, 106 n
Loisy, M l'Abbé   35 n, 39 n
Lombard, Peter, *see* Peter L
Loofs, Prof F   153 n, 156 n
Lotze, Hermann   223 n
de Lugo, Cardinal (1583-1660, Jesuit)   168 n, 169, 170 n
Luther (1483-1546)   181-2, 184
Lutheran   182-3, 240 n
Lux Mundi   57 n

Mabillon (1632-1707, benedict of St Maur)   234-5 n, 237 n
Macarius Magnes (c 350)   245 n, 304
Macarius, Bp   284 n
Mai, Cardinal   156 n
Mansi, J D (abp of Lucca, s xviii)   177 n, 178 n, 257 n, 268
Marcellus of Ancyra (s iv)   139 n
Martensen, Bp   192-3, 215
Martineau, Dr J   224

Martini (dominican, s xiii)   289
Mason, Dr A. J   231 n
Maurice, F D.   24 n
Meyer, Dr H A W   3 n
miracles   236, 249, 258 n, 261, 264, 270-1, 278 n
Missal   246, 250-1
Moesinger, Dr G   130 n, 295 n
Mommsen, Dr Th   19, 21 n
monophysitism   153, 154-6, 182, 274, 280-2
Morin, Dom G.   106 n

Nazarenes   52 n
neo platonism   173
Nestorius (bp of CP 428-431)   104, 145
Nestorianism   121 n, 144, 156 n, 160-1, 181-2, 194-5
Newman, Card   102 n, 120 n, 154
Nicolas II (pope 1059-1061)   257-8
Nicolas Cabasilas, *see* Cabasilas
Niemeyer, Dr H A   182 n
nihilianism   175-7, 279 f

οἰκονομία   151
Oldenberg, Prof   56 n
Origen (c 185-c 253)   45 n, 47, 48, 52 n, 100, 108, 114-121, 122, 132, 171, 218, 224, 291

Pange lingua   235 n
Panthera   6 n
Paschasius Radbert (†865, abbot of Corbey 844)   236-241, 243 n, 246, 282
Pearson (1613-1686, bp of Chester 1673)   196 n, 289
Perrone, F (S J)   271 n, 278 n
Petavius (1583-1652, French Jesuit)   160 n, 169, 179 n
Peter, Gospel of   48, 50

Peter Lombard (†1160, abp of Paris 1158) 167 n, 168, 175-6, 178, 260 n, 267, 280, 282
Peter the Venerable (†1156, abbot of Cluny 1122) 264
Philo († c 45) 50, 61-3, 298
Photius (c 815-891, bp of CP 857) 158, 276 n
Plato 65, 290-1
Polycarp († c 155, bp of Smyrna) 8, 44
Proclus of Cyzicus (†446, bp of CP 434) 104
Prosper of Aquitaine (c 403-c 463) 275
Psalms of Solomon 14 n, 17 n

Quadratus (s ii) 46
Quirinius, Publius Sulpicius 19

Rabanus Maurus (c 776-856, abp of Mainz 847) 237 n
239-40, 280
Rahlfs, Dr 298 n, 299 n
Ramsay, Prof. W M 15, 30 n
Ratherius of Liége (†974, bp of Verona 932) 250
Ratramn (c 868, monk of Corbey) 239 n, 240-246, 247, 249, 255
reception by the wicked, receptionist 232, 234, 237, 239, 262-3
Reformed, the 182-3
Renan, E 3 n, 6 n, 29 n, 35, 38 n, 55 n, 61 n
repraesentare 310
res and *virtus sacramenti* 234 n, 240, 255, 266
Rhys Davids, Prof 58, 59
Richard of St. Victor (†1173, prior of St V 1162) 178
Robertson, Rev A 122 n, 153
Robinson, Rev J A. 50
Routh, Dr M J. 274 n, 275 n
Rugamer, P W. 153 n, 156 n

Rupert of Deutz (†1135, abbot of D c 1120) 276
Ryle and James 14 n

Sabellianism 122
Sanday, Dr W 14, 15 n, 22, 76 n, 301
Schell, Dr H 169 n
science, physical 216-7, 222, 285
scientia beata, indita, acquisita 168
Sentius Saturninus 21
seven sacraments, the 265-6
Severians 154 n, 155
signa (of sacraments) 232, 246-7, 255, 262, 282, 312
Simcox, Rev W. H 54 n
Simeon, bp of Jerusalem (s ii) 54
Socrates (of CP, c 439) 42 n
Solomon, Psalms of, see *Psalms*
Sophronius (†638, bp of Jerusalem 634) 157
species, Christ entire in each 266 n
Stanley, Dean 29 n
Stanton, Prof V . 18 n, 52 n, 289
Stephen of Baugé (†1139, bp of Autun 1112) 268 n
Stokes, Prof Sir G G 216-7
Strauss 35
Strong, Rev. T B 224 n
Suarez (1548-1617, Spanish Jesuit) 169
'substance' 123, 194, 281
substance and accidents 242 n. 252, 272, 283
Suetonius 20 n, 31 n, 55
συνάφεια 144
supernatural and natural, the 109 273-4, 277-8, 280, 285-6

Tacitus 20, 31 n
Tatian the Syrian (s ii) 130, 295 n
Taylor, Jeremy (1613-1667, bp of Down and Connor 1660) 197

II. Names and Terms.

Taylor, Dr C 48 n
Tertullian (fl. c 200) 21,
 41 n, 44, 49, 109, 245 n,
 289–290, 303, 308–312
Testament of the xii Patriarchs 48
θεανδρικὴ ἐνέργεια 174
Themistius (of Alexandria, s. vi
 init.) 155, 156 n
Theodore of Mopsuestia (c 350–428,
 bp of M. 392) 144–5
Theodore (s vi, abbot CP) 156 n
Theodoret (c 393–c. 457, bp of
 Cyrrhus 423) 131–2, 160, 275
Theodosius (bp of Alexandria 536).
Theodosians 155 n, 157
Thomasius 189
Tobit, Book of 26 n
tradition 41, 106, 121
transubstantiare 268 n
Trench, Abp 24 n
Trypho 45, 51

ubiquity, doctrine of 182, 240 n

Victorinus Afer (fl 360) 209
Vincenti 289
Vischer, A F & F Th 248 n

Wainewright, Mr J. B 284 n
Waterland (1683–1740) 198
Weiss, Dr B 7 n, 14 n
Westcott, Bp 82 n, 85 n, 89, 93,
 146, 166, 173 n, 199, 200
Witmund (bp of Aversa 1088)
 249 n, 259–263,
 264–5, 267, 282
Wright, Mr I. 216 n

Zacharias (at Besançon 1131, pre-
 monst at Laon 1157) 264 n
Zoroaster 4

THE END

www.ingramcontent.com/pod-product-compliance
Lightning Source LLC
Chambersburg PA
CBHW072022240426
43667CB00044B/2024